Adventures in Africa

*For John + Sue –
Enjoy your trip of Adventures
in Africa!
Love, Aunt Mary!*

Adventures in Africa

Letters to My Grandchildren

by

Marjorie Sharp

SMITHFIELD PRESS
NORTH RICHLAND HILLS, TEXAS

Smithfield Press
An imprint of D. & F. Scott Publishing, Inc.
P.O. Box 821653
N. Richland Hills, TX 76182
817 788-2280
info@dfscott.com
www.dfscott.com

Copyright © 2004 by Marjorie Sharp

All rights reserved.
No part of this book may be reproduced in any manner whatsoever without written permission of the author except for brief quotations embodied in critical articles or reviews.

Printed in the United States of America

08 07 06 05 04 5 4 3 2 1

Library of Congress Cataloging-in-Publication Data
Sharp, Marjorie, 1927-
Adventures in Africa : letters to my grandchildren / by Marjorie Sharp.
 p. cm.
ISBN 1-930566-43-3 (trade paper : alk. paper)
 1. Africa, Sub-Saharan--Description and travel. 2. Sharp, Marjorie, 1927- 3. Missionaries--Congo (Democratic Republic)--Biography. I. Title.
DT352.2.S465 2004
967.51'024--dc22
                                    2004006014

For my grandchildren

Aaron, Mireille, Matt, Nicole, Zachary, and Kallianne

And for Murray

Without him this book would never have been written.

*Grandparents are proud of their grandchildren,
just as children are proud of their parents.
—Proverbs 17:6 (Good News Bible)*

Contents

For My Grandchildren — xi

1 Life on a Bush Station
New Worlds to Conquer — 1
We're on Our Way! — 6
We Made It! — 10
In the Swing of Things — 13
It's Time for a History Lesson — 20
These Shoes Were Made for Walkin' — 23
What's for Supper? — 26
It Never Rains But It Pours — 30
The Saga Continues — 33
"Bingo, Bango, Bongo"—We're Trav'lin' in the Congo — 36
We're Still Trav'lin' — 39

2 Independence
There's Trouble Brewing — 45
The Calm before the Storm — 47
The Storm Breaks — 48
Things Only Get Worse — 51
Home at Last! — 55

3 Seeing More of Africa
En route to Victoria Falls, Northern Rhodesia — 59
Let the Fun Begin — 62
Of Monkeys and Bubble Gum — 65
Watch Out for Wild Things! — 67
Was Someone Lost? — 70
Cruisin' Down the River — 72
Riding the Rails to Elizabethville — 74

4 Meet Some of Our Friends
   Where's the Huili?   77
   Retirement Zaire Style   82
   Emile   85
   Tata Joseph   89
   Special Friends, Special People   92
   Mind Your Manners!   96

5 Kaleidoscope
   Kaleidoscope   99
   The Latest "Edition"   102
   Variety is the Spice of Life   104
   Anyone for a Boat Trip?   109
   Where's the Beef?!   112
   "Band-Aids" to the Rescue!   117

6 On Safari
   On Safari in Kenya   121
   Home Sweet Home in a Camper   125
   Tsavo National Park, Kenya   126
   On Our Way to Lake Manyara   128
   Elephants for Breakfast   130
   Things That Go Bump in the Night   132
   "Boy Scouts" to the Rescue   135
   Back to Civilization   136
   We're Off to Entebbe, Uganda   140

7 Kaleidoscope II
   All that Glitters is not Gold   145
   Is Getting There Half the Fun?   149
   Partners in Crime   153
   Kinshasa Was Never Like This   155
   Tragedy on the Kwilu   160
   You Can't Get There from Here   162

8 Hostel Living

Who? Me? A Houseparent?	167
Someone's in the Kitchen With. . .?	169
Ingenuity Pays Off	173
Off to the Boonies	177
Gobble, Gobble, Gobble!	182
What Next?!	187

9 Christmas in Africa

Frog Legs for Christmas?	191
Merry Christmas in the "Zoo"	196
How 'Bout a Swim on Christmas Day?	201
You Won't Find Snow on the Equator	205
Caw, Caw, and Just Becaws	206
Diff'rent Strokes for Diff'rent Folks	208
The Twelve Days of Christmas (in Zaire/Congo) with Apologies to the Original Author	212
A Christmas Goodbye	214

10 The Purchasing Service

Oh, The Perils of Purchasing	217
Bugs, Bugs, and More Bugs!	219
Excitement on the Kwilu	221

11 Kaleidoscope III

Policemen on Patrol	227
It's Raining, It's Pouring!	231
What? No Television? No Video Games?	234
Thanksgiving Is More Than Turkeys	238
"I Think That I Shall Never See . . ."	240
Long Ago and Far Away	243

For My Grandchildren

We first set foot on African soil in October 1954. Grandpa and I had just completed a year of French study at the Colonial School in Brussels, Belgium. Our adventures in Africa were about to begin.

Having answered God's call to serve him wherever he should lead, we were on our way to the Belgian Congo. At that time it was still a Belgian colony. We had taught in public schools in the United States and would soon begin teaching in mission schools in Congo.

During the more than thirty years we lived in Congo, the name of the country changed from Belgian Congo to Republic of the Congo to Zaire and to Democratic Republic of the Congo, as it is known today. We were there when Belgium granted independence to the country in 1960; there when Mobutu Sese Seko ousted Kasa Vubu, the elected president from office and installed himself in that position; and there when a brave people struggled with tyranny, corruption in high places, and the exploitation of its natural resources. We have great admiration for a resilient people who, despite all that life has dealt them, continue to be optimistic and courageous.

Africa was in turmoil the years we lived and worked in Congo/Zaire. Many countries changed their names after receiving independence from their European governments. Throughout these letters I've tried to note those changes such as Banza Manteke/Nsona Mpangu, Elizabethville/ Lubumbashi, Northern Rhodesia/ Zambia, Leopoldville/Kinshasa. Even TASOL, the school where Steven and Susan first attended classes, is now called TASOK after the city assumed its present name. Sometimes I have used names interchangeably, particularly Congo/Zaire. I haven't tried to be historically accurate by always calling the country its proper name at the time I've written about.

You will recognize that Tata and Mama are the equivalent of Mr. and Mrs. in our society.

Your parents grew up in Congo. What was it like for them to be raised in a country and culture so different from what you know today? Did they have the same fears, hopes, joys that you experience? Why is it that today they still treasure many of the friendships they made during their growing up years? I'm sure one reason is because we were "family."

While it was always good to return to the States for a year and reconnect with relatives and friends and shop in stores where they had a choice of what they bought, it was also good to return to Congo where they were no longer in the spotlight, where friends didn't think they were weird or ask dumb questions: "Did you live in a hut?" "Did you see any tigers?" "Do you speak African?" Congo family was special. Like wearing a comfortable old shoe, it was good to be back among friends who didn't ask silly questions and who accepted them just the way they were.

Steven and Susan had so many unique experiences growing up in Congo that I've put a few of them together to share with you. Maybe you will get a glimpse of what life was like for them being raised in a different culture. I couldn't possibly include everything that happened between 1953–1987, but I wanted you to know some of the things they experienced. They have their own memories and could write their own book. Perhaps some day they will. Until then, I hope you will enjoy reading these "Letters To My Grandchildren."

Much love, Grandma

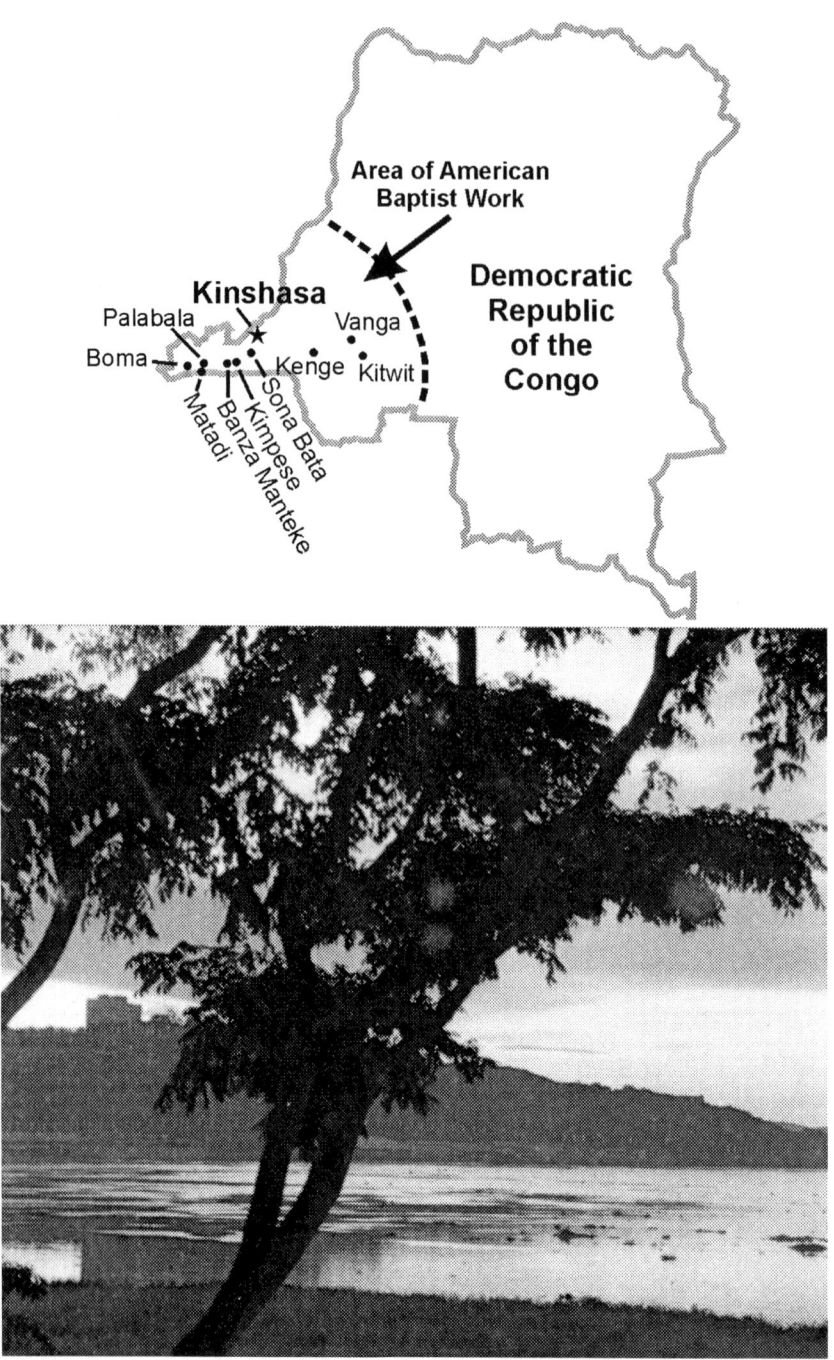

View from Kinshasa Mission Station Looking Toward Mont Ngaliema

Life on a Bush Station

New Worlds to Conquer

Dear Aaron, Mireille, Matt, Nicole, Zachary, and Kallianne,
The queen was waiting for us when we arrived in New York that day in late August fifty years ago. How proud and regal she looked sitting on her sparkling blue throne. We were just three of her several hundred "subjects," and we could scarcely control our excitement as we waited our turn to meet her. For this was no ordinary queen, this was Queen Elizabeth. The SS *Queen Elizabeth!* She would take us to Southampton, England, the first stop on our way to Belgium for a year of French study at the Colonial School in Brussels.

Never before had we been on an ocean liner sailing the high seas. But now, Grandpa, Steven, and I were embarking on a voyage that would take us first to Belgium, then a year later to Belgian Congo. We didn't know what lay ahead, but we knew God would be with us, guiding and leading us as we prepared to serve him there. Having said our goodbyes to families and friends, we traveled to New York, where we boarded the *Queen Elizabeth*. It would be five years before we returned to the United States.

While we were teaching in public schools in Kansas, a missionary from Belgian Congo spoke in our church, telling of the need for different types of missionary service in that country. Following the meeting, we spoke with him, explaining that we were teachers and that we believed God was leading us to Congo. After much prayer and thought, we applied to our mission board and in due time were appointed as missionaries to Belgian Congo. Now we were on our way.

After five days on the Atlantic Ocean, we looked forward to disembarking at Cherbourg, France, but as there were strikes in Paris, we sailed on to Southampton, took a train to London, another to Dover and crossed the English Channel by boat to Ostend, Belgium. Another train took us to Brussels. We had arrived! The stamps in our passport were evidence of that.

Our first priority was to find a place to live. With help from a colleague who had finished the year's course and would soon leave for Congo, we found an apartment near the end of Number 93 tram line. Since the 93 was near both the colonial school and our French tutor's home, I was pleased that it would be easy to get to those places from our apartment. Grandpa had another idea.

Why didn't we buy bicycles and ride to school? I hadn't ridden a bike since I was in high school and wasn't too keen on the idea. Besides, I was pregnant. However, I said I'd give it a try even if I wasn't eager to be in Brussels traffic. It wasn't long before we both realized riding bicycles to school was not going to work. On our way to a lesson at our French tutor's home one day, your grandma managed to get on the tram track and couldn't get off. Right behind her came Number 93 clang, clang, clanging for her to move out of the way. Scared to death and wobbling back and forth I finally made it to the safety of the sidewalk, vowing to never again ride that bicycle. Fortunately, my most embarrassing moment in Belgium saved me from further bike rides. It probably saved Grandpa from embarrassment as well.

There was a small playground area with a nice sand pile where we waited for the tram. Belgian mothers took advantage of this and sometimes brought their children there. Steven like to be outside in the fresh air, for he loved to play in the sand. He was just two years old and learning to share his toys with others. One day he wanted to play with a little boy's truck and picked it up. Immediately the mother scolded him, grabbed the toy and told him (in French, of course) that it wasn't his. We thought this was a good opportunity for children to learn to play and share together, but this mother evidently had a different agenda.

Near our apartment was a nursery school, Les Petits Cailleux (Little Pebbles), where we often took Steven when we were in class or had lessons with our tutor. He didn't like being a "Little Pebble." He didn't understand French while everyone else chattered away in it. It must have been difficult for a child who was learning to speak English to be confronted with this new babble of sound. However, he was always happy when Corri came to stay with him. Corri was a young Dutch woman who spoke English. She came to our apartment, taking care of him when we had classes. Corri liked children and they got along well together.

It wasn't long before we were immersed in French study, a Belgian requirement for those who would be teaching in schools or working in hospitals. As Protestant schools in Belgian Congo were just beginning to receive government subsidies, it was important our schools be qualified for this financial aid. Often it was difficult to practice using our newly acquired French, as Belgium is a bilingual country where French and Flemish are spoken. People wanted to practice speaking English to us.

During the winter, Grandpa wore a beret just like many Belgian men. Walking to class one day, he was approached by a stranger who evidently thought he was Belgian. "*Monsieur*," asked the man, "*Quelle heure est-il?"* (Sir, what time is it?) Grandpa recognized the man as a student but looking at his watch responded in French. The two men went their separate ways, pleased that each had communicated with the other. That beret did it!

Belgians dearly love dogs, and we found it necessary to watch where we stepped sometimes. A familiar morning sight was women scrubbing the sidewalk with a stiff broom and bucket of water in front of their homes. A friend was riding a tram one day when a woman tried to get on with a very large dog. She was determined to bring the animal onto the tram. The conductor, just as determined, said she could not. As the tram pulled away, leaving the woman and her dog standing in the street, the conductor turned to our friend and said slowly and distinctly in English, "That-dog-was-as-big-as-a-horse!"

Our tutor, Madame Emoidi, was committed to teaching us French. Before her retirement, she had been a translator in the Belgian law courts. She liked to remind me that she knew "well English." In my struggle to learn French grammar, I sometimes asked her why something was expressed a certain way. Her stock answer was always, "Because it was born that way." I had to be content with that.

It was discouraging when Madame Emoidi told us we would not both pass the French course. According to her, the professors never passed a husband and wife. Whether that were true or not, we successfully passed the oral and written examinations. Her students were a cosmopolitan group coming from several different countries. We were American, British, Swedish, Danish, and Dutch. After everyone passed the end-of-year exams, she invited us to her home for tea and a chance to converse together in our newly acquired language.

One purpose in spending ten months in French study was to give students sufficient command of the language so they could follow classes in the Colonial course. Students needed to learn about the country and the people with whom they would be working. There were seventeen subjects to be studied; testing would be on eleven of them. Grandpa learned about the different tribes, the school system, history and geography of both Belgium and Congo, administration of the colony, and religion. As in the French course, both written and oral exams were given. It was an intensive six-week course.

Even though we were busy conjugating verbs, writing dictations and putting our new language skills into practice, that year in Belgium wasn't all work and no play. Once a month, Mr. Coxhill, the liaison between the missionaries and the Belgian government, arranged a trip for us to different cities in Belgium. A delightful British couple, the Coxhills had served as missionaries in Congo at one time. We watched the lace makers in Bruges, the plumed carnival dancers at Binche, and sang "This is my Father's World" in the Grottes de Han as a man with a lighted torch ran from the top of the cave down to where our group stood. We visited Bastogne, where the American General Michael McAuliffe said "Nuts!" to the German general who ordered him to surrender during World War II. Visiting a different city in Belgium each month was both educational and fun, a nice break from concentrated French study.

Our trips weren't limited to Belgium, however. In the spring, we went to Holland for the tulip festival, where we saw acres and acres and thousands and thousands of tulips. We had never seen such varieties and colors. It was a cold, gray day, but even so, seeing field upon field of tulips was a never to be forgotten experience.

That year in Belgium, colleagues Jerry and Lee, their three children, and Margot and Esther, also with our mission, were studying French. During Christmas break, the ten of us rented a Volkswagen Kombi and drove to Switzerland via France and Germany. Traveling through other European countries for the first time had us glued to the windows, exclaiming over the beautiful countryside and the busy cities. Except for France, most people we met were friendly and hospitable. Maybe the French didn't like our Belgian French accent! We remember registering at a hotel in France where the desk clerk couldn't figure out where I belonged. He just knew it was one of the single ladies who belonged with Grandpa and not your Grandma who was holding Steven!

It was very cold in Europe that winter and we couldn't find a heater in the Kombi. Despite my fleece lined shoes, my feet never thawed out the entire trip. In fact, I'm not sure they warmed up again until we got to Congo! Upon returning the car to the rental agency, our guys complained that the Kombi didn't have a heater. "Oh," said the attendant, "it's right here," and he turned it on!

Our year in Belgium was fast drawing to a close. French study and exams were behind us, we were somewhat fluent speaking French, and Grandpa had successfully passed the colonial course exams. Now we looked forward to the next chapter in our lives. It was time to pack up and leave for Belgian Congo. Grandpa made reservations for us to sail on the *Baudouinville*, a Belgian passenger ship. We were ready to go!

We'll tell you about our trip in the next letter.

Love to all,
G'ma and G'pa

We're on Our Way!

Dear Grandkids,

Yes, finally! We were on board the M.V. *Baudouinville*, a Belgian passenger ship, en route to the Belgian Congo. With the help of our tutor, Madame Emoidi, we had completed a year's French study at the Belgian Colonial School in Brussels. Because we were going to teach in a mission school, Grandpa also took courses at the Colonial School which would make the mission eligible to receive government financial support. That was all behind us now and we were on the Atlantic Ocean on our way to Congo.

Grandpa, Steven, and I left from Antwerp, Belgium excited about the seventeen-day trip ahead of us. Throughout the first day, land was visible; but toward evening, as our ship approached the Bay of Biscay, the water became choppy. Some folks were beginning to feel woozy, and by the next day the thought of eating kept a lot of them away from the dining room. We took our motion sickness pills and never missed a meal.

In spite of eating potatoes twice a day, the meals were quite good. We became accomplished in the art of eating European style with the fork in the left hand and the knife in the right. The five course dinners of hors d'oeuvres, fish, entree, cheese, and dessert followed by coffee or tea kept us busy trying to figure out the maze of silverware. In the evening, each person's place was set with twelve pieces—we were really busy!

We had made friends with the large group of missionaries studying French that year, and several of them were also on the *Baudouinville*. Most of our two hundred shipmates were Belgians on their way to Congo, many to work in the government. The seventy-five children on board kept things lively. We were fifteen adults and twelve children in the group of missionaries, young families with babies and elementary school age children.

The year of study in Belgium had been a difficult one. Brussels was COLD! My feet were always cold until we got to Congo. Shopping took a lot of time and energy. Studying French required discipline and determination. We wanted to practice using French with Belgians, but they wanted to practice speaking English with us. Belgium is a bilingual country where people speak French and/or Flemish. After the difficult year in Brussels, the two and a half weeks on board ship was a wonderful time to relax.

Steven never lacked for playmates, as he spent much of the time in the nursery with other children. The lady in charge treated the children with love and patience and kept them all happy and contented. The parents enjoyed the leisure time as well, playing Ping-Pong and deck tennis, reading, swimming in the ship's pool, and playing games. Evenings we gathered for devotions and singing, even splurging sometimes for ice cream.

After three or four days at sea, our ship docked at Tenerife, one of six small islands that make up the Canary Islands. Owned by Spain, they lie off the coast of Morocco in northwest Africa. Poverty was evident at Tenerife. Many houses were in need of repair and the people were dressed poorly. Burros were used for transport. The women transported things as well . . . on their heads—baskets of bread or laundry, cases of Coca Cola, firewood. Little girls, imitating their mothers, carried things in the same fashion. Evidently it was beneath the men's dignity to carry anything.

We took an excursion into the mountains where we had a breathtaking view of Tenerife plus two smaller islands in the distance. Vendors pursued us with beautiful leather crafts. Others had drawn-lace work, a type of stitching known as Tenerife. Lovely embroidered items were for sale. At the dock, someone wanted to sell Grandpa a fake Parker pen for three dollars. When we returned to the ship, the man was still hoping for a sale. Now his price was two pens for the price of one. Women came to the ship with handmade dolls, crocheted doilies and beautiful embroidered lunch cloths to sell to passengers who had remained on board. Tenerife was an interesting and enjoyable break on the way to Congo.

On board ship, passengers who crossed the equator for the first time were initiated by King Neptune (god of the sea). We were first timers. And we were nearing the equator. What would be our fate, we wondered? At dinner we found out. We were served a small piece of toast and told there would be nothing more to eat until breakfast. Evidently going to bed without supper was part of the initiation. We ate the toast slowly, savoring every bite, expecting nothing more to eat that night. In a few minutes our smiling waiter brought the usual evening meal. The toast was part of the initiation fun. Next morning King Neptune, wearing a crown and holding a trident, summoned us on deck. From a scroll he read the charges against those who were to be initiated. We had all committed serious crimes against King Neptune.

During the voyage the missionaries were often on deck playing rowdy games of Pit. We were so noisy yelling "corner on wheat" or "corner on rye" that King Neptune ordered us to play "corn market" (his name for the game) as part of our initiation. Our faces and hair were painted with poster paint, the remaining paint poured over our feet. We were a mess. As we slapped the cards yelling "corner on wheat," "corner on corn," the jolly old king ordered us to scramble through a large canvas tube with water spraying us from each end. The "shower" washed off a lot of the mess. Finally the initiation was over and everyone was given a certificate to prove that we had crossed the equator. If we crossed again, we could watch the fun from the sidelines.

The initiation rite of crossing the equator was not funny to the children. Several of them cried seeing their parents covered with paint and water. They didn't understand that this was all in fun and no one was being hurt. Later there was a party for the children who wore costumes for the occasion, whatever we parents could dream up on short notice. Steven was a cowboy dressed in a western shirt and jeans.

Among the passengers was an artist who asked the captain to pilot the ship close to the coast of Dakar as she wanted to paint the scene. Though the country was known then as French Equatorial Africa, today we know it as Senegal. As our ship rounded the hump of West Africa, the captain piloted the ship within a mile and a half of the city. We noticed many new and modern looking buildings, such a contrast from those in Tenerife.

We were nearing Congo, but the ship docked at two more ports before we reached Matadi. We spent four or five hours at Lobito in Angola to the south of Congo. The city is small, but the harbor is large. We were intrigued by the rainbow of colors in the houses . . . green, rose, lavender, blue. Through our binoculars, it appeared that the African houses were built of sun-dried bricks with thatch roofs. Finally, all the cargo destined for Lobito was unloaded and we were on our way north to Matadi. Sometime that afternoon, we would reach the mouth of the Congo River, drop anchor at Boma and wait for a river pilot to guide the *Baudouinville* around the sandbars the next morning.

We're almost there! It's exciting! Congo, here we come!

Love you, G'ma and G'pa

We Made It!

Dear Grandchildren,

Our last night on board the M.V. *Baudouinville*, the ship lay at Boma, anchored at the mouth of the Congo River. We waited there until the next morning for a river pilot to guide us around the islands, sandbars, and whirlpools. He would take the ship up the Congo River to the port of Matadi. The seventeen-day ocean voyage from Antwerp, Belgium to Matadi, Belgian Congo had been one of new experiences. Sighting flying fish and sharks, the excursion to the top of a mountain in the Canary Islands, the initiation ceremony as the ship crossed the equator, the port at Lobito, Angola—all these memories were behind us, and we anticipated the future.

We had heard that the water from the mighty Congo was visible thirty miles into the ocean. Now we had seen this phenomenon for ourselves. It's hard to comprehend, but the river pours a million and a half cubic feet of water per second into the ocean with such dynamic force that the Congo cuts a wide path into the Atlantic. On either side is the blue of the ocean separated by the muddy brown river cutting through it.

In the morning, the pilot came aboard and we began the slow trip upriver. Not wanting to miss anything, we found a spot on deck along with other passengers, where we eagerly watched life unfold along the river. Children waved to us as the ship passed their villages. Fishermen in *pirogues*, (dugout canoes hewn from tall, sturdy trees) cast their nets. Palm trees, their fronds swaying in the breeze, grew along the riverbanks. New to us were mangrove trees. With tangled roots growing above ground at the water's edge, we wondered how they could grow.

In this area the ground was flat, and we watched women in brightly colored *minlele* (cloths worn like wrap-around skirts), work in their gardens of manioc and maize. Babies were tied on their mother's back. Little girls with short handled hoes dug in the earth beside their mothers. Scrawny looking chickens and a few goats and pigs scavenged for something to eat. Small herds of cattle stood in shallow water at the river's edge. There was so much to see!

As we continued upriver to Matadi, our pilot steered the ship around numerous eddies and whirlpools. I remember one called The Devil's Cauldron. It was well named, as the whirlpool churned with such force I wondered how our ship could avoid being sucked into it. But the pilot knew the river well and skillfully maneuvered the ship around it.

In places, the river is five miles wide and is navigable only between Boma and Matadi. The next two hundred miles inland to the capital city of Leopoldville (today's Kinshasa) is reached only by railroad or road. In the late 1890s, Belgium completed the first railroad connecting the two major cities. Between Leopoldville and Matadi are the Livingstone Falls, a series of rapids and thirty-two cataracts, where the Congo River narrows as it cuts through the Crystal Mountains on its rush to the sea. The river thunders through narrow gorges where giant waves, thirty and forty feet high, crash onto immense boulders.

A decade before Christopher Columbus "discovered" America, a Portuguese explorer, Diego Cão, took his ship upriver around the whirlpools a short distance beyond Matadi. There he was forced to turn back because of the cataracts and rapids. Diego Cão and his men etched a deep cross, a shield, and writings on the boulders to let people know they were the first explorers to follow the river that far inland. Now, more than five hundred years later, the carvings are still there to be seen by those who have the energy to trek down the mountain from the village of Palabala to view them. Even today no ships are able to go further than the port at Matadi.

On a sunshine-bathed October day, beneath a beautiful blue sky, the *Baudouinville* docked at Matadi. Standing on deck, I looked down at the black men unloading the ship and asked God if I would be able to love the Congolese people in the way he wanted me to love them. God had seen us through language school in Brussels and had given us a safe trip to Africa. Now he would continue to guide us.

Adventures in Africa

In the sea of black faces at the port there were a number of white people as well. We spotted colleagues Norm and Von who had made this same sea voyage the previous year after completing French study in Brussels. They were stationed at Nsona Mpangu where we would begin our work and had come to meet us. How good it was to see someone we knew!

By the time formalities at immigration were completed and we had collected our baggage, we were hungry. Our friends suggested we eat at The Farm, a restaurant where they assured us we could enjoy a nice meal together. As we were eating a tasty Belgian soup, I bit into something that didn't seem quite right. As discreetly as possible I put it in my spoon . . . and to my horror discovered I had bitten into a cockroach! Granted, it was only a small one, perhaps half an inch long, but still, it was a cockroach. I had never been a big fan of cockroaches anyway, and biting into one in my first few hours in Congo, didn't make me like them any better.

Grandpa, Steven and I got into our friends' van and we started the two-hour drive to Nsona Mpangu which was still called Banza Manteke at that time. The route twisted and curved its way over a bumpy dirt road through the Crystal Mountains. They were well named because we often found quartz crystals along the roads. Norm needed to make a stop at Kenge to talk with the village school director. It was dark by now, and the director came to the van holding a lantern to light his way. Their business completed, we continued to bounce and jolt around curves and hills on our way to Nsona Mpangu. I was feeling a tad green.

Mary was waiting to welcome us with a delicious dinner, although I no longer remember what it was. My head was swimming, and I felt worse with each minute. It probably was the result of several things . . . the intense heat, the lurching of the van on twisting, curving roads . . . and certainly, biting into that cockroach didn't help. After excusing myself from the table to rid my tummy of the dinner at Matadi, Mary, whom I came to love and appreciate said, "You won't last long in Congo if a little cockroach does you in!" Ha! I fooled her! I lasted thirty-three years! Later Von confided that she eyeballed a snake in the bathroom her very first night in Congo. New missionaries were not to be immune from local wildlife.

In the morning, we enjoyed breakfast with Martin and Ruth. He had spoken in our church in Kansas, telling of the need for missionaries in Belgian Congo. We didn't know at that time that the missionaries in Congo were praying for twenty-four new folks to join them in the work, nor that we would be part of the answer to their prayers. Now, here we were in Congo, eager to share in the responsibilities.

The most thrilling experience our second morning in Congo was the welcome from 350 high school students and their teachers as they marched by singing to us in French: "'Neath the Banner of the Cross." The boys, dressed in white shirts and shorts, and for the most part barefoot, sang as only Congolese can sing. What a thrill to listen to their beautiful harmony. One hundred fifty students from the elementary school and girls' homemaking school also sang as they marched. Even today, we can still picture the students as they marched by to welcome us. We felt royally received.

You'll have to wait until the next letter to learn what happened next. Till then . . .

Love to all,
G'ma and G'pa

In the Swing of Things

Dear Grandchildren,

It was October and we had been in Belgian Congo only two days. Since Steven was celebrating his third birthday that day, Grandpa and I wondered how we could observe it. As we weren't settled yet in our new home, I couldn't bake a cake; but one of our colleagues did, and we had a party. In his three years, Steven had celebrated each birthday on a different continent—his first in North America, his second in Europe and his third in Africa. He was quite a world traveler!

When we arrived in Congo, we were impressed by its beauty. Rainy season was just starting, which meant that the dry season haze had lifted, the countryside was turning green again, and trees were beginning to flower. On either side of the road leading through the station, the flamboyant trees were a blaze of orange and red. Frangipani trees bloomed in shades of ivory, pink, and yellow, lending more color and beauty to the landscape. Palm trees lined the path leading to the high school. We loved our new surroundings!

Before we arrived in Congo, we wondered what kind of house we would live in. Would it be built of mud and thatch or of cement blocks? Arriving at Banza Manteke we were pleased to see that the school buildings and houses for both missionaries and Congolese were built of permanent materials. Shortly before we arrived, Scotty and his workmen had finished building several houses and school buildings, but he and Dolores had since moved to Boko where they started building a new hospital.

Our home was quite comfortable with two bedrooms, bath, living/dining room, office, and kitchen. There was even a fireplace, as nights were chilly in dry season when there were no rains. A breezeway running the length of the house helped keep it cool in rainy season. Built from red clay bricks that were made on the station, the house had cement floors and a metal roof. When mangoes fell on it they made a dreadful racket. During the two years we lived at Banza Manteke, we had running water and electricity, blessings we never expected.

The kitchen was divided into four small rooms. Two of them were for storage. A sink and a small cupboard were in the first room. Grandpa used some of the wood from our packing crates to build more cupboards. Ants were always a problem. To keep them from getting into food we set the cupboard legs in tin cans half filled with kerosene—ants are not good swimmers. Still, it was a challenge to keep them out of food.

In the second room stood the wood stove we had ordered through the catalog. A high school boy was hired to cut wood for the stove, but it burned wood faster than Yandu's enthusiasm for chopping it. Until it arrived in our freight from the States, we made do with a two-burner kerosene stove. It was a cranky appliance which smoked badly. Cleaning soot from pots and pans was a daily chore. We ordered a kerosene refrigerator from Sweden, as electricity on this bush station was insufficient for refrigerators. Our kitties liked to curl up and sleep on the tank next to the warm chimney-covered flame.

A teenage student helped me in the kitchen. Once, curious about a tin can on the stove, I checked its contents. A tiny naked baby bird was cooking on the stove. I hadn't been in Congo long enough to realize that for Emile the bird, tiny as it was, represented a bit of protein.

One of the teachers asked me to hire his son to clean our house. Lutete was intrigued with the anniversary clock sitting on the mantel. Never before had he seen such a wonder. He spent more time watching the pendulum circle from left to right, right to left than he did using a broom or dust cloth.

We had no washing machine, but we had Edouard. His name was Ntonenedio Edouard, but when he started working for us we had barely begun studying Kikongo. It was too hard to make our tongues say Ntonenedio, so we called him by his French name. Edouard was a personable high school student who came twice a week to do our laundry on a scrub board. One day he showed me his sore fingers from using the board. I wished for him some other method of doing our laundry. There was an alternative. He could have taken our clothes to the river and pounded them on rocks as the village women did! He used an iron which he filled with charcoal—not the kind we buy in the States for cookouts, but what the women made locally. By swinging the iron back and forth, the heat in the charcoal was activated, making it hot enough to iron our clothes. The iron could also burn holes in clothes if one weren't careful.

One day Edouard showed me a viper he had killed in the grass outside our house. When I asked him how he knew a snake was there, he replied that the chickens were making an odd sound. Being African, Edouard was attuned to the noise. Had I heard the chickens I would never have guessed there was danger in the grass.

Coming from a country where people love green lawns, we missionaries always wanted to have grass growing around our homes. Not the Congolese! They knew how easy it was for snakes to hide in the grass or flowerpots. The area around their homes was swept clean every morning and was always bare of anything green.

One afternoon each week the students were required to do some kind of work, either in the manioc gardens which helped provide a part of their diet or other manual labor. High school boys were often seen swinging *coupe-coupes* to keep the grass cut short on the station. You might call it Congo's version of a lawn mower. The *coupe-coupe* is a thin piece of metal, about an inch and a half wide and forty inches long. The cutting edge is curved and sharpened on both sides. It makes a very effective lawn mower as it's swung through the grass. It was also a good muscle builder!

On the station was a narrow, two-story brick water tower. At the top was a large tank that supplied water for the station's use. Water was pumped from a nearby spring and piped into the tank. Living on a bush station, there weren't many places where we could picnic, but the top of the water tower was an ideal place. Even though it meant climbing straight up a ladder and squeezing ourselves through a narrow opening onto the roof, the view of the surrounding countryside was spectacular. The Congolese thought missionaries were crazy to go to such effort for a picnic when they had nice houses where they could eat in comfort. Why would we do that, they wondered?

Our mission headquarters in the United States emphasized the importance of language study. We were to be given time to learn the local language in order to communicate with the people. On paper this sounded good, but in practice was not possible. There were too few missionaries and too many jobs to be done. However, within a few days of our arrival we were given tutors and we began language study.

Having completed a year's French study in Brussels, we were assigned several subjects to teach in the high school. One of mine was music, using a system called sol-fa (solfeggio). I could read music from a staff, but this four-part harmony method used letters (such as "d" for "do") and punctuation marks (e.g., . or : or ') to indicate quarter notes, half notes, etc. It was like learning *another* foreign language. The students knew more than their teacher. I was more comfortable teaching home economics to the girls. At least I knew those subjects. In a year, Ruth would return to the States for a year's home assignment and I was to become the director of the Homemaking School.

Grandpa had a heavy schedule in the high school. His teaching assignment included French grammar, history, geography, algebra, and physical education. We were required to make our lesson plans in French which took considerable time, time that we would like to have used studying Kikongo.

There were several responsibilities that had nothing to do with teaching, and while they weren't difficult, they did take time from language study. Once a week, Grandpa drove to Lufu, the nearest railroad station, to send the outgoing mail pouch to Leopoldville and pick up the one that had arrived. We also sent a meat order to Kolo, another railroad town where the order was filled and sent by train to Lufu the following week.

Grandpa added overseeing the carpenter shop to his growing list of responsibilities. An African carrying a plank on his head to the shop was a familiar sight. Men would cut down a tree in the forest. That was the easy part. Sawing it into planks was not. When the tree fell, the men dug a pit under it. One person stood in the pit while another straddled the tree. Holding the saw vertically the men sawed up and down, up and down until they had succeeded in cutting a plank. Their method of sawing lumber seemed backwards to us, but we never knew them to do otherwise. When someone walked to the station with a plank, Grandpa was called to the shop where a price was agreed upon. The carpenter shop had an electric planer where the plank was then planed into useable lumber. The beautiful mahogany tables and chairs and chests of drawers for our home were made by men in the carpenter shop.

Grandpa built a tree house for Steven outside the breezeway of our house. It wasn't actually in a tree, but it did have ladder steps to get up to it. He spent many happy hours there playing with his matchbox cars, "reading" *Highlights for Children* and eating snacks. When the Clark family was assigned to Banza Manteke, Betty Sue, who was a year younger than Steven, joined him sometimes. He liked to say and do goofy things to make her laugh. She fed his little male ego by telling him, "Oh Stevie, you 'c-r-a-z-y' boy!"

Saturday afternoon was hair salon day for the girls. Sitting outside their dorms, the girls dressed each other's hair. They unwound the black thread which held the different styles in place, combed it all out, then styled it again. They had many attractive styles and each one had a name. One of the more popular ones reminded me of bottle brushes. Sections of hair were wound tightly with black thread, then the remaining hair fluffed into little tufts at the end of each section. Their hair stayed neat for at least a week.

Congolese kids had fads that they followed just the same as American kids. One that was popular when we arrived were long, wide belts, The belts were three or four inches in width and hung down several inches. The longer they were, the more stylish. The boys liked to wear mirrorlike sunglasses that caught the reflection of anyone looking into them. They were supposed to keep their hair cut short, but more than one boy had a swath cut through his hair by a teacher who thought it was getting too long.

A dam on the nearby Lunionzo River was the site of a small hydroelectric plant which provided electricity for the mission station. Crocodiles were reported to inhabit the water, though we never saw any. Even so, an African appeared at a missionary home one day hoping to sell eggs to Grace. She questioned their source and was assured he hadn't taken all of the eggs. Maybe he was concerned about the balance of nature! Nearly every time there was a storm, the lights went off, and Grandpa was expected to go to the river, tinker with the hydroelectric plant by flashlight and get electricity restored once more on the station.

With lesson plans to prepare and classes to teach, plus the other responsibilities we were given, it wasn't easy to find time for language study. There are four hundred languages spoken in Congo and two hundred of them have dialects. The four major languages are

Kikongo, Lingala, Tshiluba and Swahili. We were studying Kikongo, the language spoken by the Bakongo people, the tribal group among whom we were living.

If we thought learning French was difficult, we would discover that learning Kikongo was even more so. Kikongo grammar is nothing at all like French grammar, and we were in a sea of confusion from the beginning. There were times we thought we would never be able to pass the four language exams required by our mission in order to be reappointed after home assignment. But our tutors were patient, and we persevered. However, it was six months before the fog began to lift and the agreement of verbs, nouns, and modifiers started to make sense.

We learned to say *kiambote* (hello) when we greeted people and *sikamene?* (Hello. Did you wake up?) when we greeted them in the morning. We learned there were two ways to say goodbye—*sala mbote* and *wenda mbote*. Which form you used depended if you were the one staying or leaving. We learned the difference between *ntondele* (thank you) and *mfiaukidi* (an especially polite thank you) and when to use them properly. One banana was *tiba*, but two or more were *bitiba*. A book was *nkanda*, but several books were *minkanda*. Plurals were far more complicated in Kikongo.

The Congolese must have had a lot of laughs over our attempts to speak their language, but most were gracious about our mistakes and genuinely appreciated that we wanted to communicate with them in their language. Most Belgians never bothered to learn African languages, relying instead on speaking French.

Steven was also learning a bit of Kikongo. When he played outside with his cars and trucks little boys came along to play with them as well. He began to understand some of the language and use a few words. Just as he was becoming fluent in Kikongo we were reassigned to Leopoldville where he never had the opportunity to speak it again.

Life was certainly different living on a busy mission station. We'll write again soon.

Love to all . . . and sala mbote!
G'ma and G'pa

Adventures in Africa

It's Time for a History Lesson

Dear Brenner and Sharp Grandkids,

During the two years we lived at Banza Manteke, we didn't know its true name was Nsona Mpangu. The original Banza Manteke, established in 1879, was several miles from the present mission station. It had moved to its current location before 1930 when the original station became too small for expansion of church, hospital, and school buildings. At that time, the chief at Nsona Mpangu offered land to build a new mission station. Even though it was built on Nsona Mpangu land, people continued to call it Banza Manteke. After independence in 1960, the station resumed its authentic name, Nsona Mpangu.

To distinguish between the two areas known as Banza Manteke, the original site was referred to as Old Banza Manteke. We remember the ancient weather-beaten church, elevated on stilts two or three feet above the ground. Decades before we arrived in Congo, the lumber for the church had been imported from England. Congo had beautiful mahogany forests, and why local wood was not used, we're not sure. Perhaps it was too difficult to harvest the trees and plane the wood by hand.

Standing in front of the old church were two enormous iron wheels which, according to local legend, had been found in the nearby forest. They were said to be relics from the wagons the famous explorer Henry Morton Stanley used in the late 1880s to portage supplies around the rapids and cataracts on the Congo River. His men (Congolese) had to transport everything by land, over mountains, though forests, or at rare times, on the river in places where it was navigable. It was backbreaking work, and the wheels are a mute reminder of the difficulty in establishing an overland route into the interior.

There is also a small graveyard where several early day missionaries or their children are buried. One Banza Manteke missionary was killed by an elephant, though the elephants were long gone by the time we arrived. Life was harsh then, and many died from malaria or other tropical diseases. A few who came to Congo lived less than a year before they became ill and died. Due to intense sun and malaria, it was thought too dangerous to raise white children in Congo. In the early years, children born in Congo were sent back to America to live with extended family members or else to a home for missionary children. They were separated from their parents for years at a time. It was not until after World War II, when better antimalaria drugs were developed, that missionaries were able to keep their children with them in Congo. On the advice of senior missionaries, we bought Steven a sun helmet when we arrived at Matadi. He steadfastly refused to wear it.

Now, a bit of background about the men and women who established the mission station at Old Banza Manteke . . .

In 1879, Charles Peterson and Henry Richards, walking from Matadi into the interior of western Congo, searched for a site to establish a mission station. At that time, there were neither roads nor railroads for the traveler, only trails. Somehow the two men made their wishes known, and eventually permission was given by the chief at Banza Manteke to begin work there. From the very beginning of their arrival, the two men were faced with countless problems.

All too soon, Henry Richards was alone as Charles Peterson died in 1880, possibly from malaria. That same year, Mr. Richards married, but his wife died nineteen months later and is buried in the little cemetery. Within three years, he married again, but that wife also died after a few months. Good health was fragile for many of the early missionaries. Marrying a third time, Henry Richards and his wife Mary worked together the next thirty-four years.

When Richards first walked into the Banza Manteke area, he was alone among people unknown to him. He had no knowledge of their customs or unwritten language. How do you communicate with people if you cannot speak to them? God in his wisdom provided a black man who had learned English somewhere and had later been bought as a slave. Through him, Richards was able to communicate with the people. As he learned Kikongo, he wrote down vocabulary words, but it was several years before he became proficient in speaking the language.

People were often distrustful and some were outright hostile to the man whom many would later affectionately call *ngw'ankazi* (maternal uncle—he is the one who makes the major decisions for his sisters' children as well as other family matters). *Ngw'ankazi* is a term of great respect, and Henry Richards was the only missionary in the Bakongo area to have been given this title.

One chief, much hated throughout the region because he had shown hospitality to the white man, continued to be friendly to Richards. Another, hoping to get rid of the missionary, united some chiefs to fight the one who had befriended him. People dumped filth and trash into the spring where he drew his drinking water. They threw clods of dirt and rubbish into his house. Gobs of red dye were thrown at him and smeared on his clothes. Someone tried to shoot him. He was beaten, his clothes torn and burned. Porters who carried supplies from Matadi stole some of it for themselves. Through all the trials, he was patient and unafraid. He trusted God to help him love the people despite his persecution.

Some people thought he had committed a crime in Europe and fled to Congo to avoid prosecution. They couldn't believe he had come to teach God's Word so they could be saved and have eternal life.

For seven years, Henry Richards worked among the Banza Manteke people without winning a single convert. Then a marvelous thing happened. People began to open their hearts to God. At first, just a few were won, then it was like a flood and more than a thousand were baptized in a short time.

One day he preached from Luke 6:30: "Give to everyone who asks you for something, and when someone takes what is yours, do not ask for it back." By our standards he didn't have much, but he had a lantern, washbasin, a table and chairs, some clothes, a few tins of food. Even so, that was more than many of the people had who lived in the little grass huts.

Did this white man really mean what he said? So they asked him, and he watched the people carry away the few things he owned. The next morning he was surprised to see them returning all the possessions they had taken the day before. The chief told them they didn't need those things nearly as much as the white man did and that something terrible would happen to them if he should die. The sacrifice Richards was willing to make impressed the people. Hearts were now open to God's leading and the Pentecost of the Congo was born. (Pentecost is celebrated fifty days after Easter and commemorates the Holy Spirit descending on the apostles.) In today's expression, we would say Richards "talked the talk and walked the walk."

Scornfully at first they called Henry Richards *Lumonso*, the left-handed one, but in time with his love, patience and unfailing kindness he became their beloved *Ngw'ankazi*, their maternal uncle. Henry Richards lived his faith.

Love to our "quiverful,"
G'ma and G'pa

These Shoes Were Made for Walkin'

Dear Aaron, Nicole, Zach, Kalli, Mireille and Matt,
We had been in Congo only six months, trying to learn the Kikongo language when Ruth, our senior missionary, invited me to go on a trip with her to the village of Luanika. It was her husband, Martin, who spoke in our church in Kansas. He told of the need for teachers in Congo. God used his message to encourage us to apply as teachers in our mission schools.

Even though my ability to speak Kikongo was still limited, I jumped at the chance for this new experience. It would be exciting to see life away from the mission station. Ruth and I would conduct a Women's Institute which would include worship services, emphasis on child care, literacy classes using the Laubach method, and Bible study. Two Congolese would go with us to assist in teaching the various classes.

Since there were only footpaths leading to Luanika, getting there would be half the fun. It was somewhere near the Angola border, toward Matadi, I was told. This trip sounded like an adventure to me. Martin drove us as far as the village of Lufu in the station van. We would walk narrow trails the rest of the way. I picked up my small suitcase and followed Ruth and the others down the path to Kibemba where we would spend the night. The adventure was beginning!

Five and a half hours of walking in the hot African sun certainly satisfied my quest for adventure. We arrived at dusk at the village of Kibemba where a family had swept and vacated their two-room mud and thatch house so that we would have a place for the night. You might call it a village version of Motel 6, although bath and toilet facilities were woefully lacking. The village people expected us, and in typical African courtesy had prepared a place for us to stay. Children brought firewood. Young girls walked to the nearest stream, filled pails with water, and walked uphill, the pails carefully balanced on their heads, to provide "running water" for our comfort!

Some women brought us dinner: *sakasaka* (spicy cooked manioc greens), *mwamb' ansusu* (chicken cooked in palm oil and hot peppers), and *chikwanga* (made from manioc flour, then steamed and fermented in banana leaves). The women checked to see what else we might need, and chased away the little children who had come to watch these strange white people. We were something to chatter about! Since Kibemba was reached only by trail, probably most of the children had never seen white people before. Ruth and I lit kerosene lanterns, set up our camp cots, snuggled under mosquito nets and were soon fast asleep. That long walk in the hot sun had tuckered us out. I had had enough adventure for one day!

When morning came, we were on the trail again, accompanied by three or four children who helped carry our supplies. They quickly outdistanced us even though they carried everything on their heads. I still can visualize one barefoot girl walking up the trail, a card table balanced on hers. Children were used to these paths and had no trouble walking up hill and down in the hot morning sun. Tall elephant grass on either side of the path made it impossible to tell if wild things might be hiding out there, ready to pounce on us. We were told there were elephants in the area, even though none had been seen for several years. I half expected to be startled by one.

Someone assured me that "we go up the mountain in secret," meaning that we wound our way up the hills which was easier than climbing straight up. Whether we climbed up in secret or walked straight up those hills, it was a vigorous four-mile hike to the village of Luanika.

I had asked Ruth if it would be offensive to the culture if I wore slacks on the trip. She assured me slacks would be fine and they would certainly be good protection while walking the trails. As we approached the village, people came out to greet us. They greeted Ruth first. *Kiambote, Mama.* Then they saw me. *Kiambote, . . . Mama? . . . Tata? . . . Mama?* Those slacks had completely confused them regarding my gender!

The village nurse had moved from his home to make it available to us. His house was built of split bamboo, perfect for the children to press against and peer at us through the cracks. I saw a row of big brown eyes watching every move we made. Surely looking at us was more fun than a trip to the zoo would have been for them!

Each morning began with a worship service followed by a class on nurturing good character in children. This was a women's institute, but the men didn't want to be left out and they were invited to join us. As some of the women were illiterate, we held reading classes using the Laubach method for teaching people to read. We recruited women who could read to help. One "teacher," sitting opposite her "student," held the book so that she could read it, but it was upside down for her pupil. There were a few men who also wanted to learn to read and they were included in classes. Being able to read the Bible was important for Christian growth.

There were Bible studies, role-playing, hygiene skits, and discussions on the family throughout the afternoons. Later, everyone had a chance to say the Bible verses they had learned. One evening, there was a Festival of Lights in which a large group of women participated by lighting a candle and repeating, "I want the light of Christ to shine in my heart and in my home." They were hushed and reverent for this service, knowing the importance of their commitment.

The village people thanked us for coming to share those few days with them. They always made sure we had sufficient water for bathing, boiled our drinking water, and prepared meals for us. Each morning, several came to ask if we had slept well. We were more than repaid for our long, tiring walk by the love they showed us. Now it was time to return to Banza Manteke.

We took a different route home, but it was just as difficult as the earlier one. Going up and down hill, climbing over rocks and boulders in the hot sun was tiring. We started singing to keep up our spirits. By the time we reached the last mountain it was dark, and we inched our way along. Who knew what might be on the path? Snakes? Animals? Rocks? Finally, one of the men sent word ahead, and folks from the next village returned with a couple of kerosene lanterns to help light our way.

Grandpa and Steven (who was three and a half years old) had driven to the village and were waiting to take us home. They heard our singing and hurried in the darkness to meet us. Steven had missed his mommy, and she had missed him (and Grandpa too!). What a happy reunion to be with my family again. We had so much to share with each other.

It had been an awesome five days. I had met some fine people, had a chance to practice my Kikongo and experienced gracious Congolese hospitality. It had been a great learning experience for me. And my walkin' shoes had definitely had a workout!

Love to all,
G'ma and G'pa

What's for Supper?

Dear Grandkids,

There is an expression which says "One man's food is another man's poison." We had been in Congo not quite a year when we had an experience that reminded us of that saying.

Directly across the red dirt road from our house at Banza Manteke lay the schoolgirls' dormitories called Logani. Mary was from Logan, West Virginia, and her church had provided funds to build these dorms. They weren't as fancy as dorms in the United States, but they were adequate for the girls. They had wooden bunk beds and places for the girls to store their meager belongings. They did their cooking and eating outside over charcoal fires. Each day, the girls swept the hard-packed earth in their *lupangu* (courtyard) to keep it clean and free from trash.

One afternoon, we heard loud wailing and crying and, looking out our windows, we saw the younger girls running from their dorms "lock, stock, and barrel." Or, more realistically, sleeping mat, suitcase, and cooking pot. What could have upset them, we wondered? We had better investigate.

It was early fall, a few weeks before the rains started, and the men had set fire to the surrounding countryside in preparation for the women to plant their manioc gardens. The fire blazed behind the dorms, and although there was no danger to the girls, the younger ones were frightened. Assured that their dorms were safe, the girls gradually moved back, a bit embarrassed for their hastiness. Since the fire had covered quite a large area, we walked across the road to see what was happening. New missionaries are curious!

We walked out into the burned countryside. By now the fires had died out and only the blackened earth remained. Even through our shoes we felt the heat from the ground, but the swarms of barefoot school kids didn't seem to notice. All the children had some sort of digging tool: hoe, machete, stick or club. We soon learned they were after any 'game' that had escaped the fire. Mainly rats and mice had escaped, for they lived in tunnels under ground.

With an assortment of digging tools, the kids dug into the burrows in hope of capturing a critter before it could escape. Years of learning to cope in their environment had taught the Congolese a nifty way to assure trapping the rodents before they could get away. Several students had narrow, tubelike devices (about thirty-six inches long), a *kimpuku,* woven from reeds and grasses. It looked similar to a cane except it was hollow inside. The top was closed, but the bottom was open and a bit wider, something like a funnel. Digging furiously into the burrow, the *kimpuku* was popped over the hole when the rats or mice tried to escape. The clubs were used to clobber the hapless animal should it escape the funnel. Not only were schoolchildren enjoying this sport, but several women as well. Some had their youngest baby tied securely to their back.

Spirits were high, and there was lots of competition and laughter to see who could have the most rats or mice jammed into their *kimpuku*. What were they going to do with them we wondered? Well, there was some good eating in the dorms that night! Now lest you be turned off by this admission, we were told that never, ever would anyone eat a rat that had been killed in a house, for they were dirty. Rats and mice in the fields ate only seeds and grain, so they were clean and safe. Made sense . . . but still . . .

We were curious and wondered how this protein on the evening menu would be prepared and asked a high school student. They would singe off the hair, slit the stomach, remove the intestines, and then roast them on a stick, he said. And then, he had a question for us.

"How do you fix them in your country?"

"Well, um, . . . uh, . . . I guess we don't know how good they are."

Our student looked as though he thought we were missing a real treat.

It's easy for us to go to the store to buy any meat we might want, but people who live in developing countries are not that fortunate. Protein deficient people eat whatever is available. Even though we had been in Congo less than a year, we learned an important lesson that day: don't be critical of customs and habits that differ from yours, for there are good reasons for them. Once when Grandpa offered a rabbit to his head teacher, the man refused saying his tribe didn't eat rabbit. Many North Americans think rabbit is delicious. We tend to eat what our culture dictates.

While out in the fields watching the students dig for rodents we noticed there were a lot of toadstool-shaped termite hills. Some were eighteen inches to two feet high and eight to ten inches in diameter. Grandpa says the small ones make dandy stools to sit on when you're hunting. Although not symmetrical, the inside of the hill is similar to that of a bee hive. The ants were in various stages of development from egg, partial egg/partial ant, edible winged ants, fully developed black ones, and the queen herself. As a queen, she was pretty ugly—a large white creature with a body like a grub, but head and front legs like an ant. This queen would win no beauty contests. The eggs were the size of a grain of rice, and the minute we turned the ant hills over, each big black soldier ant picked up an egg and went underground with it. Fascinating to watch!

The grasslands around Banza Manteke held much more valuable game than rodents and termite hills. There were also buffalo, antelope, and wild pig in the grassland. African buffalo, which are called Cape buffalo, are not wooly like our American bison. After hunting with some Congolese, Grandpa came home unhappy one morning as he had just missed a shot at an antelope. Earlier he had shot a buffalo, but though the bullets hit their mark, he claimed it grinned at him and ran away. Long after that incident, the Congolese referred to the animal as Tata Sharp's buffalo. Cape buffalo are mean, and the men said that a wounded animal was dangerous; it could circle around from behind and attack. In places, the grass was fifteen feet tall, and as the men burned it, the animals ran out, giving the hunters opportunity to provide meat for their families.

We were learning lots of interesting things about life in Congo, especially in regard to diet. Most of their food we thoroughly enjoyed and had no problem eating. But hey, how 'bout ordering pizza for supper?

Till next time . . .
G'ma and G'pa

It Never Rains But It Pours

Dear Grandchildren,

Have you ever had a time in your young lives when you thought things couldn't get worse, but then they did? We had a weekend like that after we had been in Congo only one year. Living at Banza Manteke on a bush mission station was a bit restrictive at times. It was always nice to get away to see and do something different. Once a month, Grandpa had to go to the bank in Matadi to get payroll for the teachers and station workmen. Steven and I usually went along. Each time, the jolting three-hour drive over bumpy, dusty roads (and just as long and bumpy and dusty on the return trip), dimmed in my memory and I was ready to go again. Traveling on Congo roads was a jarring experience!

Sometimes we traveled by train. Twenty-five miles from Banza Manteke was Lufu, one of several railroad villages between the mission station and Leopoldville. The railroad was another link to the outside world. Though not far away, it took nearly an hour to drive to Lufu. That was where we sent and received the weekly mail sack for the station. Once a week, we sent a meat order to Kolo, another village on the railroad. Building supplies and other materials reached us by rail. It also connected us to the port city of Matadi to the south and to the capital city of Leopoldville to the north.

Gini was the missionary nurse at Banza Manteke. There was no longer a doctor at our station, and she was responsible for running the hospital with Congolese staff. Grandpa, Steven, Gini, and I intended to catch the train at Lufu and ride it to Kimpese where there was a large hospital. Grandpa and Gini planned to have their eyes checked by an eye specialist who was volunteering his services in Congo for two weeks. This hospital was a joint medical effort of American, British, and Swedish missionaries. I looked forward to going to Kimpese and seeing some of our colleagues.

An hour before we were to leave to catch the train, Tata Hezekiah, a nurse, informed Gini that the wife of one of the station workmen had delivered one baby the day before but was unable to deliver its twin. It was now twenty-four hours later. Since there was no doctor at our station, we quickly changed our plans and took the mother to Kimpese in the hospital ambulance (a small Ford pickup truck). There were doctors at Kimpese. It was a two-hour drive over bumpy, rutted, dusty roads. Gini was prepared to deliver the baby en route to Kimpese, but eventually the mother gave birth to the twin, a nice healthy baby, at the Kimpese hospital.

The next day, before returning to Banza Manteke, we stopped at the hospital to pick up some medicines. We were surprised to see Nurse Hezekiah, and Nkubi, the Congolese chauffeur (driver). They had brought a woman who had been unable to give birth in her village. Her family had taken her to Banza Manteke, but she needed a doctor's attention. Sadly, by the time the mother arrived at Kimpese it was too late to save her baby. We switched vehicles with Nkubi and Hezekiah, and they started back to Banza Manteke in the ambulance. With them were the newborn twins, their mother, and family members who had gone with her to Kimpese. We planned to stay overnight at Kimpese and return home the following day in the van.

A few kilometers from the Kimpese hospital was a pastors and teachers training school where colleagues invited us to spend the day. Phil and Rose suggested a picnic at Vampa Falls on the Bangu, a prospect too good to resist. While no one who lives in the Rocky Mountains would consider the Bangu a mountain, it rises one or two thousand feet above the surrounding countryside and is considered a mountain by everyone around. Its flat top reminded me of Grand Mesa, visible from my home in western Colorado.

Hiking through the tall elephant grass, we came to a swinging bridge several feet above a stream. With good reason it was called a swinging bridge—every step we took that bridge swung back and forth! Made of vines and tree limbs, it was a flimsy-looking structure at best and certainly didn't inspire much confidence as the way to cross from one side of the stream to the other. Safely across, I was glad to put my feet on firm ground once more. On that side of the stream were huge rocks and boulders where the water from the falls above tumbled into a deep pool. What a marvelous place to swim! Grandpa, remembering his youthful days swinging from grapevines in Kansas, cut a vine to the desired length. Then he and Phil courageously swung out over the water, and with Tarzan-like yells let loose of it and dropped into the pool. What fun! Steven had just celebrated his fourth birthday, and he and his friend Doug played in the water to their hearts' content.

It was time for lunch and folks were getting hungry. The "Boy Scouts" in the group gathered sticks for a fire. Canned hot dogs don't compare with those we buy today in grocery stores, but even tinned ones were tasty roasted over coals. Hot dogs and potato salad were delicious. While we were eating, the blue, blue sky overhead began to darken, the clouds opened, and the rain poured. No way could a tropical rainstorm dampen our spirits! We transferred our fire underneath a rocky ledge, crawled under it and continued to eat our lunch and sing together.

It was a short rain, and when the blue sky returned we hiked three hundred yards upstream to view the beautiful falls where the water plummets down from the top of the Bangu. A long, moss-covered boulder sloped into the water making a wonderful slippery slide. Time and again we slid down the boulder, only to go back and do it all over again. Dripping wet from our swim, we hiked back to the mission station, crossing the flimsy bridge one more time. It had been a great afternoon of fun and satisfied our desire to have a break from our usual daily responsibilities.

After the concern for the two mothers giving birth and not knowing that the next twenty-four hours would bring even more disturbing events, picnic and swimming at the Bangu were a wonderful time of relaxation. That good time was sandwiched between two days of serious incidents.

I'll tell you about them in the next letter.

Till then—love you,
G'ma and G'pa

The Saga Continues

Dear Grandchildren,

In the last letter I told you there were more things that happened that weekend that made it one we would never forget. The story goes on . . .

Sunday, after attending morning worship service and eating lunch with our friends at Kimpese, we jolted our way home to Banza Manteke. Sixteen miles from the mission station, we came upon an accident. It was a Ford pickup truck . . . the hospital ambulance! Nkubi and Hezekiah were taking the mother and twins home when a Portuguese driver in a five ton truck rounded a curve and plowed into the little pickup. Its windshield was knocked out, both the fenders and left front door demolished. Although the woman's husband and older daughter had head wounds, the mother and babies were lying unhurt on a stretcher. What a traumatic experience for the newborns. We thanked God no one was seriously injured.

Meanwhile, in our absence, things were happening at Banza Manteke. With only a twenty-four hours' notice, forty former students descended on the station to welcome back their former teacher. He had just returned to Banza Manteke after studying four years at a university in Belgium. On a bush station there are no motels nor restaurants, no stores of any kind to accommodate travelers. Where would they sleep? Where—and what—could they eat?

There had been a heavy rain, the muddy road was slippery, and the travelers arrived after dark. Of the six missionaries living on the station only Mary was there that weekend. Being very resourceful, she rallied support from the teachers, who found places for everyone to sleep. But they still had to eat.

On the road to Lufu lies the village of Kitomesa. Surely there would be bread for sale at the little store. A few of the teachers ventured out on the muddy road, but when they arrived at Kitomesa, they discovered the store had sold all the bread earlier. Mary did the next best thing. She made pancakes. Dozens of pancakes. It took a lot of them to satisfy the appetites of forty hungry Congolese.

While Mary was in the kitchen making pancakes Martin and Ruth returned from Leopoldville with devastating news. The government had cut off money to pay teachers' salaries for several of our schools. Among them were those on the Bangu. The Belgian school inspector had paid a surprise visit and found two of the teachers gone and only half the students in class. This was a serious situation since government subsidies paid the teachers' salaries.

By the time we arrived home, Mary had supper waiting for us (not pancakes!), and we learned all that had happened while we were gone. In one weekend, there had been two medical emergencies, the ambulance pickup had been in an accident, the government had withdrawn its financial support from some of our schools, and forty former students had arrived at the station needing lodging and meals for the night. Surely that was enough excitement for one weekend. What more could go wrong? We were soon to find out.

While we were eating, we heard someone gently cough outside the door followed by *kokoko* (hello). A man stood there reporting that he had brought a fellow who had been injured that morning in a hunting accident. He was at the hospital waiting to see Nurse Gini. She examined him and discovered the shot had gone into his buttocks and lodged in the groin. Obviously, the man needed to see a doctor. We would have to return to Kimpese.

Soon we were on the road again, driving the injured man and his friend over the same bumpy road we had traveled just a few hours earlier. We awakened the doctor who said to take the man to the hospital. Finding a bed for the patient was not easy as all the beds were occupied at that time. A Congolese nurse found a patient who had recuperated enough that he could be moved elsewhere (on the floor, actually), and his bed was given to the injured man. Sometimes it was necessary to do things like that.

In the morning, Dr. Glenn operated and found a little treasure of grass and tiny stones that had been blown into the gunshot wounds. The man's bladder had also been pierced, but it could be repaired. We left the man in stable condition, though he might need a blood transfusion. We were so thankful for the hospital and caring medical staff, for without proper treatment he would have died.

The return trip to Banza Manteke the next morning was uneventful. That is, until we arrived at the site of the ambulance accident. The badly damaged Ford pickup was no longer there. Another van had been sent from Banza Manteke and had picked up the mother, babies, new father and their daughter. They had returned to the station. The accident had to be investigated by the territorial agent who had come from Kenge, which was halfway to Matadi. The Portuguese driver lied that he had run into the pickup. Our driver had returned to the station, and the agent was quite irate. He insisted that our chauffeur meet him at Kenge no later than 2:00 PM that afternoon.

Now we had a new problem. For various reasons none of the station vehicles were available, yet the Banza Manteke chauffeur had to be at Kenge by 2:00 o'clock. The only vehicle left on the station was the ambulance. It would run, even if it didn't have brakes or lights. He would have to drive it. In the meantime, we returned to the station. By seven o'clock, we were concerned that the driver hadn't returned from Kenge to meet with the territorial agent. Remember, the ambulance he was driving was without brakes, lights, a windshield, and had a caved-in door.

After fixing sandwiches and a thermos of coffee, Grandpa and I set out in the rain to search for them. On the other side of Lufu we found them creeping along the muddy road, the pickup's lights no brighter than candles. We drove down the road to turn around—and got stuck in the mud on a hill. The Lord proved his faithfulness by sending several men out in the rain to push us out. We returned safe and sound to the station thankful to be home again. It had been a long weekend. You might even call it Congo's version of a soap opera.

The next morning Grandpa took the battery from the van and sent it to the five-ton station truck which was stranded at the Lunionzo River. The truck had been sent out to buy lumber, but on the return trip it had run out of gas. Now its battery was dead as well. Arriving back at Banza Manteke with the lumber, the truck then drove to Lufu to buy rice for the school children. With forty extra people on the station over the weekend, there was nothing to feed the children. The cupboards were bare!

With everything that had happened, we found the words in Matthew 6:8 very true: "Your Father knows what you need before you ask him." In spite of all the calamities of an action-packed weekend, he supplied everything we needed to face each situation with strength, compassion, and humor. We hope your weekend will be calm and uneventful!

Love you,
G'ma and G'pa

"Bingo, Bango, Bongo"—We're Trav'lin' in the Congo

Dear Mireille, Matt, Aaron, Nicole, Zach and Kalli,

It was February, and we were well into the short, dry season. It was hot, and there wouldn't be any rain for a few weeks. We had been in Congo almost a year and a half when senior missionary Martin invited us to make a trip with him to the Bangu to examine village schools. Along with evangelism, education was a high priority in our mission work. To enable young people to compete for jobs, education was a must. For church members to grow in their knowledge of God's love and plan for their lives, being able to read the Bible was equally important. Throughout the mission, adult literacy classes were held for those who had never had the opportunity to go to school.

Life at Banza Manteke was "very daily" as one of our colleagues often remarked, and we looked forward to the change of pace. Steven was four years old, too young to be helpful in school inspections. Colleagues Rose and Phil, who had a son Steven's age, invited him to spend the week with them. We settled him with Doug at Kimpese and left on the six-day trip.

When we weren't bouncing and jolting our way to the Bangu over a narrow, rutted, dusty road, we enjoyed spectacular scenery. Lush green hills dotted with darker green forests were before us. Even in dry season, the countryside was beautiful.

"Look for antelope and monkeys as you drive," we were told, "and if you're really lucky you might see an elephant." That sounded exciting, something to write home about! Surely there were animals just waiting for us to find them. Surely we would see that elusive elephant. Although we scanned the horizon for signs of wild life, the only creature that resembled any was a *ngwadi*, similar to a guinea fowl, as it scurried down the road in front of us. How disappointing!

We slept the first night at Mukimbungu, formerly a Swedish mission station, where there was an upper elementary grade school. Touring the station, we came upon a small cemetery, the gravesite of fourteen missionaries and children who had died many years earlier. In the days before sulfa, penicillin, and especially malaria medicine, death took its toll of both missionary personnel and Congolese. We were glad to sleep under mosquito nets that night. The mosquitoes were fearsome.

While Martin inspected schools the next morning, Grandpa and I studied Kikongo. Preparing lesson plans in French so that we could teach our classes at Banza Manteke left almost no time for language study. To be free from classroom teaching was just what we needed. While we tried to learn the difference between saying *luka* (to go up, as a mountain) and *luka* (to throw up, vomit), Martin questioned the teachers about their responsibilities.

Evidently a new missionary, preaching about Jesus climbing a mountain to teach his followers, mispronounced *luka*. A few giggles, mingled with looks of disbelief greeted the unfortunate preacher. How could Jesus vomit a mountain, they wondered? We weren't anxious to make similar mistakes. We wanted people to understand us and not snicker because we mispronounced words. Naturally, we made our share of mistakes over the years, (and people did snicker on occasion), but folks genuinely appreciated our efforts to speak to them in their language. They were very forgiving of our mistakes.

Meanwhile, as we worked to improve our language skills, Martin talked with the teachers. Were the students attending classes regularly?

Did the younger children have slates and slate pencils? Why were there so few girls in school? Had the villagers made enough desks for the children? No child had one to himself. Three children crowded into space meant for two. The desks they had were crude by our standards as they were made by village men. Cutting a tree down first and sawing it into planks to be made into furniture took a lot of time and energy. Were the teachers keeping lesson plans to present to the Belgian school inspector when he came? Government subsidies depended upon each school's evaluation by the inspector.

Some school buildings were built of red clay bricks, as was this one at Mukimbungu. The villagers had used the dirt in their area to make sturdy classrooms for the children. In poor villages, the schools were crudely built of local materials: sticks, mud and grass. With a dirt floor and thatch roof to keep out the sun and rain, the schools were nothing like the beautiful buildings you are privileged to attend. Can you imagine plywood painted black for a chalkboard? A dusty rag for the eraser? Even chalk was scarce and had to be carefully hoarded. No child had the luxury of textbooks. Teachers wrote lesson material on the blackboard. The children then copied it onto their slates or into thin notebooks. Unless they attended classes on a mission station where schools were built of permanent materials, the facilities were quite primitive.

In the morning, we awakened to the aroma of coffee brewing. Tata Ngila, the Engwalls' cook who always traveled with Martin, was fixing breakfast. Now, with the school inspection completed, it was time to say *sala mbote* (good-bye) to our hosts and move on to the next village—but not before the school boys gave us a royal send off. They had decorated the van with red hibiscus blossoms and brilliant orange and yellow flowers from the flamboyant tree. Then they gaily waved us on our way. Had anyone written "Just Married" on the van we would have looked the part!

As the trip had just started, we'll have more to tell you in the next letter.

Till then, G'ma and G'pa

We're Still Trav'lin'

Dear Grandchildren,

From Bidi to Mamianga, from Kasi to Nsala Kimoko—"far away places with strange sounding names"—those were all villages where we stopped to examine schools. It was extremely rare to meet other cars or trucks on the way. As we drove through villages, barefoot children ran out to chorus: *Tala mundele! Tala mundele!* (Look at the white person!) If I had a dollar for every time I heard that the years we were in Africa, I would be a rich grandma today! Some people might find it tedious and monotonous to drive on narrow dirt roads from one village to another inspecting schools, but not Grandpa and I. We didn't like the bumpy roads, but we were meeting courageous people who were using their limited resources to the best of their ability.

The villagers dealt with a variety of problems. A school had not received government financial aid, but the local people had worked hard to bring it up to standard. Could they now request subsidies to help them pay the teacher? Another school had to be closed as there was a serious moral problem with the teacher. What would happen to the children who had no place to go for further education? Could teachers be juggled around so classes would be covered? Most of these schools were built by the local church people who also assumed responsibility for paying the teacher. If a school met government requirements and could be subsidized, it helped ease the villagers need to dip into their own meager resources to support the teacher's salary.

People were unfailingly kind and generous, moving out of their homes so we might have a place to sleep, providing water for drinking and bathing. The hard packed village dirt was swept clean each morning (women's and girls' work), and the villagers were genuinely glad to see us. No doubt our presence was a bright spot in their day to day sameness.

Some of the villages were nestled in a small forest where nearly every home had banana, mango and *nsafu* trees (a local fruit that I can't describe because it tastes like nothing you've ever eaten). More prosperous looking homes were built from red dirt bricks, while others were made from the usual bamboo and thatch. In one village, the pastor and his wife graciously vacated their mud brick house with cement floor and thatch roof for our comfort. Congolese are a generous people and are known for their hospitality.

Our mission had begun work in this area many years earlier, and although we were new, Martin Engwall, our senior missionary, was well-known. Driving from village to village, men working on the roads and women hoeing in their manioc gardens would stop to call, "*Aiee! Tata Engwalli! Yandi kwandi!*" (It's him!)

Each evening, villagers and missionaries gathered together for a time of worship and praise, sometimes in the little mud brick church lighted by a kerosene pressure lantern, sometimes outside under the stars, our only light coming from a campfire. Martin preached in Kikongo, and it was said his pronunciation of the language was so correct that people could not tell a foreigner was speaking. That couldn't be said of Grandpa and me, but even so, people appreciated our efforts to speak their language. Grandpa prayed in Kikongo and I read scripture from the Bible which had been translated years earlier into Kikongo. Later, sitting around the fire, palavers were settled. Matters of church discipline, building a school, and hiring teachers were items of concern to the villagers.

Even though we rarely met another vehicle, one morning, on our way to another village, we came upon an accident which had happened a day and a half earlier. A seven-ton truck with its too heavy load of manioc, tomatoes and bananas lay overturned on the road, the produce rotting in the hot, tropical sun. Several passengers who had been riding atop the load managed to jump off the truck before it overturned. The driver, now in the hospital in Leopoldville, had started up a hill, but the truck was so heavily loaded it began to roll back and he lost control. Had it not been for so much weight, it could have rolled down the hillside into a ravine. Trucks were always excessively crammed with people and things, but other than walking a hot dusty trail, there was no way for village folks to get themselves or their produce to market.

Arriving at the village of Paza, we drove to a home where Martin had stayed previously. Maybe we could stay there again. However Plan A was quickly switched to Plan B, for directly across the road a woman lay dying. Mourners were arriving and, although she was still alive, wailing had begun. There would be no sleep for us that night. Someone else offered their home, a stuccoed cement house with dirt floor. Soon our camp cots and mosquito nets were set up, and Tata Ngila, Martin's cook, was preparing supper.

That evening under a beautiful Congo moon and star-filled sky, we sat around a campfire singing and praying with our village friends. They didn't need hymn books; they knew all the words by heart, their rich voices filling the night air in praise. Men sat on chairs brought from their homes, while the women sat on low stools or reed mats on the ground. Each village had a church building, but it was much pleasanter to be outside in the cool night air gathered around the fire, sharing our faith with one another. At one village where I was not present, a woman asked Martin if Tata Sharp (your grandpa) had given birth yet! We thought that was a quaint way to ask if he had any children.

Someplace along the way, the van picked up a nail in a tire and it went flat. Your grandpa had changed and repaired many a tire on occasion, but Tata Ngila was anxious to help. Grandpa changed the tire, then handing Ngila a wrench, asked him to tighten the bolts. Happy to oblige, he did as requested, and we were soon on our way again. En route to the next village we heard a loud knocking noise. Grandpa got out and checked but could find nothing wrong. The noise continued. Grandpa checked again.

Finally, the noise was so loud we knew something was seriously wrong. It sounded as though the van was going to fall apart. That time Grandpa discovered that the rear wheel was about to fall off! Unfortunately, he hadn't realized he should have checked Ngila's work to be sure that the bolts had been tightened properly. One of them had broken off the rim and the others were all chewed up. God protected us from what could have been a serious accident. Poor Tata Ngila! He was a much better cook than auto mechanic!

At Nsala Kimoko, we inspected a regional school that was in good condition with adequate teaching staff and materials for its 250 students, mostly boys. Students came to this school from nearby villages, some living with relatives in Nsala Kimoko during the week, and others walking daily to school from their villages. Martin planned to send us to examine schools in two nearby villages, but it would have meant a long walk uphill and down in hot sun to reach them as there were no roads. We used the time to study Kikongo instead.

Kimbanza, a rather dirty and untidy looking village, was the last stop of our five hundred kilometer, six-day trip It took time before it was decided where we should stay, and a house was swept out so we could set up our camp cots and mosquito netting. A Motel 6 would have been nice at that point! Like many others, that evening was spent around the campfire singing and sharing our faith and listening to palavers. Some girls asked us to teach them a song. The only one we knew in Kikongo at that time was "In My Heart there Rings a Melody." We sang it until everyone knew it.

It had been a busy day and we were tired, ready to get under our mosquito nets and go to sleep. The house had no door, and there were many interested onlookers who followed us. Imagine all those little eyes peering at us through the slats in the bamboo, all that whispering going on as the children noted our every move! Although they didn't mean to be impolite it was a bit irksome. Wanting some semblance of privacy we hung a blanket over the doorway. Shivering would be preferable to having the whole world watch us sleep! Finally, a kind woman came to our rescue, placed a sleeping mat over the opening and shooed the children away. And so to bed.

It was time to return to Banza Manteke. Visiting in the villages, we learned more about the Congolese people in those six days than we did in six weeks on the mission station. We had seen them go out of their way to extend hospitality by moving out of their homes so the three of us would have a place to sleep. We had seen their sincere appreciation for the gifts of clothing Martin gave to those who had befriended us. We had witnessed their joy as we visited and sang around the campfire. We had seen others place their faith in Christ and pledge themselves to follow him. Our ears were more attuned to the Kikongo language. It had been a memorable week.

Driving back to Banza Manteke, a man, live chicken in hand, flagged us down. Could we give him a ride to Lufu, he queried? We said yes and to hop in. Then he presented us with the chicken. Better to wait until permission was granted than to risk losing both the chicken and transportation!

A few hours later we arrived at Kimpese, delighted to see our four-year-old again. In spite of being busy every minute, we had missed him. Steven and Doug had had a good time playing together, that is, until Doug developed mumps. Now we had something else to look forward to!

Love you all,
G'ma and G'pa

Independence

There's Trouble Brewing

Dear Grandchildren,

It happened while we were on home assignment in the States. In January 1959, there was rioting in Leopoldville, the capital city of the Belgian Congo. The Congolese were insisting that Belgium grant them the right to self-government. All over Africa, there was serious unrest as more and more countries demanded independence from the European nations which had colonized them. Independence was coming to Africa, ready or not. In the 1800s, Belgium had colonized Congo and now the Congolese were demanding they have the right to govern themselves. Their determination sparked the riots. Ultimately, Belgium agreed to grant independence and set June 30, 1960 as the date.

There was a lot of tension during the eighteen months prior to independence. Would the transition from colony to self-government go smoothly? Would there be serious problems? Everyone was nervous and concerned about what might happen. Many people did not understand what independence meant, but they knew they wanted their share of it. Political parties were organized along tribal lines as each group worked to get their people elected to positions of leadership and authority.

In the weeks preceding independence, there were numerous festivities to herald this important occasion. There was to be a grand celebration in the stadium and the Protestant young people wanted a piece of the action. With youth leaders representing the different church groups, it was decided some of the missionaries would teach the young people to dance the Texas Star. This was quite an undertaking for kids who had never square danced. While dance was a part of Congolese culture, square dancing was not. (After independence, we were scolded by some of our leaders. We didn't need to teach them to dance, they said, they know how to do that.) We borrowed records from the United States Information Service (USIS) and we were in business. For several weeks the kids practiced allemande left, do-si-do and all the other calls . . . and got hopelessly mixed-up. At times, we wondered if they would ever learn, but eventually they got the hang of it and were ready to perform.

On the day of the parade, along with many other groups, five hundred young people representing Protestant youth marched into Tata Raphael Stadium. And two hundred of them made quite a stir when the music came on as they ran onto the field to perform the Texas Star. The boys were dressed in white shirts and black denim jeans, called Flamys, and the girls wore white blouses and brightly colored full skirts. As a gift from Bata shoe factory, all the dancers wore tennis shoes, the kids' one request for this important event. They danced their way through the different calls and had a great time. The folks in the stands clapped loudly when the young people finished and ran back to the bleachers. This was indeed a festive occasion.

But there were troubles ahead. Although the election for a president and cabinet went smoothly, there was still much unrest. In the next letter I'll tell you about a bizarre incident which Grandpa and Steven witnessed when they went to a parade.

Love you all,
G'ma and G'pa

The Calm before the Storm

Dear Brenner and Sharp Grandkids,

Congo's election had taken place peacefully and the newly independent country now had its first president, Joseph Kasavubu. As part of the festivities, there was to be a parade downtown. King Baudouin, king of the Belgians, and President Kasavubu of the Democratic Republic of the Congo, would stand together as they rode in a convertible. King Baudouin had come to free the country from colonial rule and turn it over to the newly elected government. Great throngs of people lined the street to witness the king and president riding together. Grandpa and Steven were part of that crowd.

The convertible approached with the king and president, and Grandpa, poised to take a picture of this history-making event, stepped into the street. Just at that moment an exuberant Congolese snatched King Baudouin's ceremonial sword and ran down the street with it! *Life World Library* captured that picture which is recorded in *Tropical Africa*, page 156. Grandpa recorded it too, but unfortunately his film was lost during the army revolt that plunged the new nation into chaos a few days later. In *Tropical Africa*, however, Grandpa's head is visible as he snaps his picture. Not recorded in the picture is Steven, who was there nonetheless, standing on the curb waiting for his dad to come back from the photo op.

While no one knew what might happen at independence, all of us were committed to carrying on our work as normally as possible. As June 30 had passed without incident, the three cooperating mission groups

(Presbyterian, British Baptist, American Baptist—we had worked together teaching the young people to dance the Texas Star) decided to go ahead with plans to hold a youth camp at Bibwa. This was a campsite near a village of the same name thirty-five miles outside the city.

Camp Bibwa had none of the conveniences of camps in the United States. The young people slept in tents, their sleeping mats on the ground. Respecting Congolese culture, they bathed in a nearby stream, girls at one time, boys at another. They carried water up the hill from the stream, and all cooking was done outside over wood fires.

It took a lot of rice and mackerel, bananas and bread, milk powder, tea and sugar to feed this large group of hungry teenagers. As food supplies were getting low, Grandpa and I volunteered to drive into town and buy what was needed. Mulueme, one of the Congolese youth leaders, accompanied us. We left Steven, eight years old at the time, in camp with the young people. Susan went with us. She was three years old.

En route to town we noticed a few vehicles abandoned along the road. We wondered why they had flat tires and shattered windshields, but we weren't greatly concerned. After all, things were calm.

We soon learned that just the opposite was true.

In our next letter we'll tell you what was happening.

Till then, much love,
G'ma and G'pa

The Storm Breaks

Dear Grandchildren,

It was at Limete, the area of Leopoldville where the Presbyterians worked, that Grandpa and I first learned disturbing news. During the night, the army had revolted against their Belgian officers at Thysville (today called Banza Ngungu), a small town thirty miles from Leopoldville where there was an army camp. While Belgian Congo had received its independence from Belgium, none of the Congolese soldiers had been promoted in rank and they were angry. They wanted their independence, too. The country might have a president, they said, but the army still had its Belgian officers. Just barely a week after a calm turnover in leadership, the army revolt threatened the fragile peace. Within a few days, there were army revolts throughout the country.

We were concerned about driving across town to our mission headquarters. With so many uncertainties, should we risk trying to get to our home? A telephone call to our mission headquarters advised us to stay where we were, buy what we needed in Limete and return to camp. We bought the necessary food supplies, and then started back to Bibwa with our youth leader. Someone gave us an American flag to display in case there should be any problem. We didn't want anyone to think we were Belgians!

There was little traffic on the road as we drove back to camp. But suddenly we were stopped by soldiers at a roadblock. There had been none when we drove to town a few hours earlier. When we explained about the camp, the soldiers lifted the barrier waving us on through. A few miles later, we came upon a second roadblock. More soldiers. More explanations from us and again we were allowed to continue toward camp.

About ten miles from Bibwa, we came to the Ndjili airport and a third roadblock. These soldiers acted mean and threatening as they held their guns on us. We were ordered out of the car at bayonet point. Sent to Ndjili to guard the airport, they had been drinking and everyone talked at once. No one would listen to us. And they certainly were not impressed with the American flag. Our friend Mulueme tried to explain in Lingala about the youth camp as did Grandpa in Kikongo. Finally, a Kikongo-speaking soldier from the Sona Bata area where one of our mission stations was located, explained to the others that we were missionaries. We were there to help the people, he said, and told the others to let us go. With grateful hearts for God's protection, we got back in the car and returned to camp. Thankfully, although Susan was only three years old, she was not upset by the loud voices, guns, bayonets, and confusion.

It was almost dusk. Cheers and shouts were raised as we drove into camp. Shortly after we left for town that morning, men from the village of Bibwa, hearing the radio report about the army revolt, came to advise everyone to stay in camp. The youth leaders protected Steven from this news, telling him that we might be delayed in getting back, but he could sleep in the tent with them. For an eight-year-old this was heady stuff! It would be far more exciting to sleep in the tent with the big boys than to sleep with Dad and Mom in theirs. To the music of drums and whistles, all the campers snake-danced and sang around the campfire and flagpole, thankful that we had returned safely.

Yes, Steven did get to sleep in the youth leaders' tent while Grandpa, Susan, and I spent a miserable night battling mosquitoes and tried to sleep in the station wagon. July in Congo is the dry season, the coolest time of the year. Because it was chilly, Susan was wearing her nearly outgrown sleeper pajamas which gapped between the top and bottoms. The next morning she had a solid band of mosquito bites, in front and in back, where those insects had feasted while she tried to sleep. Thankfully, God protected her from a bad case of malaria.

Sometime during the night, a jeepload of soldiers drove into our camp, perhaps to see if we had told them the truth earlier, perhaps to see if we were hiding anyone. Because they had been drinking, we knew they could be unpredictable. Our camp was too near the airport for comfort. In the morning, after discussing the situation with the other missionaries and youth leaders, it seemed wise to break camp and send everyone home. It was a disappointment to all of us, for they were a nice group of young people with leadership abilities which they would put to good use in their local churches.

Although we were a bit anxious about the possibility of encountering roadblocks on our way back to town, it was a relief to return home safely without soldiers stopping us. Driving past Ndjili airport, we could see the Russian aircraft which had brought the Soviet delegation to the independence celebrations.

There's more to tell, but it will have to wait for the next letter.

Love,
G'ma and G'pa

Things Only Get Worse

Dear Grandkids,

We were thankful to be back in our home, safe and sound after the experience with the soldiers while we were camping with the young people. There was a great deal of tension as everyone wondered whether we would be able to stay and continue our work. We wanted to stay if at all possible.

As you know, our mission station was situated on the banks of the Congo River overlooking Stanley Pool, today called Ngaliema Bay. On one side was CHANIC, the Belgian shipbuilding company where riverboats were made. Its Belgian director and family lived on the other side of mission property. As the political situation worsened and people continued to flee the country, the CHANIC director offered guns to the missionaries to protect themselves. The general secretary for the mission declined, explaining that our work would be finished if we ever took up arms against the very people we had come to work with and serve.

Several young children lived on the station and they were affected by all that was happening. The parents tried to keep everything as normal as possible, yet nothing was normal. Some of the kids played in the sandbox outside our house, while others spent happy hours creating Matchboxville from the little cars and vehicles that all of them owned. They were good at making their own entertainment.

Things were happening so fast it was hard to know what to do. In case we might have to suddenly leave the country, I packed a small suitcase with a change of clothing for each of us, plus a few food items in a basket. A few hours later, I told myself we would never have to leave—and put everything away. The next day it seemed wise to repack. Then again, I convinced myself it was unnecessary to prepare for a sudden departure, and the suitcase was unpacked a second time. Finally, I had the good sense to pack once more and leave things where they were. The uncertainty of the situation made it difficult to make a decision and stick with it.

In the midst of the unpredictable situation, there were some amusing moments. Our general secretary regularly cabled the mission headquarters in Valley Forge, Pennsylvania, to keep them aware of the situation. The headquarters then contacted the State Department in Washington, D.C. to learn what they knew about the conditions in Congo. Even the State Department wasn't sure what was happening. They in turn cabled the American Embassy in Leopoldville for information. It went full circle when some of their personnel came to the mission to find out what the missionaries knew that they didn't!

With things so uncertain, the station families felt it wise for everyone to sleep in the two-story house where we lived. Normally, there was a closed-off inside stairway separating the two floors which gave more privacy to the two families who shared the house. Now, the connecting door between the upstairs and downstairs was removed so that everyone might have easy access to either floor. The kids took advantage of this and had a ball. Running upstairs and down had never been such fun! While I don't remember where everyone slept nor how many of us there were, the Presbyterians from Limete accepted the invitation to join the Baptists, and we were all together our last forty-eight hours in Congo.

After the army revolt, most of the Europeans and Americans still living in Leopoldville, particularly women and children, hurriedly left the country. By now, the missionaries were the largest American group still in the city. We were trusting things would settle down and we could continue our work. In addition to those of us living in the capital, there were several families with young children working on our seven mission stations in the interior. There was twice-daily radio contact with them to keep everyone aware of the latest developments.

Barely a week after independence had been granted to the Belgian Congo, the army continued its rampage. Answering the office telephone one morning, Grandpa learned that soldiers who had lost a battle at the port city of Matadi heard there were white people at Nsona Mpangu (Banza Manteke). Assuming they were Belgians, a few of the soldiers made their way to the mission station where they rounded up all the missionaries, beat the men with rifle butts and molested some of the women. The Congolese were horrified at what was happening to their missionaries. Ironically, one of the teachers who had frequently given a lot of trouble, courageously defended the missionaries, telling the soldiers who they were and to stop abusing them. Finally the soldiers left.

Someone in the American Embassy called to say they had a helicopter ready to fly to Nsona Mpangu, but they needed someone who knew the area to go with them. As we had lived there our first two years in Congo, Grandpa said he could find the mission station from the air. He crossed the river by ferry to Brazzaville where a U.S. soldier, a reporter with Stars and Stripes, interviewed Grandpa regarding the reason for his going downcountry. He got into the waiting helicopter and the pilot took off, following the Congo River south toward Nsona Mpangu. Susan was only three years old, but she remembers my pointing to the helicopter as it flew from Brazzaville across the river, telling her that her daddy was up there.

Grandpa spotted familiar landmarks, then scanned the countryside until he saw the red roof of the Nsona Mpangu church. The pilot settled the helicopter down in a grassy area at the edge of the station. One of the missionaries ran from her house, waving her arms. The soldiers were gone, but in the few minutes it took the pilots to refuel, the missionaries quickly gathered their children and a small suitcase apiece and boarded the helicopter. One of the children was barely a week old, having been born June 30. Many of the Congolese were weeping as their missionaries flew away. It was a sad day for everyone.

During World War II, in the Philippines, the Japanese killed several of our missionaries and Filipino Christians who were protecting them when their hiding place was discovered. After that incident, our mission headquarters determined that never again would the lives of national Christians be endangered by protecting their missionaries. With this in mind and because of what happened at Nsona Mpangu, it was decided that we did not want to jeopardize the lives of our Congolese. We would return to America until the country was stable again. It was with heavy hearts that the decision was made, sad for the missionaries as well as the people with whom we worked.

Grandpa was still at Nsona Mpangu when those of us in Leopoldville were taken to the American Embassy. A large group had assembled there waiting for transportation to the port where we were ferried across the river to Brazzaville, the capital of French Equatorial Africa, today Republic of Congo. Thankfully, I had not unpacked that suitcase a third time! We left our home with clothes drying in the sunshine and our African gray parrot in its cage on the back porch. One of our resourceful colleagues, not wanting to leave her trumpet behind, stuffed underwear in its bell and layered herself with as many clothes as possible, removing a layer each day on the trip home. Another refused to leave his beloved cello behind and though it was bulky, he got it safely home to the States.

Brazzaville was abuzz with people fleeing Congo. Steven, Susan, and I spent the night in a Catholic school where cots had been hastily set up in a classroom. I remember it being very crowded and that the room was full of men. They had already sent their wives and children to Europe before the situation worsened. As the children and I had been separated from the other families from our mission station, it was comforting to find one of our families who had just arrived from the bush. At least we were in the same room with someone we knew. Meanwhile, Grandpa and the Nsona Mpangu people rescued by helicopter spent the night in a Catholic convent in Brazzaville.

Imagine the confusion of trying to provide food and water and bathroom facilities for several hundred people set adrift by the events that were happening in Congo. It seemed ages before we had anything to eat. When "supper" finally came, it was a small serving of cold macaroni with no cheese or meat sauce of any kind. Just plain, cold macaroni. Grandpa had gone downcountry without any water or lunch, and when he returned he was both hungry and thirsty. He remembers drinking the half glass of water he was given, then chided when he asked for more so he could take a malaria pill. All water had to be boiled. Things may not have been what we were used to, but we appreciated the efforts of those who were trying to meet the needs of this horde of people who had descended on them. We thanked God for his continued care and protection in a very tense situation.

Independence

The next day we found Grandpa . . . or maybe he found us . . . and we were thankful to be reunited. By now, several of our families from the upcountry stations had been rescued as well, and there were joyful reunions with our colleagues. The kids, hyperactive from the drastic change in their daily routines, had fun reconnecting with their friends as they ran and played in the school yard.

Now we waited. Would we be able to return to Congo? Would the situation there improve so that we could stay? What was happening to our many Congolese friends? We had so many questions.

There's more to come. . .

Love you, G'ma and G'pa

Home at Last!

Dear Grandchildren,

The decision had been made. We were going home, home to America. French military vehicles transported us to the Brazzaville airport where a US Air Force C-124 Globemaster waited to fly us back to the States. This huge, ungainly looking double-deck aircraft was a cargo plane, large enough to accommodate tanks or helicopters inside. Its unpadded, bucket seats were not built for comfort. Several of the kids visited the cockpit and were fascinated by all the instruments.

The Globemaster was a terribly noisy mode of travel, making it difficult to talk above the roar of the engines. Once, on liftoff somewhere on the trip home, crewmembers scrambled to get the open door set back in place. In the morning, we landed in Accra, Ghana. At the airport, we watched Ghanaian troops as they boarded planes that would take them to Congo as part of the United Nations efforts to restore order.

While in Accra, we had an amusing incident at the hotel where we stayed. At Brazzaville, Grandpa had bought two oil paintings with his remaining Congo money. One of the pictures was a market scene with elongated figures of women buying produce. We didn't want to damage the painting and took it out of the suitcase and propped it on the dresser in the hotel room. The teenage chamber boy checked it out from every possible angle. Then, quite seriously, he turned to us and inquired, "Ees dat peeple?" Evidently those tall, skinny figures didn't look like people to him!

People in Accra were very gracious to these refugee missionaries, taking us to church on Sunday, then treating us to an afternoon at the beach. While at Accra, two of our doctors decided to return to Congo, as they felt their services would be needed there.

Airborne again, the Globemaster flew us to Casablanca to another American airbase. En route to the States, most of our meals were C-rations—military fare. Due to the stress of the past several weeks, fatigue was catching up with me, and my memories of Morocco are hazy. About all I remember of that stop are the camels I saw in the distance, reminding me of Bible lands. Also, I remember being awakened from a deep sleep and told to hurry and get dressed because the plane was leaving shortly. It was pitch black outside and it was ages before we finally left. The strain was beginning to show when Lee fainted in the hotel lobby. Jerry was one of four men who stayed behind in Leopoldville to hold things together. Traveling alone with their six children, the youngest a toddler, was stressful for Lee.

Airborne again, our next flight took us to the Azores where this chain of islands in the mid-Atlantic was home to another U.S. airbase. We were treated royally and showered with attention. Laundry facilities were made available, television cameras captured us. We were given something to eat and a place to sleep. Steven remembers getting a real haircut (Grandpa was the family barber in Congo). Later he says they walked to the end of the runway to watch the sun set in the Atlantic Ocean.

In the Azores, people couldn't do enough for this large group of children who had flown into their airbase. The kids, plied with ice cream, candy and rich food, thoroughly enjoyed all the attention lavished on them. However, it had its price.

The next day, airborne once more, and on the final leg of the journey home, most of the children succumbed to airsickness. They were sick. Very sick. Kids were throwing up all over the place, and what was worse, it was running from the upper deck, through the cracks, down on folks below. A double-deck airplane is not the place for sick children! It was not a happy experience for children or parents. And especially not for those on the lower deck. A combination of excitement, rich food, and travel fatigue had finally caught up with our children. Steven says he waited to get sick until we arrived in Kansas City a week later.

We were almost home. God had cared for us during those tense days in Congo following independence, provided safe travel and caring people along the way, and (other than upset tummies) had kept any of us from being seriously ill on the trip back to the United States. Much as we hated to leave Congo, it was good to be back on American soil. The Globemaster landed us safely at Andrews Air Force Base in Washington, D.C. in early August.

In the past few weeks, Belgian Congo had received its independence followed by the army revolt just a few days later. We had been evacuated from the country, traveling from Leopoldville to Brazzaville, from Accra to Casablanca, and from the Azores to Andrews Air Force Base. We had been several days on the way, but now we were home.

The press and television crews, as well as the Red Cross, were on hand to welcome us. But before any of us were allowed to disembark, this rather bedraggled looking, smelly bunch of travelers suffered one final indignity. Men came on board and sprayed the aircraft. With all those sick children we had the fragrance of a zoo!

The Red Cross took us to a department store where everyone was able to purchase a change of clothing. As we had been permitted to board the Globemaster with only a small suitcase apiece and had been several days on the way, it was good to have something fresh again. The children were each given a small drawstring bag with a few toilet articles, notepad, pencil, etc., compliments of the Red Cross.

We were thankful to be citizens of a country that cared about us and provided the means to rescue us and bring us home safely—even if our government did later bill the mission headquarters thousands of dollars for our flight home!

After we returned home, people asked us how we felt during those tense days following independence. Living it, the experience didn't seem that bad. It wasn't until we arrived back in the States that I realized how serious the situation had been. Yet God was with us the entire time.

I was anxious to let Grandpa Stewart know we were home safe and sound. I telephoned him and said, "Dad, it's Marji. Guess where we are?" Very nonchalantly he replied, "You're in Washington, D.C., I suppose." He had been following the news from Congo on TV and knew all about our rescue!

It was good to be home again.

Love to each of you,
G'ma and G'pa

Seeing More of Africa

En route to Victoria Falls, Northern Rhodesia

Dear Mireille, Matt, Nicole, Aaron, Zach, and Kallianne,

After arriving in the United States following independence, we were home only six months when we looked forward to returning to Congo. We spent that time in California, then drove to Kansas to spend two weeks with your Great Grandma Sharp before boarding our flight back to Leopoldville. In that brief time, the situation worsened and International Ministries advised us to delay our return. We went back to California, and within a day or two, two things happened: Lumumba, the elected prime minister, was assassinated, and our Sabena flight crashed on landing in Brussels. We don't know why God spared our lives and not those of others, but we are grateful he gave us another twenty-six years to serve him in Congo. It was six months later before we were able to return.

Arriving back in Congo in June 1961, we were welcomed by our Congolese coworkers and, at the request of the pastors, established a Christian Center program. Some time during the cool, dry season, we tried to have a break in our responsibilities and go on vacation. Usually that was at another mission station, but one year we spent several days at Moanda on Congo's few miles of coastline. It was such a relaxing time we decided to return two years later.

Our reservations to return to Moanda fell through at the last moment. That was a big disappointment, for we loved being at the ocean where we could swim and relax. We liked to take long walks along the beach, fish, go on picnics, and bargain at the market for fresh fruit and vegetables. It was fun to swat crabs with beach towels as they scurried sideways and tried to dig themselves into the sand before we could nab them. As it turned out, we had a most wonderful vacation, not at a beach, not even in Congo. Our destination was Victoria Falls, on the border between Northern Rhodesia and Southern Rhodesia. Today they are known as Zambia and Zimbabwe.

It was a cloudy, dry season day in June 1964 when the Sharp and Clark families boarded the Sabena flight to Elizabethville (today's Lubumbashi) in southeastern Congo. Jim and June, our colleagues, and their three girls, Betty, Jeanie, and Sylvia, and we four Sharps were on our way to Victoria Falls, known by the Africans as "The Smoke That Thunders."

Probably the first white man to ever view this spectacular sight was David Livingstone, the intrepid missionary explorer, who discovered the falls in 1855 and honored his queen by naming them for her. With a height of 355 feet, the falls thunder into the Zambezi River on the border between Zambia and Zimbabwe. Now independent African countries, they were still British colonies when we were there.

It was a five-hour train ride from Elizabethville down to Sakania where the Congolese border patrol had all passengers get off for luggage inspection. For some reason, the soldiers wouldn't let the women and girls be present for the inspection and sent us off to another area. Jim and Grandpa stayed with the luggage and watched as the soldiers went through everything in our suitcases. The men even had to remove their shoes and socks and empty their pockets. No doubt the border patrol was looking for diamond smugglers, as diamonds are one of the country's natural resources. We wondered about a man on the train who refused to take his hat with him although Jim said, "Sir, you've forgotten your hat." The border officials even cut through the bread and lunch meat of some passengers in their search for gems.

Having determined we were not diamond smugglers, the soldiers finally Xed our suitcases with chalk, and we were free to get back on the train. Forty-five minutes later, we arrived at Ndola in Northern Rhodesia, where another train waited to take passengers south to Victoria Falls, a trip of twenty-four hours. What luxury! Pullman accommodations, snowy white table linens, a wonderful four-course dinner for less than a dollar and even half price for the children. We were not used to such comforts.

Our first view of Victoria Falls was breathtaking, as there was a full moon that night. Only people who have lived in Africa can appreciate how truly bright a full moon can be. As the engineer stopped the train on the bridge over the Zambezi River that separates the two countries, we stepped outside and felt the spray from the falls in our faces. The water thundered over the falls into the chasm below to throw mist hundreds of feet into the air.

What a marvelous way to begin a vacation that would be full of awesome experiences! The psalmist expresses it so beautifully: "Oh Lord, our Lord, how majestic is your name in all the earth!"

You know how Grandpa loves his coffee first thing in the morning. We were still asleep the following day when we were awakened by a loud knock at the door. It was six AM. Barely daylight! As I sleepily opened the door, there stood our smiling British steward holding a tray with coffeepot, cups, sugar, and milk, inquiring ever so cheerfully, would we like coffee?

"Yes, please," said a still groggy grandpa. "We'd like two cups."

Coffee at six AM must be a British custom we'd not heard about we decided, and having finished drinking it, we concluded the only thing to do was to try and go back to sleep. Just as we dozed off there came another knock at the door. Our steward was back!

"That will be two shillings, sir."

Thus we learned about wakeup coffee service on a British railway train.

I'll tell you more about our trip in the next letter.

Love to all of you,
G'ma and G'pa

Let the Fun Begin

Dear Grandchildren,

It was already dark by the time we arrived at the railroad station in Victoria Falls. The men looked for a taxi that would hold the nine of us and our luggage and take us to the camp where we had reservations. Somehow we managed to squeeze ourselves and luggage into a four-door sedan. It was a tight fit. The taxi driver delivered his load and we untangled ourselves and walked into huts P and Q . . . adequate for people bent on safari, but definitely not the Hilton Hotel. June, south of the equator, is cold and the three heavy wool blankets on each camp bed were most welcome.

When morning came, we were all feeling rested and ready for adventure, but a surprise awaited us. In the dark the night before, our taxi driver had taken us to South Camp whereas our reservations were for North Camp. The lady in charge at South Camp fussed about these travelers who didn't know the difference between the two camps. While the men went to find some means of transportation to take us to our rightful destination, June and I repacked the suitcases. A bit later, the men returned driving a little rented British Zephyr which would involve much squeezing of the nine of us into space meant for four or five. But the real challenge was yet to come: driving a right-hand-drive vehicle on the left-hand side of the road in good British fashion.

Even though it was a nuisance to repack our suitcases, the drive to North Camp gave us our first daylight view of magnificent Victoria Falls. We settled quickly into our proper accommodations and were soon ready to go exploring. Somehow we squeezed ourselves into the car again and were on our way.

Each time we crossed the border from one country to the other, certain formalities had to be observed. On the Southern Rhodesia side, the guards required the driver to go into the border patrol office and declare how many people were in the car. Maybe they wanted to be sure no one sneaked into the country and stayed illegally. On the return trip to Northern Rhodesia we merely waved a permit.

We had heard about "Big Tree," a huge old, ancient baobab tree and wanted to see it. Signs warned travelers:

"Beware of crocodiles. Bathing and paddling strictly forbidden."

This reminder was sufficient to keep us all safely squashed together in the car, though we did manage to peer out the windows and watch antelope and flocks of guinea fowl running along the road.

Big Tree is well named, for it measures sixty-six feet around the base. Baobabs can grow to enormous heights and widths. Before a bad storm blew out the top, it was 150 feet high. There is a fence around this particular tree, put there no doubt to discourage people from carving their initials on it. Steven was chagrined that he couldn't add his name to those already there. It was obvious the fence hadn't stopped everyone.

There are many both beautiful and interesting trees in Africa, but the baobab is one that always fascinated me. Legend says that when God created this tree it did not want to grow as trees do with their roots in the ground. The baobab persisted in pointing its roots skyward. In exasperation God turned the tree upside down with its root-like branches in the air and said, "There now. You just grow that way!" And it has, ever since.

Also known as the traveler's tree, the baobab's center is usually hollow, and water collects in it for the thirsty traveler. We know this is true, as we tossed a rock into the one at the vacation house at Nsiamfumu and heard water splash. We have been told the fruit—large sausage-like appendages dangling from its branches—is one source of cream of tartar. Fishermen split the "sausage" in half, clean out the pithy center and use the shell to bail water from their dugout canoes. Sometimes they strip bark from the trunk and beat it into sturdy "rope." At night, huge, white blossoms open so quickly you can almost see it happening. It's like watching something photographed with a time camera.

From Big Tree, we drove nearer to the falls to see the monument erected in honor of David Livingstone, British doctor, missionary, and explorer. He stands, cane in his right hand and Bible in his left with a finger in between some of the pages, overlooking the Devil's Cataract. There the water churns and boils with fury. The Africans have named it well, "*Mosi oi Tunya*," the smoke that thunders. At the six-sided base of the monument, the carver has inscribed: 1813 (birthdate), Livingstone, 1873 (death), missionary, explorer, liberator.

Walking along the trail overlooking the falls, we saw beautiful rainbows arched over the river as millions of gallons of water tumbled and roared over the cataracts. Steven was twelve that summer and wondered how the power of the falls compared with that of the atom bomb.

Under an intense blue sky, the spray was so high and dense at times it obscured the falls. The sun glistened like diamonds from the spray on the leaves of the trees. What a magnificent sight! Walking through this rain forest left us dripping wet with soppy shoes and hair falling in our faces. A large tree had fallen across the path. As it was too big to move, someone had sawed a chunk from the part of the trunk covering the path and rolled it to one side.

The return trip to North Camp took us through Livingstone Game Park. It's small and is where we sighted our first African animals. Packed as we were in the car, we had to swivel and turn to see them all. Near the entrance, a herd of zebra grazed, a wart hog off to the side of the road snuffled a grunt as he hustled over to inspect us. A waterbuck stuck its head in the open car window and Jim had to push it out. Giraffes stopped their feeding long enough to gaze quizzically at us, different species of antelope raced across the plain. We never saw such sights in Leopoldville. As we were leaving the game park, the guard told us an elephant was coming down to the water. We spotted him at a distance on an island in the river. Finally we had seen an elephant.

Returning to North camp, we roasted hot dogs over the coals and enjoyed fresh tomatoes, cucumbers, and potato chips for supper, apples for dessert. Hard to get items in Leo were king's fare to us. What a treat! Yum!

It was quite a day!

Love you,
G'ma and G'pa

Of Monkeys and Bubble Gum

Dear Aaron, Nicole, Zachary, and Kallianne,

It happened during our first trip to East Africa, destination Victoria Falls, separating what at that time were Northern Rhodesia and Southern Rhodesia. Today we know them as Zambia and Zimbabwe.

Did your mom, who was seven years old at the time, ever tell you about the day a monkey jumped on her back and stole two little packets of sugar she was saving?

Monkeys roamed freely at the camp where we were staying, but they were especially pesky outside restaurants and snack shops. We had just finished eating a picnic lunch on the terrace of a restaurant, where for once, they had left us alone. As we were leaving the area Susan tossed a bread crust to one of them. Not content with a bread crust, what did that rascal do but jump on her back and snatch the sugar from her hand! She was quite indignant and mad, even a bit scared. She cried too, more mad than scared, because that scamp of a monkey had the audacity to steal her packets of sugar.

And did she ever tell you about the time she spent an entire shilling on bubble gum? At age seven, Susan dreamed of having all the bubble gum she could chew. Especially since it was never available back home in Leopoldville. Skipping along one morning what should she see at her feet but a shiny shilling, at that time worth fourteen cents in American money. What good fortune! There was a little shop with all kinds of wonderful things to buy in the camp where we were staying, and among the treasures were pieces of bubble gum. Susan could scarcely wait to spend her shilling.

A very proper looking British gentleman seemed to be in charge, and as we approached the counter Susan said she wanted to buy bubble gum. He reached into the case, retrieved one piece and laid it on the counter. Susan was crestfallen. One piece didn't look like much bubble gum to her.

"Oh, no." I explained, "She wants to spend the whole shilling on bubble gum."

Startled, the shopkeeper exclaimed, "Disgraceful!"

I agreed it probably was, but replied that she hadn't had bubble gum for three years and that her heart's desire was to buy *lots* of bubble gum. Slowly he counted out a shilling's worth of the chewy stuff, all the while shaking his head and muttering, "It's a disgrace!"

No doubt the shopkeeper had private thoughts about a mother who would allow her child to buy a shilling's worth of bubble gum. He probably went home that day telling his wife about the dreadful American woman who indulged her young daughter so disgracefully. But without a doubt, Susan was the happiest, chewingest, bubbliest child in all of Northern Rhodesia that day!

Love to our Brenner grandkids,
G'ma and G'pa

Watch Out for Wild Things!

Dear Grandkids,

Seventy-five miles south of the falls is a game reserve where we had enough thrills and excitement to last us for a long time. It's called Wankie, and, although it's a small park, many animals make it their habitat. Since we also wanted to see the big animals on this trip, the nine of us wedged ourselves once more into that little British Zephyr and headed south. The drive through the wooded hills reminded us of a gorgeous fall day in the States. There was beautiful color in the leaves plus an incredibly blue sky overhead. Finally the paved road ended and we bounced the rest of the way over a dusty, bumpy road.

Entering Wankie Game Reserve, a welcoming committee of three elephants greeted us. Also a sign warning people to stay in their car! By unanimous vote we declared this to be the start of an exciting trip. So

Large Elephant at Wankie Game Reserve

that we wouldn't be attacked by the hungry munchies, we stopped at Robins Camp to buy picnic supplies. Protected by a wire fence, Robins Camp boasted a little store, ranger headquarters, and thatched roof rest huts called *rondavels*.

We hadn't driven far, before we saw several species of deer. Since there were no signs posted giving their identity, we had to guess the species of these beautiful, graceful creatures. Ostriches that had survived the era of plumes for ladies' hats paid no attention as we drove slowly through the reserve. Although their bodies look too bulky for their spindly legs, the ostrich runs with amazing speed. We've been told their kick is worse than that of a horse. Imagine the size of an ostrich drumstick!

Then there were giraffes. There were so many we finally gave up counting after twenty-five, but the most exciting "find" was the one we came upon right in the middle of the road as we rounded a curve. We stopped to watch him while he posed for us along with four nearby friends intent on reaching the topmost leaves of the trees. Even though giraffes are rather ungainly looking when they bend over to drink water, they move with grace. They watched us with liquid brown eyes before resuming their afternoon snack.

At a waterhole, waterbuck and impala were quenching their thirst. Were they aware that a lioness was crouched behind a nearby mound? Jeanie spotted her, and, when Grandpa backed up the car a bit, we all saw her. Actually that was the only lion we saw that day, but one was enough for our nervous, rather scared children. There were guinea fowl with their pretty blue topknots and wart hogs so ugly only a mother wart hog could love them. In spite of their appearance, they're fun to watch as they run with their tufted tails sticking straight up in the air. A massive hippo surfaced from the water at one of the dams. A three-foot long monitor lizard rested at the dam as well.

Dusk comes about six-o'clock in most of Africa south of the equator, and by now it was time to start back to Robins Camp. We had been warned that if the rangers had to go out and search for late arrivals a heavy fine would be imposed. Even more worrisome was seeing the gas gauge hover near empty on the Zephyr. We had visions of being surrounded in the dark by red-eyed wild things as we waited for the rangers to rescue us.

To our disappointment, we had seen no elephants other than the three when we first entered the reserve. As we drove back toward Robins Camp, we counted eight shy ones, but they wouldn't come out in the clearing to give us a better view.

Time was growing short, and we were becoming more anxious that we would be stranded with an empty gas tank when we came upon a huge herd of mean, treacherous looking Cape buffalo. We estimated there were three or four hundred. They wanted the road, and, since there were more of them than there were of us, we weren't about to argue. Edging slowly along the road, we got through the herd only to come upon another, possibly half as many. It's wise to respect their might and strength. African hunters will never go after a wounded buffalo, for they are known to circle around and attack from behind.

The afternoon shadows were growing longer, the gas gauge registering empty when we came upon enough elephants to last us for a lifetime. We counted sixty then lost count. At that time, it was estimated there were four thousand in the park with some herds numbering 150. There were big ones, papas, mamas, teenagers, little ones. To the right of us, left of us, in front of us. They were as intent on going to the waterhole as we were in getting back to Robins Camp on time. The children were scared and five-year-old Sylvia was terrified, her screams competing with the noise of the elephants. When one huge, trumpeting bull started toward our tiny car with its nine very small, very scared passengers we had visions of being squashed flat by this elephant determined to let us know who was boss. Grandpa put the car in reverse and v-e-r-y s-l-o-w-l-y backed up. At last the elephants had all crossed the road and we began breathing again.

By now the sun had slipped below the horizon. We came upon another herd of elephants, only twelve or fifteen this time, but enough to set the kids howling again. We waited respectfully while the elephants ambled across the road, in no hurry or concern for a 6:00 PM deadline, let alone an empty gas tank. Due to our precarious situation, we had to forego a stop at the crocodile pit, and even though there was a beautiful sunset, we were too anxious to think of much more than a stalled car in a game park after dark.

The lights of Robins Camp finally came into view. What a relief! We checked our names off the guest register, filled the gas tank and headed back toward Victoria Falls.

Only a few miles out of the park our lights picked up a zebra crossing the road. "Oh, no!" wailed Sylvia. "We're back in the zoo again!" What an incredible day!

Love, G'ma and G'pa

Was Someone Lost?

Dear Mireille and Matt,

The first family trip we took outside Congo was the year the Sharps and Clarks went to Victoria Falls. Other vacations had been in Congo, either at another mission station or at Moanda on the coast. After poring over maps of Africa, we set our sights on Victoria Falls. After all, if you live in Africa you can't afford not to go there was Grandpa's philosophy. So, with great anticipation, we flew from Leopoldville (today's Kinshasa) to Elizabethville (Lubumbashi), then by train to the Rhodesias which were still British colonies. We've already told you some of the adventures we had that time, but did your dad ever tell you about the time he got lost?

Actually, he was good at that, although it likely depends who is telling the story to know who was really lost. How well we remember the first time! Your dad was six years old, and we were in Belgium on our way back to the States for our first home assignment. Your Aunt Susan was thirteen months old. She had just started walking, taking her first steps all alone in our hotel in Lisbon, Portugal. Now we were in Brussels attending the Exposition, the World's Fair.

Because there were thousands of people at the fair, we felt it wise to have a meeting place in case we should become separated from one another. The Atomium, a huge metal structure several stories high and easily seen from any point at the fair, would be a good landmark, we decided. Susan was in the stroller, but it was a lot of walking for six-year-old legs and your daddy got tired. Susan was grumpy about letting her brother stand on the back of the stroller.

Suddenly, we realized Steven was no longer with us. There we were, in the Russian Pavilion! We searched . . . and searched . . . and searched. Had the Russians kidnapped him and taken him off to Russia? Probably it was only a matter of minutes before we finally found him in the crowd of people, though at the time it seemed heart-stopping forever. What a relief to find him and know that he hadn't wandered off alone to the Atomium. Or worse yet, been kidnapped!

Your dad remembers that at Victoria Falls he was not the one who was lost. He knew exactly where he was he says, but he lost us. I guess that means we were lost! We were near the Livingstone Monument and he had followed a trail leading into the rain forest that faced the chasm overlooking the falls. In the mist, visibility was greatly reduced, and it was not easy to see one another. At some point, we became separated, and when he retraced his steps he found the rest of us gone. He started walking along the road back to our camp, figuring he would find us there. Meanwhile, as we left the rain forest, we realized Steven was no longer with us. Not knowing if he had fallen over the precipice into the gorge below, we nearly panicked. Only a few minutes earlier we had read a lurid account of various deaths and suicides connected with the falls.

As we started walking back to the camp, hoping to find Steven there, a car stopped and the driver asked if he could give us a lift. We explained our concern to him. He was most solicitous and determined to stay with us until we found our son. In a short time we found Steven walking along the road ahead of us and we were thankfully reunited. What a relief! At age twelve, Steven only remembers the driver's pessimistic comments about Northern Rhodesia's approaching independence from Britain. We remember the driver's kindness for staying with us until we found Steven. Now who was lost do you think?

Something else happened on the trip that your dad may or may not remember. Ask him if he remembers the treasure he found when we went down into the third and fourth gorges where they were building a new underground pump to provide water for the city of Livingstone. We had to walk quite a distance before we got a trolley, a little open tram with roof overhead. It descended into the gorge at an almost perpendicular decline. It took eight or ten minutes to make the trip, but then we were free to roam around on the rocks and let the kids dabble their feet in the chilly water.

When we returned to the first and second gorges Steven struck out on his own. When we found him again he had a great big smile on his face. In his hands, he carried a baboon skull! Excitedly he showed us how one tooth went in and out. A perfect treasure for a twelve-year-old boy! I don't remember that it found its way back to Leopoldville so his killjoy parents probably convinced him it was not something he wanted to put in his suitcase. It certainly didn't go in ours!

In our next letter, we'll tell you about a sundown cruise on the Zambezi River.

Love you,
G'ma and G'pa

Cruisin' Down the River

Dear Sharp and Brenner Grandkids,

When we heard about a two-hour cruise on the Zambezi River, we thought that sounded like fun. Evidently other people thought so too, for by the time the cruise started there were sixty or seventy eager passengers on the launch. Our captain, sporting a short mustache and goatee, was dressed in typical British safari outfit of shorts, belted jacket, and knee socks. His appearance was the perfect advertisement for an African travel magazine.

The first eight miles of the cruise was on the Maramba, a tributary of the Zambezi River. From there, we had a good view of the falls with the "smoke" rising above them. Several islands dot the Zambezi, and the captain, knowing the sites and habitats of the animals and vegetation, frequently indicated points of interest to us. A Goliath heron, well-named for its size, flew up as we motored by. Crocodiles slithered into the water. One enormous croc was at least ten feet long.

The captain called our attention to a number of ivory palm trees growing on the islands. We had never seen that variety before, as it doesn't grow in Congo—at least not in the area where we lived. This tree bears a fruit that is inedible for humans, but it's a tasty snack for elephants. Known as vegetable ivory, elephants and ivory carvers compete for it. We watched an elephant pound her trunk against a tree to shake the palm nuts loose. On another island, we watched as four elephants foraged among the palms.

The launch stopped at Palm Island where we enjoyed that delightful British custom of tea time. Two teenage African boys prepared the charcoal fire. Soon the kettle was boiling for tea served with "biscuits," known as cookies by Americans. We were free to hike on the island, but were cautioned by our captain not to scream, please, if we saw elephants or other animals. Just be quiet and let them pass! After our experience at Wankie, the prospect of meeting face to face with an elephant was not a comforting thought. While we didn't see any critters on our hike, there was plenty of evidence they were on the island. Animal droppings and large tracks in the mud let us know we were on their turf.

There were lots of vines hanging from the trees, a perfect invitation for Grandpa to try them out. Even though he looked longingly at them, playing Tarzan wasn't on the agenda for the day and he had to resist the temptation.

Tea time and hike finished, the passengers got back on the launch when the captain called "all aboard." It had been a wonderful excursion cruising on the Zambezi River enjoying again the beauties and wonders of God's creation. However, not expecting Rhodesia to be so cold, the Clark and Sharp families shivered their way back to port!

We return to Congo tomorrow. And that's another story.

Love you,
G'ma and G'pa

Riding the Rails to Elizabethville

Dear Grandchildren,

Our two-week vacation was almost over, and it was time to pack the suitcases in preparation for our return to Elizabethville. Although the taxi arrived in time to take us to the train station in Victoria Falls, the waiting room was not open and we had a chilly wait, even in the sunshine. It was so cold, we could see our breath on the air. Even in dry season, Leopoldville was never that cold. It was June, but it was winter in the Rhodesias.

On the train that Sunday evening, the Clark and Sharp families met for worship, singing hymns and choruses, reading scripture, and having prayer together. Looking forward to a good night's sleep and breakfast the next day, we anticipated a pleasant, uneventful trip to Elizabethville. Little did we know!

Arriving at Ndola right on schedule the next morning, we hoisted the luggage through the train compartment window assuming the electric train to Sakania would be along in a few minutes. That was a mistake. We stood outside for two hours in the cold—not the happiest way to begin the day. It seems the train would not start and a "trailer" was being sent in its place. The person sharing this bit of discouraging news indicated that only a fool would ride that train. It wasn't long before we knew what he meant.

Down the track huffed an ancient car with wooden benches, canvas doors opposite every other seat, and a roof overhead. A cozy electric train it was not. It resembled an old-fashioned street car in its very open, definitely breezy, absolutely cold, and exceptionally rocky forty-five minute trip to the border.

Evidently the border patrol didn't consider us potential diamond smugglers this time and made only a minimal check of our luggage. There was even a decent train waiting to take us from Sakania to Elizabethville. Things were looking up. However, after making sure all the passengers and baggage were comfortably settled aboard the train, the authorities came and informed us the train wouldn't be making the trip to Elizabethville after all. Everyone would have to get off and wait until the next train arrived. There would be one that evening at 6:00 PM, they assured us. For cold, hungry passengers, this was not good news. It meant a seven-hour wait in the boonies. Sakania boasted neither hotels nor restaurants.

The Silesian fathers (I remember them as "elderly") at the Catholic mission heard of our plight and invited our party of nine to come for lunch, which was a wonderful Belgian soup. They seemed especially delighted to have children at their table. Most of these men had spent their lives in Congo, never returning to their homeland to visit their families as we Protestant missionaries did. Their hospitality was indeed gracious to cold, hungry strangers, hovering over us to be sure we got enough to eat. They had created a bit of heaven in that rather forsaken place with beautiful gardens, lovelier than any we ever saw in Congo.

While we were enjoying that delicious soup, word came from the station that a train would be leaving at 2:00 PM and we could be on it. Being able to leave on an earlier train was good news. Saying our good-byes and thank yous, we picked up our luggage and once more boarded the train for Elizabethville.

About halfway between Sakania and Elizabethville, the train stopped. An official came on board with the unpleasant news that all passengers were to get off the train and take their luggage with them. They were to exchange places with the passengers that had just arrived on the train coming from the north . . . Elizabethville. This meant climbing from our train down into a ditch and up the other side to the waiting train. In the confusion, people from both trains were getting in each other's way. When we were finally settled on the train expecting to continue on our way north, the official came back and announced there had been a mistake. Everyone was to pick up their luggage and return to their original train! We did just that, climbing down into the ditch again, up the other side, bumping into people who were headed back to the southbound train. Playing "musical trains" was not a fun game.

Two things stand out in my memory from that crazy experience. While we were at South Camp, we bought a twenty-pound carved wooden elephant stool that I "couldn't live without." I promised faithfully to carry it should the need arise. As you can see, the need arose several times although gallant Grandpa came to my rescue and did the carrying. He was certain, though, that that elephant gained weight each time he had to lift it. Also, there were several gun-toting soldiers on one of the trains, and in transferring from one train to the other they involved our children in passing guns. June was aghast at seeing eleven-year-old Betty nonchalantly passing rifles from one soldier to another.

All the passengers finally arrived at their destinations in spite of the crazy nature of the trip. The remainder of the trip to Elizabethville was uneventful. Our hotel reservations were honored and we had a good night's sleep.

However, the train fiasco was a good preview of what awaited us in Leopoldville. At the airport, Grandpa safely stowed our luggage . . . and elephant stool . . . on the Sabena Airlines bus which would take us into town. Then it seemed there was some mistake. Everyone was on the wrong bus, we were told! All the passengers and their luggage must get off and transfer to a different bus. Grandpa declared that elephant stool gained another pound!

What a way to end a delightful vacation!

Love,
G'ma and G'pa

Meet Some of Our Friends

Where's the Huili?

Dear Aaron, Nicole, Zachary, and Kallianne,

After Belgium granted independence to Congo in 1960, Grandpa and I worked in the Christian Center in Kintambo, one of the small cities that make up the capitol city of Kinshasa. One day, Pastor Lubikulu asked if we had work for an elderly lady who had no family to care for her. She was very poor and needed to earn some money to help with daily expenses. Perhaps she could sweep the classrooms, he suggested, or sweep around the buildings.

After talking with the woman, we agreed she could work at the Christian Center. Her responsibilities would be to sweep the office and keep the grounds outside clean and tidy. A few times we bought her large bags of peanuts to shell and roast, then sell to school children at recess. Naïvely, we thought she could save a bit of money from her sales to buy another sack, but she was never able to do that. Life was too hard.

Her name was Nsukami (meaning the last) Suzanne, and we called her Mama Suzanne. In many Congolese languages, the titles Tata and Mama are the same as Mr. and Mrs. in English. Beneath her *kitambala*, (head scarf) wisps of white hair escaped. She walked with a definite limp and she must have been in her seventies when we first met. The moment she learned we had a daughter, Susan, this lady latched onto us as though we were long lost family. (This prompted Steven to say once that she would be easier to love if she didn't like you quite so much.) She always called Susan *ndoi* which in the Lingala language means namesake. The fact that her name was Suzanne and your mom's was Susan was sufficient reason to establish kinship.

Most Congolese come from large families with parents, brothers, sisters, aunts, uncles, and cousins. But not Mama Suzanne. Gradually, we learned her story and realized what a remarkable woman she was to have suffered the hard knocks life had dealt her and still be a happy, resourceful person.

One morning, I took a crocheted doily to the Christian Center, and Mama Suzanne picked it up to examine it. After a few moments of inspection, she said, "I know how to crochet. Mama Hallo (Hall) taught me; Tata was a black man, but Mama was white like you." I knew that many years earlier, back in the late 1880s and early 1900s our mission board had appointed some black missionaries. One of those couples was named Hall. I had seen a picture of them, and yes, Tata was a black man. Mama was mulatto. In Congo, if a person is of black and white parentage, that person is considered white. So Mama was white like me.

In the late 1800s, when Belgium was building the railroad from the port city Matadi to Kinshasa, two hundred miles inland, Chinese coolies and men from Sierra Leone in northwest Africa were brought to help build it. Thousands of Congolese and many of the imported workers died as a result of the extreme heat, malaria, and hard work. Mama Suzanne's father was one of the men from Sierra Leone.

He married her mother, a Congolese, and they had two little girls. Back in his own country, he must have attended Protestant services, for he wanted his daughters raised in the Christian faith and took them to the mission station at Palabala. It was there that Suzanne and her sister learned to read and write, crochet and embroider.

Then tragedy befell the family. From the way Suzanne closed her eyes and pantomimed falling over, the sister probably died of sleeping sickness. (Sleeping sickness is caused from the bite of the tsetse fly.) Her father was crushed to death between two engines in the railroad yard.

She grew up and married, but after a time, when there were no children, her husband divorced her. Families put a great deal of pressure on couples to divorce if there are no children. Eventually, her mother died, and Suzanne was left alone. Never knowing her father's family and having neither siblings nor children, she had no near relatives. She may have been distantly related to Pastor Lubikulu's wife.

One Sunday morning, after returning to Congo from home assignment in the States, we worshiped at Kintambo church where Pastor Lubikulu was preaching. Mama Suzanne was there too. When she spotted us her mouth dropped open and she hid behind her *nlele* (three times!). The *nlele* is a versatile cloth worn by women. They may wrap it around their shoulders, drape it as a skirt, tie the baby on their back, or even use it as a covering at night.

Following the service she headed straight for us, shaking her fingers and hand in typical African gesture. After many hugs and expressions of delight that we had returned she told us she would come to see us. True to her word, the next morning she came bearing a gift of bananas and homemade peanut butter. Over and over she asked about *ndoi* whom we had left in the States for college. We gave her a picture of your mom, which she kissed repeatedly. Our friend certainly had a flair for the dramatic!

While in Kenya one Christmas, we purchased yellow and pink crochet cotton to give Mama Suzanne, knowing this was something she would like. When we returned to Kinshasa she came to see us, and we gave her the thread, expecting her to be quite pleased. She looked at it, considered it and finally asked, "Don't you have any white?" Fortunately, we had lived in Zaire long enough that we knew better than to take offense. For some reason, in their culture if you act too pleased about a gift it loses some of its value.

After finishing her first year of college, Susan came to Zaire to spend the summer with us. Mama Suzanne brought two crocheted

Susan (Ndoi) with Mama Suzanne Holding Aaron

doilies as a gift for Susan and instructed me to put them away for her until she got married, then I should give them to her. Suzanne visited our home on several occasions and she always brought a gift. Sometimes it was bananas, perhaps spinach, or maybe a small packet of green beans wrapped in a bit of paper. She couldn't afford to do that, but it was her way of showing friendship. I always sent her home with food items I knew she liked and included some money to buy anything at the market that I had neglected to include. She never failed to look things over, then ask for something more!

One day we received word that Mama Suzanne was quite sick, and I went to see her. The little room which she called home was neat and orderly, her meager possessions in place. As we visited together, she seemed troubled. Something, angels perhaps, had been singing to her she said, and she didn't understand why. Over and over she sang the tune she heard the voices sing. There were no words, just music. I told her God knew she was ill and perhaps he sent the music to comfort her because he knew she was alone in the world without family. He was letting her know he loved her and wanted her to feel his presence in her illness. She eventually regained her health and never again mentioned the music.

The biscuits were just out of the oven one morning when we heard a banging at our gate. Looking out we saw Mama Suzanne. She had come for a visit. It was Saturday and I had a long list of things I needed to get done. A visit from her was not on the list. As she came to our front door we saw that she was on the verge of tears. We greeted her and quickly learned the source of her anxiety. Just the night before a friend told her I had had an operation on my arm and that I was very sick and weak. She had cried and prayed to God all night, she said, asking him to heal me. However, her good friend Mama Marie told her to quit worrying because God was looking after me.

Not content with her friend's advice Mama Suzanne must come and see for herself. She set out on foot and limped the three miles to our home. On her way to the house as she was praying, telling God about me, she overheard a soldier say to another, "Look at that crazy old grandmother talking to herself!" While it was true that I had had minor surgery it was obvious I was neither sick nor weak. By the time she joined us for biscuits, jam, and sweet milky tea, she was in good spirits and we had a nice visit together. Before she left our home, I gathered some rice and tinned fish, milk, sugar, tea, and a bit of money to send with her. We prayed together and I sent her on her way. I had just sailed into the kitchen to tackle the dishes when I heard *kokoko* (hello) at the door. She was back! Having checked the things I had given her she discovered there was no *huili* (from the French *huile*—oil), so could she please have some? Dear Mama Suzanne! What a character! I shall never forget her!

Much love, G'ma and G'pa

Retirement Zaire Style

Dear Grandchildren,

Although Kinshasa was a city of more than four million people when we lived there, it was often referred to as "the world's largest village." There were dozens of satellite cities, each one usually settled by a different tribe. People preferred to live where others spoke their language, where tribal customs were the same.

One Sunday morning, we were invited to a special church service at Bumbu II, one of the many cities making up greater Kinshasa. People who lived there were mainly from the Moanza area and spoke Kisuku. Most of them also spoke Lingala, the language used throughout the city.

Turning from the paved street, we followed a dirt road until we reached the church. We were fortunate that day. Driving to some churches it was necessary to park the car where the road ended and then continue on foot. Upon entering the sanctuary, the missionaries and Zairian leaders were ushered to the front and seated in chairs which members had brought from their homes for this special occasion. Guests at church services were always welcomed this way. The rest of the congregation sat on planks supported by cement blocks. As churches received sufficient building funds they added a roof, benches, or whatever was considered most important at the time.

Mama Selepa, leader of the women's work, was being honored. For twenty years, she had been actively involved with the women in the life of the church. Now, at age seventy-three, she was turning over her responsibilities to younger women.

To the accompaniment of drums, rattles, shakers, and bells, the congregation sang as the women's choir escorted Mama Selepa into the church. This was no sedate walk! This was a joyful dance as they entered the cement block sanctuary. At the front of the church, a place of honor awaited Mama Selepa. An armchair, decorated with a piece of cloth bearing the message "A Christian Woman is a Light in her Home," was waiting for her. Many women in the congregation were dressed in the same material that morning. It identified them as members of our churches and gave them a sense of unity. "Women of the same cloth" they called themselves.

The blouse was made according to the woman's choice of style, but the skirt was always the same: a floor length piece of cloth wrapped around the body and twisted at the waist to secure it. Whenever I wore African dress, I always cheated and wore a string around my waist lest the cloth come loose and fall around my ankles! The third part of the dress was another length of cloth, just like the blouse and skirt. It served as an overskirt or the mother used it to tie her baby on her back.

Zairians love to sing, and several choirs were on hand to lift their voices in praise to God that morning. The choir leaders or members often wrote their own music and passed the anthems along from one church to another. Usually there were many verses to a song, and the pastors asked the choirs to sing only three verses. But that was no fun! The choirs found a way to get around that request. They remained seated while singing a shorter song, then stood up to sing their three-verse anthem. Sitting down while singing didn't count as the anthem! With choirs from several churches singing that morning, Selepa got up at times from her place of honor to dance in rhythm to the music.

At the close of the service, everyone was given the opportunity to express their appreciation to this woman who had shared her leadership ability with them for so many years. As the rattles and bells continued to make music, and the choirs continued to sing, we danced—two steps forward, one step back—to present her with gifts. Even though people were poor, the women from Selepa's church gave her a small hand operated sewing machine and a set of dishes, a testimony of their love and respect for her. Others brought money or other gifts which were placed in a large enamel basin decorated with a hand embroidered cloth.

Following the service, the pastor invited the guests to his home for dinner. Walking there, we picked our way through the rubbish and across a yucky, narrow stream. Garbage removal service was almost nonexistent and people threw trash anywhere. Someone carried a plank and laid it across the stream so we wouldn't get our shoes muddy in the mess. (I was reminded of Sir Walter Raleigh laying down his cloak for his queen so she might avoid stepping in a mud puddle.) Returning to the car after dinner, we didn't have the plank, and guess who stepped in the mess and wished she hadn't!

Even though we didn't deserve special treatment, the Zairian leaders and missionaries were served dinner first. While the other invited guests waited outside, we enjoyed a delicious meal of rice and beans and chicken cooked in palm oil. As we were leaving the pastor's home, I noticed the cooks were taking the remaining chicken from the bones and putting it in the sauce so that others might have a bit of meat as well. We had been served whole pieces. It was humbling to see their hospitality when they had so little.

∽

Even though we lived in Africa many years, we never ceased to be amazed that the people shared so willingly the little bit they had. A brief encounter with a woman I had never met before taught me a lesson in giving one day. Our Zairian youth leader wanted a project for the young people. He learned of an extremely poor woman whose home could only be called a hovel. He wanted us to go with him to see if the youth might be able to build her a house of some kind.

We were totally unprepared for what we saw. Perched on a sandy drop-off, the house was made of sticks and flattened cardboard boxes. We wouldn't have put an animal in such a place. During the rains, she would have been drenched as her house would have fallen apart. A squatter, she was a small woman, but even so she had to bend over to get inside her tiny hovel. Her only garment was a dirty piece of cloth tied around her waist. At one time it had had a message printed on it, but that message was no longer readable. In Kinshasa, we never saw women without a blouse, yet this woman was so destitute she lacked even that.

Did she see the pity in my eyes? Did she have a proud spirit that made her resistant to help? She disappeared for a moment behind her shack, then reappeared with a handful of peanut plants, peanuts still clinging to the roots. She had plucked them from her tiny "garden" then offered them to me. How could I possibly take this gift from one who had absolutely nothing? Yet I dared not refuse. I clapped my hands twice according to culture and accepted her gift. Poor as she was, and for whatever reason, she shared what she had.

God taught me a lesson that day. I was to freely give, just as this poor woman had freely given to me.

Till the next letter—
G'ma and G'pa

Emile

Dear Grandkids,

We first met Emile when we were teaching at Banza Manteke. She was fifteen years old and in fourth grade. Girls often did not have the same educational opportunities that boys had. They worked in the gardens with their mothers to help provide food for the family. Many were needed at home to look after the younger children. Some parents didn't realize the importance of girls getting an education. Others lacked enough money to send both boys and girls to school, and boys were given priority.

Emile worked in our house after school, which gave me opportunity to practice speaking Kikongo. She was pleasant, and we enjoyed having her in our home. I will admit to being a bit startled once when I checked the contents of a tin can on the back of the wood stove and discovered a rather naked baby bird. Tiny as it was, it meant a bit of protein in Emile's diet. When we moved to Leopoldville two years later I lost track of her.

Afterwards, I learned Emile had finished primary school, and then became a student in the Home Economics school. She and Jean (John), one of our former students, became engaged. After graduating from high school, he furthered his education at Kimpese and became a teacher there. Even though some family members opposed the marriage because Emile had some health problems, she and Jean were married at Banza Manteke among family and friends. Then came 1960 and independence from Belgium.

Jean was one of four young men from our mission who had the opportunity to study in the United States in the early 1960s and receive a university degree. Emile and baby were to follow when Jean was settled.

Emile's family never wanted her to go to the States; sometimes people fear the unknown. The day she was to leave for America it was discovered she lacked a certain document required by our government. When the photocopy was received from the United States and another plane reservation made, Emile was no longer in town. Her father had taken her to the village. While there she evidently was given medicine which made her extremely ill, and when she and the baby arrived back in Leopoldville she was quite sick. Her feet had been cut, infection had set in and she was weak from loss of blood. Instead of getting on an airplane to go to the States to meet her husband she entered the hospital.

For a while, Emile's sister cared for the baby, who was now eleven months old. But the sister had to return to her family and Emile asked me to take care of her daughter. She did not want her baby taken back to the village.

The little girl was named Théodora, but five-year-old Susan found it hard to remember the name and pronounce it. "What's her name, Mama?" Susan would ask. Since she found it difficult to say Théodora, I told her she could call her Teddy. And so this charming little girl became Teddy to all of us. Her charm fell apart when I wouldn't carry her around on one hip as she was used to! She yelled and cried and was not impressed that the *mundele* would not do what she wanted. But she was a sweet baby and Susan loved playing with her.

I made daily trips to the hospital so Emile could see her little daughter, hoping this would give her the determination and will to get well. Her condition worsened, and, on the advice of our mission doctors, we took her and Teddy to Kimpese to the intermission hospital staffed by European and American missionaries. Jean was advised to return to Congo. We were all encouraged when Emile began to gain weight and respond to the good medical care she was receiving at Kimpese. It was a shock when she died suddenly.

Even though most Congolese do not believe in autopsies, against family opposition Jean insisted that the doctors learn the cause of Emile's death. The autopsy revealed that heart and lung and liver damage were the result of the severe infection and were not due to any long-standing illness. Her family always insisted she was sick, but until this last illness our doctors had never found any physical reason for her problems. If you tell someone something long enough they will often come to believe it. Jean wanted a Christian burial at Kimpese, but Emile's family overruled and took the body to the village to be buried.

Had our mission known a certain document was required for Emile's arrival in the States, she would have been on the plane and spared those months of suffering. When Jean returned to the university, he took Teddy with him, then later remarried and went on to seminary.

There are times we don't understand why things happen as they do, but we have the faith to believe that God knows things we can't know. His ways are always right.

Another little girl we knew was rescued from a very bad home situation. Her name was Nasha, and although she was almost three years old when we first saw her, she was more the size of a one-year-old. The

Lindland family heard about her and were able to care for her until she was strong enough to go back to her own family. She weighed only eleven pounds, but dropped to ten pounds after being given a worm cure. The child was totally listless, with arms and legs like matchsticks.

Nasha was the sixth child in the family, but while the mother was expecting her, the father took a second wife. Nasha's mother blamed her unborn child for that, although the father continued to be interested in each of his children. Plural marriages were not uncommon in Congo.

Very likely, all those parasites created feeding problems for Nasha, but she had managed somehow to survive on bananas and dried fish. Now, with lots of love, good care and good food she began to thrive. She started to pull herself up and everyone was encouraged that some day she would walk.

A missionary nurse who worked at several clinics tried for six months to get the parents to let her find a home for Nasha until she was

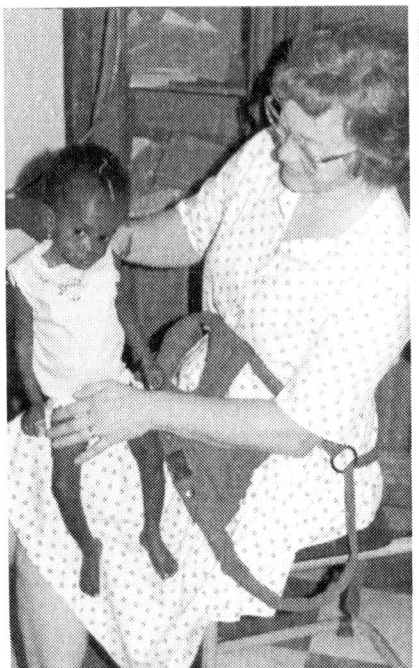

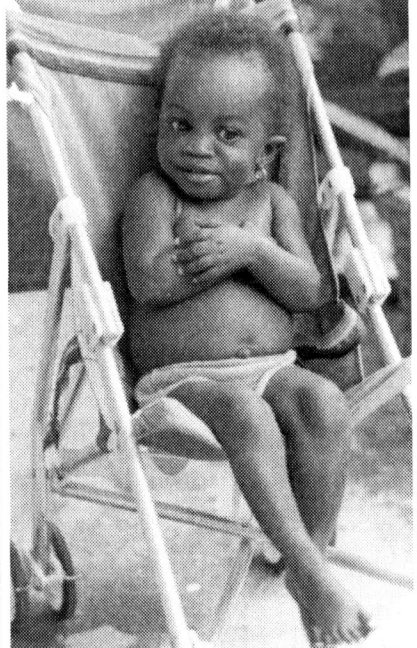

Sigrid and Nasha, Before and After

strong enough to return to her own family. At last they agreed, and an extremely sick little girl was given a new lease on life. Maybe God had something special for Nasha to have spared her life until the parents were willing to let the nurse find a temporary home for her.

There are lots of Nashas in the world. We try to help when we can.

Love you all, G'ma and G'pa

Tata Joseph

Dear Grandkids,

His name was Nkelani Joseph, although we called him Tata Joseph. He worked in our home in Leopoldville for a few years. Although slow as the proverbial molasses in January, Tata Joseph always stayed to finish his work and was totally honest. He was a cheerful worker, and our family thought a great deal of him. He was extremely bowlegged. Perhaps as a child he had developed rickets, a bone disease caused by a deficiency of vitamin D.

Joseph Nkelani came to our home on the recommendation of Tata Ngizulu who worked at the Christian Center with us. The two men were good friends, both from the Bakongo tribe. At one time, Joseph worked for a Belgian family, then came independence and many Belgians left the country never to return. Tata Joseph needed a job. We needed someone to work in the house while I was at the Christian Center. With Tata Joseph washing and ironing our clothes, preparing the noon meal and cleaning the house, I was free to write a kindergarten curriculum in Lingala for the Christian Center.

While working for the Belgian family, he had learned to make a wonderful pureed vegetable soup. Steven and Susan loved it and often asked for "Tata Joseph soup." The name stuck and whenever any of us make it today we still call it that. Joseph also made good pies. Grandpa liked that!

Tata Joseph and his wife, Mama Marie, had a large family. Seven or eight children were considered the perfect number by Congolese. As many children did not survive childhood, parents desired large families to help with the work. It was also hoped they would care for their parents when the parents were no longer able to care for themselves.

One year, one of Joseph's children died of sickle cell anemia. This is an inherited form of anemia found mainly in people of African descent. Naturally this was a very tragic and sad time for the family. It was customary to hold a wake (a vigil over the body of someone who has died), usually outside in the family's courtyard. Tata Joseph sent word to Grandpa asking him to come to their home and help set up a light for the benefit of family, friends, and neighbors who would be there. The body lay on a bed, and four candles, one at each corner, were lit. In Christian families, there was often all night singing and praying, while among non-Christian families there was weeping and wailing. Sometimes, even in Christian families there was weeping and wailing because a strong member of the extended family insisted on following the old ways.

When Grandpa arrived, he discovered that a neighbor had taken a long electrical cord connected to an outlet in his house and had stretched it across the dirt street to Joseph's home. Now the Nkelani family did not have electricity, but from somewhere Joseph had found a cord and light bulb and the men were tying the two cords in a knot hoping to provide light for the mourners when we arrived. Grandpa had the necessary tools to splice the wires and join them properly so that there would be light for the wake.

Among Joseph and Marie's children were twin boys, Nsimba, the first born, and Nzuzi, the second born. Twin girls are also called by the same names. (Grandpa Sharp is Nsimba and Uncle Maurice is Nzuzi.) One day Nsimba got into big trouble. He was four years old and probably bored.

A friend came to our home to inform Tata Joseph that the little boy was being held at the police station in Kintambo. For whatever reason, Nsimba lay down in the unpaved street and didn't get up when a truck came along. Fortunately the driver saw him, stopped and picked up the child, then took him to the police station. Due to a death in the family Mama Marie was in another part of the city, the older children were at school and Tata Joseph was at work. A friend was supposed to be looking after the twins.

The friend went to the police station to get Nsimba but the police refused to release the child. Then the man came to our house to inform Tata Joseph. By the time Joseph reached the police station two women had been successful in getting the child released but he had to pay a $4.00 fine. That's not much to us, but it was a sum Tata Joseph could ill afford to pay.

One day Tata Joseph did not come to work, and because he was always faithful we knew he must have had a good reason. When he returned to work, he related the past day's experience with his usual cheerful good humor. Learning that a relative living in another part of the city was ill, Joseph wanted to go visit him. There was a problem however. He wasn't sure of the exact location. He set out on foot with his ten-year-old daughter who knew the way, but they hadn't gone far before a soldier stopped them asking for their identification papers. Joseph's were in order, but Monique had left her school identification card at home.

Joseph was given permission to go on, but Monique would have to go to a place some distance away where people without proper identification were being detained. She was terrified. Joseph persuaded the soldier, who of course was hoping for a bribe, to take him and let his daughter go home to get her card. He spent the next several hours confined with thirty others in an extremely small room with neither toilet facilities nor food. Some people had been there for three days, he said. Imagine how frightening that would have been for a child. When Monique returned home, she was so frightened she couldn't talk, but gradually her mother learned what had happened. She got the necessary identity card and 1000 francs ($2.00) to pay the fine, and in due time Joseph was released. What a harrowing and agonizing experience for both parent and child!

I was impressed with Tata Joseph's spirit. He didn't appear to have any hatred or vengeance regarding the soldier who had stopped him. Rather, he was saddened. "What is our country coming to?" he said. "Children have always been able to accompany their parents without identification. The idea of taking a little girl like that away from her father is horrible."

Soldiers in the Zairian army were poorly paid and often went weeks without their salaries. Bribery was a way of life for many of them. All people, Zairians or expatriates, could be stopped on a false charge, the soldier hoping he would be given a bribe. It wasn't only soldiers who expected them. At an annual meeting one year, our Zairian leaders wanted to include a certain sum in the budget for bribe money as they knew that was the only way to get things done when they had to do business at some office. "Beans for the children" was the term they laughingly called a bribe.

We were very privileged to have had Nkelani Joseph work in our home. His faithfulness and loyalty, his faith in God, his gentle spirit, his ability to deal gracefully with all that life handed him were an inspiration to our family. He was a good friend.

Till the next letter,

Love to all, G'ma and G'pa

Special Friends, Special People

Dear Mireille, Nicole, and Kallianne,

While we lived in Zaire, we met many people who became friends and taught us a lot about Zairian life and culture. Two of those friends were a mother and daughter, Mama Ngunga and Mama Mattie. Let me tell you about them . . .

Ngunga was an elderly lady when we first met her at the village of Ngombe, several miles downriver from the city of Kinshasa. By the world's standard she didn't have much going for her . . . her house was no mansion, her wardrobe was very simple, her education quite limited. People were drawn to Ngunga because she cared about them. As a young woman she married, and she and her husband had one child, a little girl, Mattie, named for an early Sona Bata missionary. When her husband died, Ngunga was left a young widow with a small child to raise. She later remarried, becoming the wife of the Ngombe pastor. They had no children of their own, but their home was a place where children felt welcome; some even lived with them.

In addition to Mattie, Mama Ngunga nurtured many children and young people in the Christian faith. Girls and women came to trust Jesus as their Savior because of her faithful example and witness. Since girls often lacked the same opportunity for an education that boys were given, Ngunga patiently taught many women to read. She believed it was important for them to be able to read the Bible if they were to grow in their faith. One time we attended a service where some of the women she had taught to read were baptized in the Zaire River. Later that day, dressed alike, they proudly stood reading Scripture together, a tribute to the soft-spoken, modest little woman who had shared her faith with them.

As a small child, Mattie did the things that little Congolese village girls still do—march off to work in the gardens with hoe balanced properly on her head in imitation of her mother, run and play with friends, carry water from a nearby stream, sweep the ground around the house with a handmade broom, and even "babysit" someone's child tied on her back, Congo fashion.

Ngunga was a woman of vision. Some girls might not get to go to school, but her Mattie would not be one of them. When Mattie and a few other little girls enrolled in primary school, the boys poked fun at them. They didn't think girls could learn! Mattie worked hard and finished primary school. Some mothers thought that a girl with six years of schooling was well educated. After that, it was time to think about a family arranged marriage. But not Mama Ngunga.

Mattie had done so well in grade school that her mother encouraged her to enter the nursing program offered by the Sona Bata hospital. Mattie and a friend were the first girls in all of Belgian Congo to enter the field of medicine. In those days, nursing was strictly men's territory. Mattie listened to the boys' taunts that "girls are stupid as chickens" and would never be smart enough to earn a nursing diploma. Then, their crowning insult... "The instruction is in French and you'll never be able to keep up." They couldn't believe God made girls as smart as boys! When they saw that Mattie was a good student and would earn her diploma, they tried a new tactic. "Ah, Mattie," they said, "You may graduate, but you will just get married and never use your nurses training."

Mattie and her friend fooled all the doubters. It was a proud and happy day when they stood in line with the other graduates at Sona Bata to receive their nursing diplomas. They were the first women in the entire country to achieve this recognition! Their example encouraged other young women to enter the nursing field, and today, throughout Congo, young women are working as nurses and midwives or in other medically related jobs in clinics, hospitals, and dispensaries. Mattie was a trailblazer.

Some of the young men's predictions came true. Mattie did marry shortly after graduating from nurses training. However, for many years she combined a career and family. At that time, very few women worked outside the home. They might eke out the family income by selling vegetables or bread at the market, or have a little store in their yard where they sold soap, matches, or tins of tomato paste. But they were not career women.

Mattie served as head nurse at the Kintambo church dispensary for many years, frequently being called at night to care for a sick person. Mama Ngunga always supported Mattie in prayer as she used her talents to bring physical and spiritual healing to those she treated and cared for.

As God developed Mattie's natural leadership abilities, he gave her opportunity to gain further training. Mattie went to Nigeria as a delegate to an all-Africa women's meeting. She returned to her local church full of enthusiasm and eager to use the new ideas she had learned. She encouraged the women to assume responsibility and leadership for their weekly meetings. Her enthusiasm was infectious. "You can do it," Mattie told them. And they could. When we first arrived in Congo, women's meetings were always led by a missionary. It was great to see our African sisters taking charge.

When new churches were started, Mattie and her committee met with the women and helped them organize meetings of their own, giving encouragement and assistance. She was responsible for organizing the women from our Kinshasa churches into groups that could work well together in spite of tribal differences. Largely through her efforts, the Protestant women in Kinshasa were organized into a fellowship that took as their motto, "A Christian woman is a light in her home."

Although Congolese women like to show their solidarity by dressing alike for special occasions, it's not that way if two American women appear anywhere wearing the same dress. (I know from experience. Once, a woman wearing a dress identical to mine walked into a dinner where I was the guest speaker. On seeing me she hastily turned around and walked out!) Think of the sight: several hundred Congolese women dressed in a distinctive cloth bearing their motto, "A Christian woman is a light in her home," as they attended meetings and services throughout the city.

Mattie was tireless in her efforts as she encouraged the women to look beyond their own immediate concerns to see that there were those whose needs were greater than theirs. After the Biafran war, which left thousands homeless in Nigeria, the women, following Mattie's suggestion, used many of their sewing supplies to make garments for needy Biafran refugees.

In 1967, following the rebellion in central Congo that took such a toll of human life, many areas were vandalized and looted. Under Mattie's guidance, the women collected food and clothing, small notebooks and ballpoint pens to send to the boys and girls in that area so they might have something of their very own when school started. The women themselves were poor, but they cared about children who were even poorer than theirs. Even a little thin notebook and pen could bring happiness to a child who had nothing with which to start the school year.

Mattie's efforts bore fruit as she directed women's leadership training institutes at both the upcountry and downcountry mission stations. Whether leading the women in song and dance around the campfire at night, teaching them health and childcare, conducting a Bible study, or just visiting with the women, she witnessed to her faith in God.

She had the opportunity to visit or attend conferences in several African countries, the United States and Europe. Wherever Mattie went, she shared her faith with others, using the opportunities to teach and encourage her Congolese sisters. She tasted the excitement and honor of meeting several heads of state when she accompanied the Kasavubu family (Congo's first elected president) to Europe as their private nurse. It probably took courage, but in each country Mattie asked to worship in a Protestant church. She wanted to know what Christians were doing so she could share with her own people when she returned home.

Like her mother, Mama Ngunga, Mama Mattie was an example of God's love in action. She was influential in helping many women understand that God means for them to use the talents and abilities he gives them, and that being "only a woman" doesn't make them a second class citizen in his sight.

How privileged I was to know these two outstanding women!

Wherever we are, we can be a witness for Christ. I pray you also will develop the talents God has given you and that you will use them to honor him.

Love you, G'ma

Mind Your Manners!

Dear Mireille, Nicole, and Kallianne,

You may remember in a letter from Banza Manteke I wrote that among my responsibilities was teaching sewing in the girls' Homemaking School. Much of their sewing was done by hand as few, if any, had a sewing machine in their home. Only the older girls were privileged to use the hand operated sewing machines. In my very first class, one of those girls was Bwamutala. A teenager at the time, she had a nice spirit, a good sense of humor and was always cheerful.

When it was time for Bwamutala and the other girls to make their graduation dresses, I learned something about the way they thought. The girls wanted to have white dresses. No problem. That sounded all right to me. Then they asked for long sleeves . . . very long sleeves. Well, it was a hot climate, but if long sleeves were what they liked that would be okay too. Then they told me the reason. When they played basketball they wanted to be sure their sleeves didn't come above their wrists! That wasn't okay! It wasn't that the girls were exceptionally modest. They just happened to like long sleeves at the time. That was the style. I had to tell them that you didn't play basketball in dresses with long sleeves.

Bwamutala graduated and I lost track of her when she moved away. After two years at Banza Manteke, we moved to Leopoldville, today's Kinshasa. I didn't expect to see her again. Then, after several years, we rediscovered each other. She had married, had a family, and was very active in women's work at the Bandalungwa church in Kinshasa.

One day, I went to a meeting where women from most of our forty-four city churches were in attendance. Each of them had brought their choir to sing. Can you imagine how long it would take for that many choirs to perform? A long time, believe me! The meeting was completely organized by Zairian women. I remembered that when we moved to Kinshasa twenty-seven years earlier our mission had only two churches in the city. Most of the women at that time were too timid to be in any leadership role. I realized how God had blessed his people and that he was developing women to become leaders in their local churches.

Mama Bwamutala, my homemaking student that first year in Congo, was now the very capable president of all the Kinshasa women's groups. She was married and envied by other women for her large family of nine children.

Presiding at the meeting that day Bwamutala explained that we were about to watch a little play performed by women from one of the churches. Zairians have a great flair for the dramatic and we were in for a treat. The subject was how not to act when you are invited to someone's home. As the "husband" and wife approached their hosts' door the man nudged his wife and told her to put on her shoes. She searched in the bag she was carrying and found her flip-flops.

When dinner was ready it was evident that "Mama" didn't know anything about good table manners. She ate with her fingers. She wiped her hands on her clothes. She stood up and reached across the table to get food from a bowl. Everything she did was rude and impolite. When the guests finished eating "Mama" stood again, took some banana leaves concealed in her skirt and proceeded to gather up all the leftovers. The women were delighted and howled with laughter. It was all in good fun. Bwamutala was a good leader and she knew how to inject humor into the meetings to keep the women's interest alive.

Now then, be sure you mind your manners when you're invited to dinner at someone's home!

Till the next time,
G'ma and G'pa

—5—

Kaleidoscope

Kaleidoscope

Dear Brenner and Sharp Grandchildren,

You probably have played with a kaleidoscope and know that it's an optical toy with mirrors and colored shapes inside. Shake it and different patterns emerge. This letter is a kaleidoscope because it has changing patterns.

Dignitaries were coming to Kinshasa. Most of the American community were invited to a reception at the ambassador's residence to meet Vice President George Bush and wife Barbara on their tour of African countries. It was one of those stand up affairs where your feet got tired and you wished you could take off your shoes—or else sit down. The event started late and there were few chairs . . . you get the picture. Ronald Reagan was president at that time.

The TASOK music director wrote to the ambassador asking if the school band could play for the occasion. Permission was granted, and the kids put on a great show. Someone informed the vice president that there was a large missionary community living and working in Kinshasa. A large group of us were invited to the reception. I introduced myself to Mrs. Bush and shook hands with her. Then, wanting to meet the national Peace Corps director, who was traveling with the official party, I went in search of Ms Ruppe. A secret service man barred my way.

Explaining to him that my son and daughter-in-law had served in Zaire with the Peace Corps and were now in staff positions in Washington, D.C., he let me pass to continue looking for the director. Another secret service man stopped me. This was your harmless grandma just trying to have a few words with the national Peace Corps director! The security gentleman personally escorted me to Ms Ruppe, introducing me as a Peace Corps mother. Good grief! That made me feel a tad ancient! Ms Ruppe and I had a short visit together, and she indicated she knew Melanie and Steven. The best part was saying she would be happy to take a letter to them.

Sending and receiving mail through the local post office was often a problem. We frequently relied on friends to carry mail for us when they returned to the States. A friend went to the post office to buy stamps for a letter he needed to mail. However, since only those of low value were available, he bought the necessary postage and pasted it all over the envelope. The clerk weighed the letter again and stated that he now needed more stamps because of the added weight! One year, a Christmas package was five months on the way. But that was okay—Christmas at Easter was fun, too.

Overseas telephone calls were made from the post office. There were little cubicles where we could place a call, then wait until the connection was made. Sometimes it was a matter of minutes, sometimes hours. On occasion we would be told, "The United States is broken down," or "The United States does not answer." Did you Brenner kids know that the first time we met your dad was via a telephone call from

Kinshasa? One year some of our colleagues came from their stations in the interior to spend Thanksgiving with us. As we sat around the table after dinner, more stuffed than the turkey, we decided to go to the post office to call our children. In forty-five minutes, we had completed our calls, then had the rest of the afternoon to talk about what we had talked about! That was a memorable Thanksgiving Day.

Following a reception at the American Embassy one year, a group of us decided to go to a restaurant to eat. The hors d'oeuvres served at the reception were no substitute for supper. It was suggested that we eat at a recently opened Chinese restaurant which appeared to be run by Europeans rather than Chinese. The food was quite mediocre, but the music was memorable. We expected to hear oriental music, but over and over a tape played "Put Your Little Foot." Years earlier, Grandpa and I used to dance to that music and we considered getting up from the table and putting ours, but the better part of decorum prevailed.

Hearing that unlikely music in a Chinese restaurant reminded us of another occasion when the music seemed out of place in Congo. We were eating at a restaurant in Matadi when we realized the music coming over the loud speaker was none other than "You Are My Sunshine." Later, at a major hotel in Kinshasa, we were surprised one evening to see a Congolese decked out in Mexican sombrero, a serape thrown over his shoulder, strumming a guitar. As he strolled among the diners, we fully expected him to do the Mexican hat dance. Even though we were in Africa, life still held surprises when we least expected them.

Once, at a retreat, we were served rice and boiled kidneys. Kidneys were not on my "to-die-for" list, but I was gamely doing my best when I bit into something that crunched. (I confess to hoping it wasn't a kidney stone!) That took care of my appetite for that meal. I guess the retreat was on a tight budget because the next evening we were served tripe and rice. I didn't think I could eat tripe and Lee didn't think she could watch anyone eat it so we beat a hasty retreat and dashed home and fixed waffles. We learned later that a lot of Zairians weren't pleased about eating tripe either.

Zairians had a joke they liked to tell about a village bride whose husband sent her to the market to buy tripe. Being unused to the ways of the city, the new bride didn't know that tripe is the lining of a cow's stomach. Its rough texture is similar to a terry cloth towel. They call it *sume*, (pronounced soomay) a corruption of the French *essuie main*, a hand towel. The bride, wanting to please her husband, bought a towel at the market, took it home, cut it up, boiled it for hours and served it to him. He may still be trying to digest that *sume*!

This is enough kaleidoscope for now. Whatever you do, don't buy tripe!

More later, G'ma and G'pa

The Latest "Edition"

Dear Aaron, Nicole, Zachary, and Kallianne,

She was to be named Carol Susan or maybe even Jon Phillip. And then, wouldn't you know, when the baby arrived, your grandpa got so excited about his little daughter he wrote Susan Carol on all the announcements! But that was okay—we liked that better anyway.

Your mom was born in Belgian Congo in the hospital at the Sona Bata mission station, an hour-and-a-half-drive from Leopoldville (today's Kinshasa). The road was still unpaved. It was a bumpy ride. I had been at Sona Bata two or three weeks when it became obvious that your mom was ready to greet the world. Someone sent a radio message (our interstation means of communication) to Grandpa telling him to come to Sona Bata.

He stopped first to pick up Steven from kindergarten. In his excitement, Steven forgot an important ritual in leaving the classroom. Well-brought-up Belgian children always bowed or curtsied to their teachers when leaving, but Steven "garbaged up" his papers (his definition) and almost made it out the door when his teacher called, "Stephan, *saluer*!" ("Steven, bow!") So he did, but with his back to the teacher as he ran from the room, his bottom facing her! Steven had more important things to think about than observing Belgian niceties!

One nice thing about having a baby at a mission hospital is that it's a family affair. Thirty minutes after Susan was born, Steven was holding his baby sister. Like all newborns, she was a bit red, but her big dark eyes and lots of dark hair prompted our friend Lee to call her Pocahontas. Tata Lulendo came by to see the latest *mundele*, and his astonished comment, "Why, she looks like our babies!" amused us. Since most missionary babies born at Sona Bata were either bald or blonde, he evidently thought all white babies were that way at birth.

Children born overseas have their birth registered with local authorities as well as with their embassy. On our return to Leopoldville, we stopped by the district government office at Kasangulu to register Susan's birth with the Belgian authority there. The gentleman must have had a bad day as we discovered he had written the name of a Sona Bata missionary as the father! We finally got that corrected and continued on home. Fortunately, there was no problem at the American Consulate office and her birth was properly registered.

When we arrived home, friends came to welcome the new baby. One of my Congolese friends brought a coconut, another delicious bananas. Later, she made dresses for Susan and me from material which had a large footprint and a tiny one imprinted on it. Malela, one of our students, was working in our home at that time, and to everyone who came he asked, "Have you seen our baby?" Susan was quite a sensation! She was definitely a "keeper."

The year your mom was in seventh grade, we were in Wichita on home assignment. It was the first year the schools there were integrated. The opening day of school, she was assigned to a table with some black girls. They were to fill out information regarding birthday, place of birth, etc. One of the girls noted Susan had written Sona Bata, Africa as her place of birth. The black girl indignantly exclaimed, "You're not black! You're not from Africa!" Seventh grade was not your mom's happiest year of school. She was relieved when we returned to Leopoldville where her friends accepted that even though she wasn't black she was indeed born at Sona Bata, Africa. So now you know how your mom came to join our family.

Our love, G'ma and G'pa

Variety is the Spice of Life

Dear Grandkids,

Sometimes, funny things happened which can give you an idea of what life was like living in the tropics. Most of the years we lived in Congo, rats and mice were never a problem. But that changed one year when I went to the storeroom to get some potatoes for supper. I surprised a rat ... or did he surprise me? I screamed, just like they do in cartoons. Not that it did any good, for Grandpa was sick in bed with malaria. He just let me scream.

A day or so later, I noticed a small piece of soap on a cabinet. It should have been at the kitchen sink. I returned it to its proper place, but the next day the soap was missing again. By then we decided it was time to buy a rat trap. At two o'clock the next morning, we were suddenly awakened by the unmistakable sound of a trap being sprung. We bounded out of bed, and sure enough, there was Brother Rat. We discovered he had built himself a cozy nest in the insulation at the bottom of the refrigerator. And talk about cheeky, we found the soap there, too. We concluded he was a tidy type and wanted to keep his whiskers clean.

We thought that was the end of the rat episode, but we were wrong. The next day I saw another huge one in the storeroom. The trap was baited once more. In the night we heard it snap and we ran to see our catch. Was it the big one? Nooo. To its great misfortune a fat toad had hopped into the trap. Exit one mosquito-catching toad!

When Steven was five years old, we decided to do something fun and drove to Leopoldville's port where we took the ferry across the

Congo River to French Congo's capitol city of Brazzaville. We checked out the rapids from that side of the river, visited the zoo and did a bit of sightseeing. When we got hungry, we looked for a restaurant. Finding one that seemed like a good choice, we went inside and were seated by a waiter. In a few minutes we were joined by a fourth "diner," the cutest little chimpanzee we had ever seen.

He was about the size of a two-year-old. He had spotted Steven and climbed up in the chair beside him. Of course, no animal would ever be allowed in a restaurant in the United States, but this was Africa and things were different.

This cute little guy stayed with us while we ate our dinner. He had found a buddy not too much bigger than himself and he wasn't about to let him get away. It was hard to keep our minds on dinner with this bundle of cuteness at our table. There's nothing like sharing your meal with a toddler chimp to put sparkle in your dinner!

Steven had never had such fun in a restaurant in all his five years. As we finished our meal and walked out of the restaurant, so did baby chimp, trustingly placing his little black, hairy paw in Steven's hand. Walking down the sidewalk together, Steven put his arms around the chimp, patted him on the head and talked baby talk to him. They were kindred spirits, each having found a new friend.

Finally, we escorted the little guy back to the restaurant lest anyone think we were trying to "chimpnap" him. Evidently the owner wasn't concerned that his clients might make off with his chimp. I think the little fellow would have happily gone home with us.

No stories about Africa would be complete without one or two about snakes. One night, a nine foot python was caught in a chicken house, but in his greed to devour Tata Boko's chickens, he didn't see men descending on him with rakes and machetes. The men quickly killed the writhing python and divided the meat to take home with them, for python is good to eat. Some people in America think rattlesnake is delicious, although I ate some once and didn't think it was that great. Grandpa always liked to try something new and asked our cook to fix some. Tata Danny stewed it with onions, greens, and *pilipili*, an extremely hot pepper that Congolese use as a seasoning. It chewed something like turtle said Grandpa, a little like the stew his dad made when Grandpa was a boy.

That python was a tough critter, so Lee tenderized her family's quota in the pressure cooker. Then she dipped it in egg, floured it, and fried it. Something like chicken fried steak. It was "less worse" that way, but still, my tribe isn't crazy about python!

When Susan was two and a half, we had another snake encounter... this time in our house... in the middle of the night. Earlier, we had been at the Niles' for prayer meeting and they had served sodas afterwards. I drank more Pepsi than I should have that late at night and as a result I woke up and had to go to the bathroom. Padding out in my bare feet, I turned on the bathroom light. While going about my business something came wiggling under the door. It must be a centipede, I thought, but it kept coming... and coming... It was a snake!

Somehow I got out of the bathroom, awakened Grandpa, and told him ssssnake! The closest weapon at hand was his shoe, which he picked up, ready for battle. The snake was no longer in the bathroom. We looked and looked—both in our bare feet—and finally found that it had slithered into another room. There it was, all eighteen inches of it, partially coiled through the spokes of Susan's tricycle. With a good swat Grandpa killed the snake and we cleaned up the mess. That was enough excitement for one night. We started back to bed.

Just then I yelled, "MURRAY, THERE'S ANOTHER ONE!" Grandpa grabbed his shoe again, but this snake wasn't going to give up easily. He hid. We finally found him under a sofa where he had slithered to get away from Grandpa's shoe. It appeared to be the same variety as the first one we killed, although larger. In the morning, we showed the snakes to one of the workmen who, in a most unconcerned voice, declared them to be poisonous and said he would go bury them. It was raining that night and we decided the snakes had come under the screen door to be inside where it was dry.

Now you know your grandma does not like snakes at all. Not even harmless ones. It was rare that I had to go to the bathroom during the night, and for me to do so at the precise moment when there was not one, but two snakes in the house was uncanny. It was the only time in all the years we lived in Congo that we had snakes in the house. Thank goodness! Surely God was protecting us.

Chipper joined our menagerie one year, shortly before we left Congo for home assignment in the States. She was a cute little bush baby, a lemur, with bright, beady eyes, ears that opened and closed like a fan, tiny little paws with tiny little fingernails, and needle-sharp teeth. Her long, bushy tail was the same length as her body. Lemurs are nocturnal animals and spend their days sleeping and their nights cavorting. Our Chipper was no different. During the day she liked to sleep on top of the curtain rod in the living room, but at night she came down to be a part of the family.

Chipper especially liked Susan and Steven. Perhaps because they were children, she related well to them, just as the little chimpanzee had with Steven a few years earlier. In the evening, if they were doing homework at the dining table, Chipper pranced on her hind legs to get them to play with her. If they were playing on the floor, she wanted to join in their fun. Hopping on her hind legs, arms outstretched, she was fun to watch.

At bedtime, we always put Chipper in her cage, as we weren't keen on rude awakenings; but one night I couldn't find her. She found me! In the middle of the night, something furry jumped on my head. It was Chipper wanting to play. She seemed to say, "Wake up sleepyhead! It's playtime!"

When it was time to return to the States for a year's home assignment, we decided to take our bush baby with us. We arranged for Pan American Airlines to fly her to San Diego where we would claim her when we arrived in California. We made sure she had hard boiled eggs and apples to eat on her flight across the Atlantic, but a Pan Am attendant scorned those and provided Chipper with grapes. We never, ever bought grapes—too expensive!

Unfortunately, Grandpa had not warned Aunt Maxine that Chipper was coming. She received a call from the airlines saying she should come to the airport and feed her monkey. (Animals had to be in quarantine for a few days.) "What? Feed my monkey? I don't have a monkey." "Well," said the airport official, "It's got your name on it. Come down and feed it."

Now Chipper was a very bouncy animal and Aunt Maxine was wearing a cervical collar for a whip lash she had gotten a few days earlier. She wasn't excited about having a bouncing bush baby in the house. But Uncle Henry and the Grebbien cousins thought Chipper was neat and they enjoyed playing with her until we arrived to fetch her. We took Chipper to Berkeley with us and enjoyed her the year we lived there.

One day I took her to Susan's third grade class for Show and Tell. Of course the children were excited and they wanted to touch and pet her. Unfortunately, their excitement upset her and she bit my hands until they looked a bit like raw hamburger. Lemurs' teeth are very sharp. Our Chipper had had enough education for one day. When we returned to Congo, we left her at the Children's Zoo in Oakland to entertain other children as she had our family. She was the most fun animal we had all the years we lived in Congo.

Jocko was given to us while we lived at Banza Manteke. He was an African gray parrot with white feathers on his throat and a short red tail. These parrots are very good talkers, and Jocko was no different. In fact, we thought he must speak Swedish, as an old Swede had given him to us. When we moved to Leopoldville, Jocko went with us and quickly learned to imitate the sounds he heard. He copied me calling Steven to come home in the evening: "Stee-ven." He imitated the crying baby that lived in the upstairs apartment. Next door to the mission station was the shipyard where river boats were built. Jocko did an excellent imitation of the workmen hammering on steel. During the day he chattered to himself, holding long conversations with some imaginary parrot friend.

It was Steven's responsibility to clean the parrot cage every day, put clean newspaper in the bottom, and give Jocko peanuts and fresh water.

Steven took a dim view of this as the parrot's bill had nipped him several times. We enjoyed Jocko until we were evacuated from Belgian Congo in 1960. We left him in his cage on the back porch, and of course, when we returned the following year he was no longer there. African gray parrots brought a good price and someone profited from our departure. We used to enjoy watching a pair of them fly from one palm tree to the next when we lived across the street in a house facing the Congo River.

Throughout the years, we were entertained by cats and kittens, dogs and puppies, chameleons, an owl, a genet cat or two, parrots, and Chipper. What a menagerie! How lucky we were!

Love from your Grandma

Anyone for a Boat Trip?

Dear Brenner and Sharp Grandkids,

Menno Travel in Kinshasa was an agency that most of us used to make arrangements for vacations or travel to the States when it was time for home assignment. One day, they planned an outing for an afternoon of fun for those in the missionary community who lived and worked in the city. That afternoon turned out to be an experience none of us would ever forget.

The travel agency arranged to hire one of the boats that daily ferried passengers across the wide Congo River between Kinshasa and Brazzaville. The trip would take us a few miles upriver; our destination was a small island (actually a large sandbar), surrounded by the dark brown waters of the Congo. During rainy season, the sandbar disappeared, but our trip was scheduled for dry season when the river was lower. Seventy of us signed up for the outing. As space on the ferry was limited, Susan's age group wasn't included. This brought cries of "It's not fair!" from the younger kids, especially when Steven and Ted and their girlfriends got to go. Ted's parents were still in Sweden and he lived with us until they returned to Congo. The lucky high school students were included in the excursion.

It was a gray day, as though the skies might open and drench us with rain, but the river was fairly calm as we started upstream toward the small island. Menno Travel spread a table with munchies to add to the festive occasion. There were sandwiches, cookies, sodas, mounds of carrot sticks. Someone even made great quantities of potato chips. What a treat those were—it was impossible to buy them in the stores. The travel agency did business with all the airlines operating in and out of Kinshasa, and several of them had contributed door prizes for this occasion.

Arriving at the island, the captain anchored the ferry at the dock. In a few minutes, folks were diving from the boat or swimming in the cool water. Someone brought along a soccer ball and a lively game was soon in progress. We weren't sure of the reason, but the captain set the tall grass afire. When the smoke settled, our faces were spotted with sprinklings of ash and scattered raindrops. However, the real excitement was about to start.

Because the Congo River widens into a large pool between Kinshasa and Brazzaville, it develops whitecaps during a storm. A storm was now threatening. The sky darkened, the clouds looked heavy with rain, the whitecaps grew more intense. Farther out in the river, we noticed a dugout canoe, its nine passengers in serious trouble as they battled the increasing waves.

At one time the canoe, about fifteen feet in length, was a beautiful tree in the forest, but it had been cut down, hollowed out and carved into a boat for river traffic. We are told never to stand in a canoe as it might tip over. However, Congolese frequently stand in theirs to guide them. Long poles or oars are used to propel the canoe across the water. The owner of this one was more sophisticated—he had an outboard motor on his.

The high wind blew choppy waves, swamping the canoe as folks bailed water as fast as they could. Heavily laden with passengers and their purchases (for they likely had come from a shopping trip to Brazzaville), the boat began to sink right before our eyes.

It took a moment for folks on the ferry to recover from shock and yell to the captain to go to their rescue. And it seemed forever before the captain backed our boat away from the island, got it turned around, and headed toward the capsized canoe. Congolese had also seen the canoe sink and hurried to rescue the passengers. Coming from opposite ends of the island, one fisherman rowed out to help while another in his motor-powered canoe sped toward the sinking boat.

Two men from the capsized canoe started to swim against the strong current to the safety of the island. Two others held aloft a baby, only a few months old, while other passengers clung to the overturned canoe. People on our boat threw life jackets to them. Ted jumped into the water to save the baby, protecting it with a life jacket. Grandpa and Steven were aiding in the rescue as well, helping get folks to our boat and retrieve what things they could.

Floating in the water were several *baguettes*, skinny loaves of French bread, which one of the women probably intended to sell in the market in Kinshasa. In spite of the seriousness of the situation that bread bouncing on the waves looked pretty funny. Some of the folks aboard our boat, remembering a verse from the Bible, joked about casting your bread upon the water and it would come back to you. (Eccles. 11:1 KJV)

Of the nine passengers rescued, four were women. One was several months pregnant. When they were safely aboard our boat, prayers of thanksgiving were said on their behalf. We took an offering to help them replace some of their things that by now had sunk to the bottom of the Congo River.

The story isn't quite finished, however. The owner of the canoe retrieved his boat, got it turned right side up and tied it to the ferry. Trailing behind us, it broke away and he jumped back in the water to recover it a second time. Maybe his canoe did not want to be rescued. Maybe it would have been easier to chop down another tree and carve a new canoe! He managed to rescue the motor, but after being submerged in the river it would take a lot of work to clean out the water and sand, dry it, and get it running again.

Menno Travel had planned an exciting afternoon of fun for all of us, but little did they know just how exciting it would be. What a memorable excursion!

Till the next letter—

We love you, G'ma and G'pa

Where's the Beef?!

Dear Grandchildren,

After we moved to the capital city of Kinshasa, there were few opportunities to experience life in the bush. That changed one year when four other women and I were asked to participate in a women's institute at Mbonga Mbanza, located upcountry in the Kikongo area. I was eager for the opportunity. To this city lady, Mbonga Mbanza was definitely "bush."

In addition to Rose, Lee and myself, two Congolese women leaders, Mattie Nsingani and Suzanne Dungu made up the team from Kinshasa. John fetched us in the little Cessna and flew us to Kenge. Looking down on the forests as we flew above the treetops, their curly leaves reminded me of giant heads of broccoli. What a difference to travel by plane. That fifty-minute flight would have been a jolting, five-hour ride by pickup.

The Boko and Kenge women delegates and the Kenge pastor were waiting for us when the Cessna landed at the airstrip. Everyone piled into the back of the waiting pickup, and, with Dick at the wheel, we started out. It was only seventy-five miles to Mbonga Mbanza, but it took six hours of bouncing up and down the dirt road before we arrived.

I didn't know what to expect at this village where our mission had an elementary and middle school, but I soon discovered the school director was a man of ingenuity. In anticipation of the women's institute coming to his village, he had organized the school children and villagers to make necessary preparations. Women in leadership roles in their local churches were coming from all over the Kwilu area, and he wanted to be ready for them.

Outside the cities, there is nothing in the wilderness that even remotely resembles Holiday Inn or Motel 6. So how do you provide facilities for fifty women? You build them! From dormitory to dining room, from kitchen to bathrooms, you build them. Mbonga Mbanza, situated in a grassy plain, had no forest nearby, but the village men under the leadership of the energetic school director, constructed crude but adequate housing for us.

Going some distance to cut down small trees and returning with them to the village, the men built a six-room mud and stick walled dormitory with thatched roof and dirt floor. Walls were plastered with clay, taken from a large pit that was about ten feet deep by the time the buildings were finished. They even made beds for us. Beauty Rest mattress company need fear no competition from the villagers. These beds were made from narrow tree limbs laid lengthwise, tied together with vines, and supported on forked poles a couple of feet off the ground. We're not talking comfort here! The sponge rubber mat I took along did nothing for the bumps and lumps. After sleeping three nights on that bed I understood what the psalmist meant when he wrote about vexed bones! Mine were sorely vexed! Even so, that bit of creature comfort between me and the tree limbs had to have been better than the thin reed mat most of the women brought to put on their beds.

For our meetings, the director had built another structure, a long room with thatched roof overhead to protect us in case of rain. The gracious villagers had loaned much of their meager furniture for the comfort of women who had left their homes to travel to this special meeting. Probably the villagers sat on mats on the ground while we sat in their "easy chairs" or straight back chairs.

Bathing facilities were certainly unique. Some distance from our dormitory was a three-sided thatch bath shelter with little stalls to accommodate two or three persons. The fourth side looked out on tall grassland—and, we hoped, nothing else. We assumed that what we couldn't see, couldn't see us! School kids brought buckets of water from a nearby stream, emptying them into barrels for chilly baths. We lathered up with soap—and kept a wary eye on the tall grass!

To help extend the food the village people were able to provide, the Kinshasa women brought rice, cracked wheat and cartons of delicious beef canned by Canadian Mennonites and sent to Congo. The village women were highly suspicious of meat in a tin can. Most had neither seen nor tasted meat processed that way. Mackerel and pilchards could be bought in tins, but not beef. They much preferred their dried caterpillars. Those were familiar. Later in Kinshasa, this beef was highly prized and pastors frequently came asking for "food," their name for it. The women served *luku* made from manioc flour, *sakasaka* made from pounded manioc greens, and *makemba*, plantains fried in palm oil.

One evening, our supper meal was only luku and dried caterpillars cooked in a sauce. *Sakasaka* and *makemba* were a treat, but, unlike many of my missionary colleagues, I had never developed a taste for *luku*. And I definitely had never sunk my teeth into a caterpillar, dried or otherwise. I was about to go to bed hungry.

Sitting on an uncomfortable bench made just like the beds, I had this little battle going on as one of the cooks approached me with a ladle of caterpillar sauce. Would I or wouldn't I eat it? She served my bowl with an ample portion and I hesitantly tasted the sauce. Hmm. Tasted just like a musty gunny sack smelled! That figured. No doubt the caterpillars had been stored in a musty gunny sack. It's now or never, I thought and spooned up a tidbit, prepared to eat it. At that very moment the lantern hanging overhead ran out of kerosene and we were plunged into darkness. Oh joy! I was saved! But I'll never know if I would actually have had sufficient courage to put my teeth into that bit of protein.

Caterpillars for supper weren't the only unusual experience at the women's meeting. A very pregnant lady from Moanza hadn't told anyone that her baby was due in two months, and she had bounced thirteen hours over very bad roads. She started into labor after she arrived at Mbonga Mbanza. Fortunately, a nurse from the village was present, but unfortunately he goofed and gave her an injection to move things along. Thankfully, nurse Mama Mattie had medicine to counteract that, and the baby decided to wait a bit longer before making its appearance, an answer to our prayers.

In the midst of injections and concern for the expectant mother, Ruth organized the women, and we began stitching a tiny layette. We even improvised an incubator. When the would-be mama's condition stabilized, Mattie rode with her to Kenge in Doris's camper where she was then flown to Moanza in the little Cessna. Through daily radio contact with our mission stations, people knew she was flying home and Moanza folks met her at the airstrip to welcome her back. As far as I know, the baby waited until its due date, deciding it wasn't in any hurry to be born after all.

I was asked to present children's work, using visual aids and stories that the women could duplicate in their churches. The women in this area spoke Kituba, which is similar to Kikongo. My knowledge of Kituba was limited, but two of the Congolese women helped me with translation and pronunciation. Some leaders offered helps in working with teenage girls while others taught classes in child care and character development. The delegates at this meeting were leaders in their local churches and would return home with new ideas and enthusiasm.

Sunday morning we walked a mile to worship with the local village people in their thatched roof, mud and stick walled church. Seating for the congregation was as rustic as the building. Sturdy tree limbs wedged into forked poles in the ground did get quite uncomfortable after sitting on them for two or three hours! The music was terrific. Congolese have beautiful voices and they love to sing. Singing to the beat of a drum and small gourd rattles was a nice change from the little pump organ used in one of the Kinshasa churches.

You likely know the expression "getting there is half the fun." Well, getting home did not fit that description. During the meetings, it had rained heavily and the roads were a mess. The six hour drive from Kenge to Mbonga Mbanza didn't compare with the twenty-six hours it took to return to Kenge. We spent eleven of those hours trying to climb about fifty feet of a very muddy hill. Heavy rains had washed out the road and Dick and local men had to rebuild it with tree limbs.

It was dark by six o'clock, and while the men continued to repair the road, we women walked to the nearest village. (I half expected to meet that long dead, intrepid explorer Henry Morton Stanley trudging through the wilderness!) Campfires provided the only light, as there was no kerosene for lanterns. All the villagers came out to welcome us, keeping up a loud, running commentary on everything we did!

The women had worked hard all day in their gardens and they were tired. They didn't appreciate the men ordering them to fix us something to eat. Even Mattie and Suzanne wouldn't eat what they brought. It was some kind of meat, perhaps buffalo, which, shall we say, was "ripe." The luku had sand in it. There was also a large fern that grows in the forest. We know it as a fiddlehead. The fronds resemble the head of a bass fiddle and are considered a delicacy. Pineapple and bananas were lifesavers. A little boy brought me freshly shelled, green peanuts wrapped in a leaf. In their unfailing hospitality, people brought chairs and tables from their homes for our comfort. After we had eaten, the Kenge pastor's wife told them about the meetings.

Unaccustomed to the rigors of bush life, we three *mindele* (white women) were tired, and, following the service, Suzanne told us to go to bed; she and Mattie would stay up and talk with the women. We were offered a house—it had a smoky fire inside and no windows—but we preferred to sleep under the gorgeous starry sky where the Southern Cross, visible only in the southern hemisphere, shone brightly. We went to sleep with all the villagers looking on. No doubt they have dated everything since then from the night the white women slept in their village!

Having finally repaired the road, the men arrived back at the village at eleven o'clock. Five hours later, awakened by thunder and an imminent downpour, we dashed to the pickup just as the rain started. Soon, mired in sand, we were stuck again until daylight when men came to push us out. In places, the road was so badly washed that we got out and walked lest the truck turn over. While we were stalled on a hill, it seemed wise to give the right of way to a column of driver ants. Their stings are vicious. The only other wildlife we saw were partridges and a cobra that the pickup ran over. We crossed two rivers by ferry, driving onto iron boats that were pulled across the river by means of cables to the opposite shore. During the entire trip we met only two trucks.

Not only was the road practically impassable, we were almost out of gas. Trying to climb the muddy hill hours earlier had used most of a tank of gas. Dutch priests at a nearby Catholic mission sold us fuel and a loaf of bread, our breakfast for twelve adults and three toddlers. We reached Kenge by noon, enjoyed lunch with our colleagues and radioed John to come and get us in the little plane. By the time I got home, Grandpa had fixed chow mein for supper. Life in the bush had been an unforgettable experience, but this city lady's desire to taste bush life had definitely been satisfied!

Till next time, G'ma

"Band-Aids" to the Rescue!

Dear Grandkids Six,

The Congolese never ceased to amaze us with their creativity. What they lacked in material possessions was often a way for them to put their ingenuity to work. It might be a "Band-Aid" but their solution usually worked until they could do something better. We even got quite good at Band-Aids ourselves.

From time to time, there was a leaky water pipe across the street from us. Since water pressure was never good, Grandpa would contact the Water Company to report it. After he had made two or three trips to remind them of the problem, men would arrive finally to repair the leak. Imagine our surprise to see them plug the hole with a small piece of wood cut to fit the diameter of the hole! It worked, for awhile at least, and surely was much cheaper than replacing the pipe. Perhaps not as efficient, but definitely cheaper and easier. There was always plenty of wood to replace the plug when it rotted out.

One night, Grandpa and I were awakened by an odd noise. It sounded a bit like someone humming. We traced the sound to our water heater, which had sprung a leak in the middle of the night. It was really quite funny to see a stream of water arching from the water heater into the storeroom. Grandpa found a screw and metal washer and quickly stopped the leak. It was quite a while before we were able to replace the water heater, and by then it had several screws and washers to stop other spurts of water. With all those spots, it looked as though it had some infectious disease.

Children didn't have a wealth of toys like so many American kids do. Little girls rarely had dolls, and we shuddered to see some white child's cast off blue-eyed, blonde doll passed on to a little African girl. It looked so out of place. Little girls often helped care for the younger children, and it was not unusual to see them with a little brother or sister tied to their backs. Maybe those were their little dollies.

The frangipani tree has exquisite five-petaled blossoms of pink, yellow, or white, which provided little children with a toy. By threading a thin reed into the end of the blossom, the kids would run and watch the blossoms twirl like whirligigs in the breeze. Another toy was a truck or car made from a rectangular margarine box. The wheels were soda bottle caps attached to the box with a thin reed. Not very many children had a ball of any kind, so the more creative kids made their own. By using narrow strips of cloth wound round and round into a ball, it satisfied their urge to practice soccer maneuvers. More than once, we watched boys do fancy footwork with mangoes as if they were soccer balls.

The most intriguing toys were wire sculptures. I'm not sure where the wire came from—maybe someone's fence—but those toys were amazing. Although they were crude looking, they were mini-versions of motorcycles, bicycles with riders, helicopters, or trucks. The wire was intricately bent and formed into the proper shape for whatever vehicle they were making. Wheels were often wrapped with a thin slice of inner tube to make them look more authentic. Each toy had a steering wheel wire extending to the chassis so that the boy could guide it. Those handmade toys provided hours of fun for kids.

Another favorite toy was one that boys in America played with years ago. Often we watched a young kid run down a dusty street behind a bicycle rim. He used a stick inside the rim to keep it revolving.

For a time, people made toys from balsa wood. These were not from purchased kits, but were thin slices of wood from the balsa tree. The wood was carved and designed to make intricate copies of passenger boats, Volkswagens, airplanes, and trucks. It took a lot of patience and of course glue for those creations. We bought a large boat for Steven one time that looked like an ocean liner.

A lot of the guys liked guitars and often they made their own. Once we saw a marimba someone had made using varying sizes of hollow gourds for the pipes. And we even discovered a new use for empty sardine tins. A young man had attached thin wires to each end of the can and strummed it with a short stick!

Ingenuity extended to the working world as well. A truck pulled into the station one day with a large engine in the bed of the truck. We wondered how the driver would unload it as the workmen had gone home for the day. Tying a rope around a large tree and the other end to the engine, the driver drove forward slowly and the engine settled gently to the ground. At times, we ordered twenty-five or thirty barrels of fuel to be sent to the upcountry stations. The workmen had their own way of offloading the fifty-gallon drums until the time they could be sent to the interior on a truck. The men covered the ground with old tires, then rolled the barrels off the truck, thereby cushioning the drums.

Few if any vehicles have radiators today, but once we saw a driver repair a leaky one. Can you guess what he used? Not chewing gum! He stuck a wad of *chickwangue* (stiff "bread" made from manioc flour that is a staple of the Congolese diet) into the hole and continued on his way.

We applied a "Band-Aid" once when we were miles from a gas station and the gas tank of our car sprang a leak. We discovered that toothpicks are handy for more than just cleaning teeth!

Much love to all, and keep your own ingenuity dusted off. You never know when your creativity might be needed!

Miss you,
G'ma and G'pa

On Safari

On Safari in Kenya

Dear Grandkids,

Imagine arriving at the airport excited about going on vacation only to discover that your name wasn't on the passenger list. That happened to us in July 1972 when Grandpa, Susan, and I were anticipating a two-week vacation in East Africa. Steven was in the States at college.

Someone failed to include our names on the passenger list, but Mr. Mbondo from the travel agency quickly came to our rescue and saw that we got on the flight. Soon we were on our way, destination Nairobi, Kenya. It had been eight years since our trip to the Rhodesias. Now we looked forward to seeing more of the African continent. In the years since that first trip, several African countries had received independence from their former colonial rulers.

Our flight to Nairobi took us first to Bujumbura in Burundi, then later to Entebbe in Uganda. It was quite startling to look up and see machine guns mounted on the airport terminal roof at Bujumbura. Soldiers patrolling the rooftop with machine guns didn't inspire confidence either despite a huge sign at the terminal entrance proclaiming WELCOME. We felt better about the welcome sign after we were inside and were treated to delicious Burundi coffee, one of their chief exports at that time. Round, thatch roofed huts were built of mud and wattle (stakes interwoven with branches). Seven foot tall Watutsis were like pictures we had seen in National Geographic magazine. French was the official language. By contrast, Entebbe in Uganda was much greener and much cooler than Burundi, and having been a former British colony, people spoke English.

Kenya had also been a former British colony, and many customs from England carried over into this now independent nation. Driving a right-hand-drive vehicle on the left side of the street was one thing that hadn't changed. There were harrowing moments, particularly in heavy city traffic. However, Grandpa carefully avoided driving on the "wrong" side of the street and got us safely around Nairobi without any accidents.

Nairobi was quite different from Kinshasa. Living in a French speaking country, we now appreciated speaking English to shop keepers and reading newspapers in English. We were intrigued by the names of some of the streets. There was Uhuru Highway. *Uhuru* means freedom in Swahili, East Africa's major language. Haile Selassie Road honored the deceased Ethiopian emperor by that name and Kenyatta Road honored Jomo Kenyatta, Kenya's first elected president.

In 1972, Kinshasa stores didn't have much merchandise on the shelves. Nairobi stores were well stocked. Susan and I discovered a Woolworth store, a smaller version of today's Wal-Mart and had fun shopping. We discovered too, that the Colonel had made his way to Kenya before our arrival and we ate lunch at Kentucky Fried Chicken. We even indulged in banana splits at Hotel Intercontinental, Susan's treat after an afternoon of shopping. We liked Nairobi!

People watching was an interesting pastime. Nairobi seemed to welcome all nationalities: turbaned Indians, gracefully dressed Hindu women in their colorful saris, an occasional Masai wearing beaded earrings and necklaces, tourists from many countries, and Africans from all walks of life. We thought our Zairian women back in Kinshasa were much more attractive in their dress than were the Kenyan women dressed western style. We heard a multitude of languages as well: several local African languages, French, German, and English.

Nairobi was a truly beautiful city. Because the climate there is better than that of western Zaire, plants grew profusely. Huge, gorgeous roses bloomed everywhere. Large painted daisies, shades of bougainvillea not found in Kinshasa, velvety scarlet poinsettias unlike our rose red variety, beautiful flowering shrubs, green lawns. Nairobi was such a contrast from Kinshasa.

We made arrangements to rent a Volkswagen Kombi camper for our trip to the game parks, which involved a stop at a bank to cash traveler's checks. Imagine our surprise to find two uniformed guards, each holding a baseball bat at the entrance! We could only conclude that the bats were to discourage any would-be thieves who might have thoughts of robbing clients or of holding up the bank.

Having completed our shopping, we hassled our way onto a very crowded bus with our packages and in good time arrived at the mission guesthouse where we were staying.

Tomorrow we leave on our safari, which will take us through three East Africa countries. We'll have lots of new experiences to share with you.

Love you,
G'ma and G'pa

Adventures in Africa

On Safari in Kenya

Home Sweet Home in a Camper

Dear Mireille, Matt, Aaron, Nicole, Zachary, and Kalli,

We were on our way. The VW Kombi camper was delivered to us as promised, and the next morning we eagerly set out for a week's safari visiting game parks in Kenya and Tanzania. Prior to independence, Tanzania, a former German colony, was known as Tanganyika. Later we would spend another week in Uganda.

Grocery shopping for this trip was fun as the stores had so much more to buy than we ever saw in the groceries in Kinshasa. We stocked up on things we couldn't find there. There were some tense moments driving on the "wrong" side of the street, but Grandpa skillfully maneuvered through the traffic. Before long, we were on our way out of town.

Five miles outside the city, but still within sight of Nairobi's skyline, lies Nairobi National Park. Although there are no elephants in this park, there were plenty of other animals to keep us glued to the windows. We saw deer, giraffes, zebras, baboons, rhinos, several species of antelope, brightly colored birds and ostriches. By the time we arrived at Hippo Pool we figured the hippos would be waiting for us. However, they must have been out for lunch since there were none in sight. We decided to eat ours there instead.

We thought Hippo Pool was misnamed and should have been called Monkey Pool. There were plenty of those rascals around. One saucy fellow snatched a bag of cheese crackers from Grandpa's hand and dashed away with it. Your grandpa, not to be outsmarted by a sassy monkey, took off in hot pursuit. The monkey was most furious when Grandpa retrieved the bag. It came charging back, sassing and scolding for all it was worth.

Driving farther into the park, we approached Lion Dip, thinking there would be a lion or two to reward our having come all the way from Zaire. We were disappointed. When we saw a large carcass, however, we knew lions were in the area as it was a recent kill. Still farther down the road, we came upon an animal orphanage where there were leopards, a cheetah, serval cats, otters, and even an injured rhino with only one horn. At the orphanage, the animals were cared for until they were either well or old enough to be released back into the game park.

We certainly saw a lot of animals that day. But it was getting toward dusk and time to find a place to camp for the night. We drove to the security of Rowallen Boy Scout camp, situated in a nice wooded area. Eating our first meal in the camper was a major disappointment. Tough steak, rice, and peas are not exciting dinner fare. But when you're tired, it doesn't matter much what you eat. After making our beds, we settled down for a good night's rest. Susan, a bit fearful hearing all the night noises, imagined all kinds of beasties out there sharing our space, but I drifted off to sleep with the sound of a train whistle in the background. Surely, civilization couldn't be far away.

Tomorrow we're off to Tsavo. We'll tell you about that in the next letter.

Love to all of you,
G'ma and G'pa

Tsavo National Park, Kenya

Dear Grandchildren,

After a good night's sleep and breakfast of sausage and eggs the next morning, we were eager to leave Nairobi Game Park and drive to Tsavo.

In Kinshasa, our Pakistani and Indian friends had introduced us to *samosas*, those little triangular-shaped, curry-flavored meat goodies that we liked so much. To our delight, a lady was selling them outside Tsavo where we stopped to buy gas. No way could we resist buying *samosas*! We purchased a few, eager to enjoy our snack. After the first bite, we discovered they were hot, hot, hot!

A few minutes after entering Tsavo National Park, we were rewarded with our first sighting of elephants. A family of five was headed toward the water. Perhaps we appeared threatening, for they protectively placed the baby in between them while the largest stood guard and watched us. Little "Babar" was well protected from tourists! Throughout the park, tree trunks were coated red with dust where the elephants had rubbed against them. When you itch, you scratch! Baobab trees were stripped of bark, uprooted, or limbs broken as they foraged for food.

We looked forward to seeing Kenya's world famous Mt. Kilimanjaro, easily visible from Tsavo Park. Many people are challenged to climb this mountain, but we were content to view it from the windows of the camper. Occasionally the clouds parted and we could see its snow-capped head; but for the most part, Mt. Kilimanjaro kept itself hidden in the clouds.

Poachers Lookout has a fantastic view of a large area. We scanned the distant horizon below us, but failed to see animals anywhere. When the ranger invited us to look through his telescope we were amazed to discover that the place teemed with animals. Looking across the plains and hills, the animals blended in with their surroundings. Peering through the telescope, we could see elephants, giraffes, a herd of Cape buffalo—about four hundred, according to the ranger—a large herd of zebras, and three rhinos. One lazy fellow was even lying down, taking life easy. Had we not looked through the ranger's telescope, we would never have known there were hundreds of animals in the valley below us.

Toward dusk, we came upon a waterhole where elephants, giraffes, impalas, and Thomsons gazelles, affectionately known as "Tommies," had gathered to drink. Though giraffes look ungainly as they bend over to drink they are amazingly swift when they run. They are my favorite of safari animals. Their eyes are beautiful.

By now, it was time to look for a place to camp, as it would soon be dark. We found a campsite called Chyulu Gate just outside Tsavo Park. One couple had pitched their tent in a fairly open space; but, just at dusk, four elephants meandered into the area. That was scary enough to convince the campers to forsake their tent and scurry to the safety of their car where they spent the night. Since there are no fences, the animals are free to roam inside or outside the parks. And they certainly do.

Enough excitement for one day. Tomorrow will have its own excitement.

Love,
G'ma and G'pa

On Our Way to Lake Manyara

Dear Grandchildren,

In the morning, we awakened early, eager to see what new adventures we might have. By now, we were used to fixing meals in the camper and soon we had prepared a nice breakfast of sausage and eggs and crusty rolls. It wasn't long before we finished eating, cleaned up camp and were ready to be on the road.

As we were leaving the campsite that morning, tourists returning to Nairobi asked if we had enough drinking water and gave us what they had left over. On safari, we needed to carry not only drinking water but other provisions as well. Being out in the middle of nowhere, miles from the closest grocery store, there was no place where we could purchase needed supplies.

Elephants and giraffes were shy that morning and stayed out of sight, but there were large herds of impalas, water bucks, and Tommies looking for their breakfast on the grassy plain. If lions had made a kill during the night, we didn't see any evidence of animals eating the carcass. Reaching the outer boundary of Tsavo National Park, we then headed south through Masai country. We had read about the Masai in National Geographic articles and looked forward to seeing them.

The Masai are an African tribe that is fiercely independent and has steadfastly refused to adopt western ways. They are a somewhat nomadic people and are cattle herders. Masai men and boys dress in simple cloths or red blankets draped around their shoulders and tied at the neck. No blue jeans for these fellas! They herd their humpback cattle, sheep, goats, and burros all together. Each of them carried a long, thin stick and long, blunt pointed spear to keep their herds and flocks in order. The spear was also their protection against wild animals.

People appeared poor, yet we noticed that poverty didn't limit their sense of style. One lady must have been the envy of her friends as she wore an intricately designed collar of brightly colored beads that was six to eight inches deep. Someone spent hours making such an elaborate piece of jewelry. Maybe it was a gift from her sweetheart! Most of the women were barefoot, and few of them wore a fancy hairstyle. They seemed to prefer the shaved head look.

The men, however, showed far more creativity in their hairdos. Perhaps you have seen magazine pictures of some of the fancy styles the men adopt. Not content with simple earrings, many Masai men and women have huge holes in their earlobes which are decorated with beads, woven hair, and wooden disks. It takes many years to stretch the earlobes enough to insert the disks. Don't try it!

Lacking many things that we take for granted, the Masai have to be creative in using materials they have on hand to make some of the things they need. One of these is their milk bottle. They grow an elongated gourd, which when cleaned out makes a dandy container for storing milk. A mixture of cow's blood and milk evidently makes a Masai courageous! We don't recommend you try this either!

Occasionally, we saw a Masai kraal in the distance, where several huts were surrounded by a stockade. At night, the men returned their cattle to the kraal for protection from wild animals.

Leaving Tsavo, we drove through fertile country where coffee is raised. Since Grandpa loves his morning coffee, we wanted to see how it is grown. Coffee berries are red and inside are two beans. We tasted some and found they were sickeningly sweet. It's quite a process before the beans are ready for that morning cup of coffee.

By now, we had left the main road and were on our way to Lake Manyara Game Reserve, the greenest and prettiest of the parks we visited. The giraffes and impalas weren't aware they were no longer in

Tsavo Park, and it was exciting to see them along the road as we drove toward the lake.

We stopped and greeted a Masai dressed in his red blanket, ears decorated with wooden disks and carrying his ever present spear. Although the Swahili greeting in east Africa is *jambo* we discovered that nearly everybody knew "bye bye" and "okay."

Watching two flocks of flamingoes fly in formation toward the lake was another highlight of the day. In flight, their under wings are black, and it wasn't until we arrived at Lake Manyara the next day and saw them on the ground that we realized from their pink feathers that they were flamingoes.

Tonight we are camped just outside Lake Manyara Game Reserve in a lovely, wooded area. The sound of a nearby rushing stream should lull us to sleep.

Love you lots,
G'ma and G'pa

Elephants for Breakfast

Dear Grandkids,

The sound of the stream did lull us to sleep. We slept well, snug and safe in our camper. Three other groups had set up tents in the clearing where we were camped. Their fires, which they kept burning throughout the night, discouraged wild animals from venturing too close. We were thankful for those fires, as we woke up once or twice to hear hyenas "laughing." After a good night's sleep we were eager to drive through the game reserve. Maybe this would be our lucky day... maybe we would see a lion.

We were wiping away the crumbs from our breakfast of strawberry jam and *pistolets* (delicious crusty rolls) prior to driving into the game reserve when we heard loud trumpeting right outside our rented camper. What on earth was happening? We sprang to the open door to investigate the noise just in time to see a woman dash frantically for the safety of her tent. Four huge elephants burst out of the forest right through one end of our campground! Two of them stopped long enough to stare at us before crashing on their way.

Even though we were outside the game park, we were definitely on the elephants' turf. Why had they come thundering out of the forest? Were they going to come back and stomp on the tents and our camper? Were they going to stomp on all of us? It had happened so quickly! Our hearts were pounding double time. Elephants sharing your breakfast space do get the adrenaline pumping!

After that awesome experience, we drove into the park to see more of God's wonderful creatures. Rounding a curve, we came upon a fantastic sight. Standing in the middle of the road, three giraffes craned their long necks to feast on leaves from trees along the edge of the road. They eyed us with gorgeous dark eyes, then calmly continued their meal. (With that long neck, is a giraffe miserable if it gets a sore throat?)

Driving through the park, we continued to see a wide variety of animals. There were impalas, baboons, and monkeys, a large herd of mean looking Cape buffalo. There were tiny dikdiks (miniature antelopes), giraffes, and a lone, young elephant having his breakfast along the edge of the road. He stripped the tree of its leaves, then wrapping his trunk around the small tree, uprooted it. Stopping by Lake Manyara for lunch, we ate sandwiches and watched a flock of flamingos lift off in flight, their delicate pink feathers lovely in the sunlight.

There was another adrenaline moment when fourteen elephants crossed the road directly in front of us. They were all ages, from babies to adults. The little ones were kept on the far side to protect them from dangerous, pesky tourists. When a couple of adult elephants started down the road toward us Grandpa was ready to put the camper in reverse gear. They must have decided we took their warning seriously, for they turned around and followed after the others. Elephants definitely have the right-of-way in Africa!

We had heard about the tree-climbing lions in Lake Manyara Game Reserve and hoped it would be our lucky day to find at least one.

We had seen pictures of them lying lazily along lofty branches. Even though we scanned trees on both sides of the road, not one pounced on us. In fact, we saw only two lions the entire two weeks of our trip. One was the MGM lion logo on a movie screen in Mombasa, and the other was a stuffed one in the Nairobi museum. Do you think they count?

Tomorrow we're off to Ngorongoro Crater in Tanzania.

Love to all,
G'ma and G'pa

Things That Go Bump in the Night

Dear Sharp and Brenner Grandkids,

The next day found us driving to Ngorongoro Crater in Tanzania. En route, we stopped to buy gas at Kitara, a Masai village where we had an unusual experience. We had no Tanzania money yet, only Kenya shillings. It was Saturday and the banks were closed. Rules were strict about cashing travelers checks or changing money. The African station attendant deciding we looked honest said, "You can pay me when you come back from Ngorongoro." That seemed too trusting to us . . . how could he be sure we would return? This was the only road to and from the park, he explained, and we should just stop in and pay for the gas when we came back! The only information he knew about us was that Murray Sharp from Congo was the driver. People would never have been that trusting in Zaire. It was not uncommon for people in East Africa to refer to Zaire as Congo since it was only a year earlier that the country had changed its name to Zaire.

It was a steep climb from Kitara to Ngorongoro Crater. But what an enchanting drive! The trees were heavy with moss, a perfect setting for an Alfred Hitchcock thriller. (Ask your folks who he was.) We stopped at Crater Lodge and viewed thousands of flamingos, pink in the sunset, through the telescope as they settled on the lake on the crater floor two thousand feet below. There, too, Masai herdsmen tucked their cattle away for the night in round *kraals* built of branches and small huts. (Can you think of an English word that sounds very similar? Both mean an enclosure for animals.)

South of the equator, Ngorongoro Crater at eight thousand feet altitude was cold in July. It's an extinct volcanic basin-shaped depression which measures ten and twelve miles across. The crater is home to elephants, black rhinoceros, leopards, buffalo, zebras, warthogs, wildebeests, and gazelles. Large numbers of lions call it home also, although we didn't see any. The closest we got to lions was at our campsite, which was named *Simba,* the Swahili word for lion. People must like that name in East Africa, as a number of places are called *Simba*. Much as we wanted to see lions, we weren't anxious to share our camping spot with them. There was no firewood at this campsite, and, since the water was ice cold, we opted to eat dinner at the lodge where we enjoyed the local specialty: nonsweet bananas with beef, and kingfish from Dar es Salaam.

Reluctant to return to our cold campsite, we spent the evening in front of the fire at the lodge. When it grew late, we started back to *Simba*. En route, our headlights picked up the glowing eyes of a Cape buffalo right there in the middle of the road. We stopped breathing! He was huge. While meeting this dangerous animal in the darkness didn't compare with the elephant experience of the previous morning, this was still a scary moment. We stopped and waited for him to move on before we moved on.

As though meeting a Cape buffalo in the dark wasn't bad enough, we soon discovered we had a flat tire. Now changing a tire at night, possibly surrounded by wild animals, was not Grandpa's idea of a fun way to end the evening. A combination of buffalo, darkness, and coldness intimidated us enough to drive our bumpy way to camp on that flat tire and wait for daylight before changing it. When we arrived at the campsite a few minutes later we found we were the only campers. Alas, no tent folks with warm, friendly fires were there to welcome us and scare off the beasties.

Grandpa woke the next morning and with courage born only of necessity, changed the flat tire in the chilly morning air. Clouds rolled in, covering our mountaintop. Masses of Shasta daisies grew everywhere; it was so cold we could see our breath on the air. We found enough twigs to start a fire and soon hot coffee and cereal warmed us as we ate breakfast.

We spent the day driving through Ngorongoro and never saw the Cape buffalo of the previous night's experience. Watching zebras at the lodge, Grandpa wanted zebra steaks for lunch. As it turned out, they were on the menu, but only in the evening. However, by then he had missed his one chance to find out if zebra steaks are striped. We settled for braised lamb chops with fresh squash, potatoes, and cabbage at Arusha that evening instead.

Plants thrived in Ngorongoro's cold, crisp climate. Red begonias, daisies, and nasturtiums grew in profusion at the lodge. A dozen zebras freely roamed the grounds. Their markings are much like fingerprints . . . no two zebras are marked alike. Driving through the park we had wonderful views of Crater Lake and the variety of animals on the plain below.

The descent from Ngorongoro Crater to Arusha was a beautiful drive. Along the way, we stopped to have the tire repaired and discovered we had picked up a thorn somewhere. The foliage was dense and the hills were green with coffee farms. Troops of baboons and several ostriches along the road kept us on the lookout for wildlife. A Masai herding his cattle definitely did not want us to take his picture and we drove on. Three scrappy little Masai girls with decorated ears and fancy necklaces insisted they be paid before we took their pictures. We stopped at Kitara and paid for the previous day's gas. Susan and I checked out the local market and bought Tanzanian fabric. Farm produce and homegrown tobacco were sold in the market as well.

Beautiful orange tulip trees bloomed on both sides of the road leading into Arusha. What a lovely welcome. We found our campsite and settled in for the night.

Tomorrow's another day.

Love you, G'ma and G'pa

"Boy Scouts" to the Rescue

Dear Grandkids,

Morning came to Arusha, and with it, three little Indian boys bent on doing their good deed for the day. They persisted in bringing wood for our fire. So dedicated were they to their task they kept rearranging our fire! Had they been true Boy Scouts they would have earned a merit badge that day. The aroma of fried potatoes and eggs cooking over an open fire perked our breakfast appetites.

While we were at the market shopping for veggies, we were astonished to see a small, barefoot man carrying a large, ivory tusk over his shoulder. It was so heavy he was bent over beneath its weight, forcing him to walk rapidly. It must have been a recent kill, as the large end of the tusk was still bloody. Was he a poacher? Was he legally in possession of the tusk? No one else appeared to share our astonishment. There seemed to be no end of amazing sights on this safari!

Was carrying an ivory tusk on one's shoulder through the streets of Arusha an everyday occurrence? Was he going to sell the tusk? Was he an ivory carver? What happened to the elephant meat? Surely some of it would be eaten fresh. Would the rest be dried and smoked and sold in the market? And what about the tail? Would the heavy black hairs be worked into a bracelet like those we had seen in tourist shops? We wondered about so many things.

We watched another man carve African animals from wood. They are a hot tourist item in Nairobi and other major East Africa cities. With just a few simple tools the wood carvers make excellent likenesses of the animals that are so much a part of their everyday lives.

Arusha was an interesting town, but it was time to continue on our way and drive the bumpy, dirt road that would take us through more Masai country. At Namanga on the Tanzania-Kenya border, we passed through customs for both countries. Now, back in Kenya, it was a relief to drive to Amboseli Game Reserve on a nice paved road. Twenty miles later, however, we made an unpleasant discovery. We had made a wrong turn at the border and were not on our way to the Game Reserve after all. That meant backtracking all the way to Namanga to pick up the washboard, dirt road into Amboseli. What a bummer!

As we bounced along the dusty road, we saw large herds of zebra and wildebeest. If there were lions or leopards about, they kept themselves hidden from view. We stopped at the lodge where Susan had a swim while Grandpa and I enjoyed the lovely British custom called teatime. At dusk, as we drove through the park, we were rewarded with more sightings of elephants, giraffes, Cape buffalo, and a black rhino.

Amboseli was dry and barren, in places almost desertlike compared to the green lushness of Ngorongoro. How did the big animals survive in Amboseli? And how could the Masai with their cattle herds compete with the wild animals for the available vegetation? It didn't seem possible, but somehow they managed.

We found our campsite located near the woods, fixed supper, built a cozy fire, and let it burn all night. In the morning, we went in search of more animals. In addition to those we had seen the day before, we sighted impalas, Thomsons gazelles, baboons, monkeys, and ungainly looking ostriches. Still no lions. They simply eluded us. Maybe they were in the trees looking down on those crazy tourists!

We had been in "the zoo" for a week and had seen enough animals to last us for a lifetime. It was time to head back to Nairobi, hunt up a Laundromat and get clean again—which we did!

Love to our favorite six, G'ma and G'pa

Back to Civilization

Dear Aaron, Nicole, Zachary, and Kallianne,

Driving through Amboseli Game Park was a slow and dusty ride, but once we reached the paved highway at Emali, the final seventy-five miles to Nairobi went quickly. We occasionally saw animals along the road. Since fences didn't enclose the game parks, the animals roamed freely.

After a week on safari, the first thing we wanted was a Laundromat. With our clothes clean once more, we looked for a campsite and spent the night in Nairobi City Park where other campers were getting settled. Several folks whom we had met at different camps during the week had also found this place. On safari, our paths kept crossing one another.

In the morning, we returned the camper to Sea, Sun and Safari and checked into a hotel. Ah, the luxury of a real bath. Hot, running water! How good to pamper ourselves and soak off all that safari dirt. Before we went to bed that night, there was a knock at the door. When I opened it a young boy stood outside with a can of bug spray. Looking serious he said, "I have come to spray the room for mosquitoes." There was always a new experience!

Shopping in Nairobi where the stores had a wide choice of merchandise was fun. We found the Woolworth store again. Susan was eager to spend the twenty-five shillings Grandpa had given her as "mad money." She had fun going up and down the aisles of the store to make her choices. Grandpa bought shoes for climbing over coral in the ocean. And my favorite purchase? A bottle of pure vanilla. We couldn't buy it in Kinshasa, and homemade ice cream tasted much better with real vanilla in it.

After enjoying a day in Nairobi we were on our way again, . . . this time to Mombasa by train where we had a compartment for the all-night trip. Dinner in the diner was delicious, your mom and I ordering curried chicken and Grandpa choosing roast leg of lamb. The rhythm of the train lulled us to sleep, and we awoke the next morning feeling refreshed and eager for the day's activities. At sunup, we spotted a dikdik, a miniature deer, as the train made its way through Tsavo Game Park.

Our destination was Kanamai, a campground twenty miles outside Mombasa. Now, getting there posed a problem, as we had returned the camper to the rental agency in Nairobi. Leaving your mom and me at the train depot, Grandpa, ever resourceful, went in search of transportation.

In twenty minutes, he zoomed back driving a bright, canary yellow dune buggy! Pretty snazzy transportation! But your mom was horrified. "Oh, Dad!" she wailed. Even though we were several thousand miles from our home in Kinshasa, Susan was certain that somebody she knew would see us, and she would be forever humiliated to be seen riding in a dune buggy. That afternoon, her opinion of such transportation changed completely when Grandpa let her drive it.

En route to Kanamai, we drove through Fort Jesus, a fifteenth-century Portuguese fort with a beautiful view of the bay. Finding an outdoor market, we bought fresh vegetables and fruit before continuing on our way. There were even two toll bridges crossing narrow streams before we finally reached our destination.

Right on the beach, our cottage at Kanamai bore the name of *mnazi,* the Swahili word for coconut. It was well named, as the campground had dozens of coconut palms. Ours in Zaire stood tall and straight, but these skinny-trunked trees bent out toward the ocean. Our thatch-roofed cottage was cool and gave us a wonderful view of the Indian Ocean through the palms.

The shoes Grandpa bought in Nairobi were just what he needed for walking out to the coral reef some distance from shore. He and Susan made several trips there, but I was a tenderfoot, lacking beach shoes. The three of us took long walks along the beach hunting shells. Swimming in the warm, blue Indian Ocean was much different from swims in the Atlantic at Nsiamfumu in Zaire where the water was colder and riding the waves was a lot more challenging.

Long before we were ready to wake up the next morning, crowing roosters rudely awakened us. We expected to share our space with wild animals when we were on safari, but were unprepared for the domestic kind that were owned by people who lived nearby. We had dark thoughts about tracking down the culprits that had disturbed our sleep. Maybe we could have chicken and dumplings for lunch!

Later that morning, we drove to Mombasa to leave the dune buggy. But how would we get back to Kanamai? Just then, an ancient bus going that direction drove up and we flagged it down. Buses in Africa are usually extremely overcrowded with people and their belongings. This one was no exception. We were the only white passengers. An elderly Indian dipped snuff, a Moslem man embroidered a hat, black shawled women chatted. Music blared loudly from the bus radio. A quite rotund motorcycle policeman stopped the bus for a road check. For some reason, which we were unable to figure out, the driver then had all the passengers switch seats, rather like musical chairs. We would have missed that experience if we hadn't ridden a rattletrap bus.

The week we spent at Kanamai was both fun and relaxing. It was nice to be lazy and unhurried. There were long walks on the beach and refreshing swims in the ocean. We bought fresh fruit and vegetables, prawns, and other seafood. Searching for marine life, we found perfect starfish, sea urchins, tiger cowries, sea cucumbers, and sea anemones that squirted "grape juice" when we touched them. There were restaurants where we enjoyed good curry and fish dinners. At one, the owner had a cute Chihuahua with the unlikely name, *Simba*. We even found a drive-in movie theater where we saw "Good-bye Mr. Chips," the first movie we had seen in English since leaving the States two years earlier.

The day before we returned to Nairobi, we discovered Nyali Beach, where swimming, beachcombing, and people watching were more fun. As we walked along the shore, we saw African women dressed in brightly colored cloth. Many of them carried heavy loads on their heads. Moslem women were totally covered in black, and most of the men, bare chested, wore a simple loincloth tied at the waist. The weather alternated between sun and rain, but we didn't care . . . we were having a grand time!

We leave for Nairobi tomorrow. We're on our way to Uganda next.

Love you, G'ma and G'pa

We're Off to Entebbe, Uganda

Dear Grandchildren,

We had planned to return to Nairobi by train until Sun, Sea and Safari asked us to drive a car from Mombasa to Nairobi for them. We sorted through the shells we had found beachcombing, repacked our suitcases and headed back to the capital city. During the six and half hours on the road, we saw two elephants, a troop of baboons, and a small herd of antelope. Since the animals didn't distinguish between game parks and open countryside, we had more opportunity to see them in their natural environment. As usual, the lions, if there were any lurking in the underbrush, remained out of sight.

When we returned to Nairobi, some of the university students were on strike making certain demands. Among them, they wanted signs at campus intersections reading "SLOW Intellectuals' Crossing."

Mombasa, Kenya

On Safari

The next day in Letters to the Editor someone wrote suggesting the students get a sign from a local elementary school with the message "SLOW Children's Crossing." We thought that was a witty response to the students' demand.

While riding a bus one morning, we observed a passenger, an older man, wearing an extremely large headdress. It was quite similar to the lion-maned ones the Kikuyu wore and resembled one we had seen earlier in the Nairobi Museum. Quite a sight! We learned new things about Kenyan culture each time we rode a bus.

Two days later, East African Airlines flew us to Entebbe in Uganda, which was only an hour's flight from Nairobi. A short taxi ride took us to Kampala, the capital city, where we found a hotel and settled in for the night. In the morning, we rented a Volkswagen "beetle" and drove to Murchison Falls Park which is on the Victoria Nile River. Throughout East Africa, there are lodges that cater to tourists, and we found them to be a good place to eat lunch. They served wonderful curry dishes with side dishes of coconut, tomato, and papaya, chopped onion, raisins, and mango chutney. So very tasty, and so very hot! Those lodge dinners were where I later got my inspiration for making "six boy curry" as one of my friends who had served in India as a missionary called it. (She said that each dish of condiments was carried to the table by a school boy.)

En route to the park, we didn't see much wildlife. Just a few elephants, some Cape buffalo, and a waterbuck. Then we arrived at the Nile River. It looked so narrow! Could this really be the famous Nile! We expected it to be much wider. Since we were near its source, the river is narrow at that point. At the entrance to the park, we were amused at the sign instructing us to "Drive Slowly. Elephants have the right of way!" Although we didn't see many elephants at Murchison Falls, we did watch one wandering behind the lodge where we stayed. We let him have the right of way.

A motorized ferry took us across the river, where we heard hippos snorting and saw a number of them along the banks. As we drove from the ferry to Paraa Lodge, a huge hippo stood on the bank like a welcoming committee. He looked quite tame, but we knew better than to approach him more closely. Hippos need to be submerged in water or mud much of the time to prevent their sensitive skin from drying out.

The next morning, we were awakened by a knock at the door. It was only 6:45 AM. Who could it possibly be? We hadn't ordered room service. When we opened the door, there stood a smiling young African with our wake up cup of... tea! What a disappointment for these coffee drinkers! A fresh cup of coffee would have been a better way to get our morning started. Uganda, having been a former British colony, had retained the British custom of morning tea. These Americans were hopelessly out of sync.

After breakfast, we joined other tourists on the *Simba*, a motorized river launch which took us to Murchison Falls where the water plunges over the rocks into the river below. Awesome! At this point, the Nile River narrows to only twenty feet across. The river was literally full of hippos and crocodiles sharing their bathtub. Aren't they natural enemies, we wondered? Maybe they got along better than we thought... until it's lunchtime and a croc is hungry. Several of those ugly critters were sleeping along the bank with their jaws open, showing all their nasty teeth. The noise from the approaching launch sent many of them slithering into the water. In addition to the submerged or swimming hippos, we spotted elephants, giraffes, Cape buffalo, and hartebeest at a distance.

Arriving back at Paraa Lodge, a mama hippo and her baby were standing on the bank to welcome us. We ate lunch at the lodge, the cold buffet for Grandpa and Susan, the Madras beef curry for me, then started back to Entebbe for our return flight to Kinshasa. Along the way, we were stopped at a roadblock where two uniformed young men ordered us out of the car. We couldn't imagine what we had done wrong. We got out as demanded and one of the men got in... with a butterfly net! He was with the tsetse fly control department, and he was checking to be sure we were not giving a free ride to any of those flies. The bite of a tsetse fly (large as a horse fly) causes sleeping sickness in humans and cattle. Confident that we were not transporting any flies, the control officer got out of the car, we got back in, and we were on our way again.

After returning the Volkswagen to Rhino Safaris we walked to a nearby Wimpy's for hamburgers. They weren't exactly the kind we were used to, being more the shape of meatballs, but they tasted good anyway. Indians operated Wimpy's. They are the commercial people in several of the East Africa countries. The women and little girls looked so pretty in their lovely saris. There were many white turbaned men. A piece of elastic under the chin of one man held his turban in place. Another had his thick beard oiled so that it clung to his face. People watching was an amazing experience!

In Entebbe, we boarded Air Zaire's flight to Kinshasa with a short stopover in Bujumbura. We sat on the plane a long time wondering why the delay. As we learned later the band, the dignitaries, and the red carpet were all for Mobutu, president of Zaire, and his entourage.

At last, we were airborne and on our way again. Arriving at Ndjili airport in Kinshasa several hours later, we had to wait to deplane until the president and his traveling companions had gotten off. Going through customs took more time, but we were finally through the formalities and home again. Lee had supper waiting for us, a perfect welcome. After three weeks on safari it was good to be home.

Love to all of you,
G'ma and G'pa

7

Kaleidoscope II

All that Glitters is not Gold

Dear Grandkids,

When Belgium still governed Congo, people making a contribution to the life of the country were awarded medals if they had served fifteen years or more. Congolese leaders, Belgians, expatriates, government people, missionaries—those who had helped in the development of the country were given this recognition. Even though Protestant missionaries had worked in Congo from its earliest days as a colony, they were rarely included in the award ceremonies.

That changed a few years after independence. Pelenda, one of our Kinshasa teachers, felt it wasn't right that his missionaries who worked as teachers, pastors, builders, doctors, and nurses were never recognized for the contribution they made to help the country grow and develop. He wanted our years of service recognized as well.

Gathering information about our six missionary couples working in Kinshasa at that time, Pelenda presented this data to the new government. In due time, we were invited to attend an award ceremony at the *Palais du Peuple* (People's Palace). We were to be honored. Be there at seven o'clock in the morning, we were told. That seemed a bit early to us, and we wondered if any of the Congolese dignitaries would be there at that time. Nonetheless, we arrived right on schedule. Cordially welcomed by a Congolese, we were ushered to the stage where we were given places of honor. There wasn't another soul in sight.

Time passed and we wondered why others hadn't arrived. We had been sitting on stage for two hours when people began trickling into the auditorium. Curiously, most of them bowed their heads and prayed silently for a few moments. A choir began to sing. Were we at the wrong meeting? This seemed more like a church service than an award ceremony. Yes, we were in the right place and we had the correct time, but, no, the assembled people weren't there to see us receive our awards.

It was Monday following Pentecost Sunday, a legal holiday in many countries. Before Jesus ascended into heaven, he promised to send the Holy Spirit (the Helper) to those who trust in him as Savior. Around the world, Pentecost is celebrated fifty days after Easter. People from Pentecostal churches throughout the city of Kinshasa were gathering at the People's Palace to celebrate the occasion. We had stumbled into their meeting quite by accident.

Slightly embarrassed for being in the wrong place, our group went outside where a number of people were milling about. Like ourselves, they too had been summoned to the award ceremony. By now it was getting hot standing in the sun as we shifted our weight from one foot to the other and waited . . . and waited . . . Finally, someone came to inform us that an army officer had died. Therefore the band would not be coming to play for us. Evidently medals could not be awarded without proper band music!

Medals were to have been given for Longevity, Courage, and Devotion. We were to have received ours for Longevity. Even though we were courageous and devoted to our work and the Congolese people, only longevity counted!

We decided to party anyway, and when we returned to the mission station Dolores put on the coffeepot, Rose made coffeecake, and I made cheese omelet. At least we all enjoyed a victory breakfast, if no victory!

~

None of us cared whether we were recognized or not, but several years later a message was sent to the mission station that a group of us were to appear at the fairgrounds for a special awards ceremony. We were to be awarded after all. This time, several of our Congolese colleagues were to be included as well. The day came, and our Congolese men dressed neatly in their *abacosts,* a type of suit worn without ties. Men were not allowed to wear ties at that time as they were considered too reminiscent of European influence. The *abacost* was Congo's answer to men's business suits and actually came from the French *à bas costume,* meaning literally "down with suits."

That morning, thirty-five of us left at 8:30 to be present at the proper time. Congolese defined time as *mindele* (white people's), and Congolese. All the years we lived in Africa, we tried to be present when a meeting was scheduled and invariably waited and waited for others to get there. This day was no different.

When we arrived, another group appeared annoyed that ours was there to be recognized also. None of us knew why since the mission had received a written invitation to be present for the ceremony. Then we learned that someone had goofed and had not notified those in charge that our group would be present. There was consternation when we Americans appeared, even though we had been included in the invitation. Not knowing Americans were coming, the band couldn't play our anthem! The band decided they could work hard and maybe play it, but we would have to pay them! We Americans declined, having no intention of paying anyone to play our national anthem.

It appeared that those responsible for the ceremony wanted a tidy sum from our group if we were to be included in the celebration.

Unfortunately, demanding a bribe was a way of life. The previous day, the mission treasurer had sent money for our participation in the event. Our Congolese general secretary negotiated with those in charge and a sum was agreed upon. The people in the offices were expecting to have a big party as their way of celebrating for the work they had done prior to the award ceremony. They expected us to pay for it! A friend of ours once said, "If you're expecting logic, you're in the wrong country."

With all the "business" taken care of, festivities were ready to begin. Standing thirty-five minutes in the hot sun, we watched the

Receiving Our Medals

performers sing and dance and wiggle their hips to the beat of two tall drums, a whistle, and a bell-shaped instrument of some kind. The band knew how to play Congo's national anthem and did—three times. There were a couple of speeches, and finally the vice-governor pinned medals on everyone. Grandpa and I were given gold, silver, and bronze. We were well-decorated! As the vice-governor pinned a gold medal on my dress he said, *"Madame, j'ai un probleme!"* (Lady, I've got a problem!) But he managed.

Having stood four hours in the hot sun, we would have been far more comfortable at home—except for the "honor" of the thing! Even so, we were pleased that our deserving Congolese leaders had been recognized.

Till next time. G'ma and G'pa

Is Getting There Half the Fun?

Dear Grandkids,

It was August, and school would start in a few weeks. If we were going to have a vacation that summer, we needed to be on our way. In the eight years since we had first come to Congo, we had always gone to another mission station for vacation. While it was nice to spend time with our colleagues when we needed a break from our work, we wanted a totally different scene.

That's how we happened to be aboard an Air Congo DC-3 en route to Moanda on Congo's coast one morning in late August. Overlooking the Atlantic Ocean, Moanda offered just the change we were looking for. It was a three-hour flight (twelve hours by road, several miles of it unpaved) with a short stop at Matadi. We were surprised and pleased to meet Yandu, a former student of ours when we taught at Nsona Mpangu. He had also worked for us, chopping wood for our hungry wood stove. Now he was a weatherman for the airport.

Airborne once more, our pilot risked heart failure among his passengers as he flew daringly down the Congo River. Even though you would call the Crystal Mountains hills, there were times when our plane was below their tops. There were also times when we were below the tops of palm trees and baobabs growing along the riverbank. I found myself wishing the plane were equipped with pontoons—or that the pilot would gain some altitude. It was one scary flight. Steven was ten that summer, and, when we landed safely at Moanda, the pilot asked him if the flight was exciting enough for him. Flying so close to the water was surely illegal—but it couldn't be beat for getting the adrenaline pumping!

Our accommodations were in one of the little cottages at the Mangrove Hotel. Susan hadn't slept in a crib for years and she was indignant to find that was the only bed for her. After all, she was five years old and not a baby.

Meals were delicious, with lots of local seafood on the menu. The maitre d' was especially delighted the day the cooks prepared fresh sardines. As he circulated among the tables he made sure the diners were as excited about the silvery morsels as he was. We were unimpressed with fresh sardines, much preferring those tinned in oil or mustard sauce, but assured the eager maitre d' they were indeed quite tasty. He was so pleased with the "catch of the day" we didn't want to disappoint him. In the dining room, a cat roamed from one table to another hoping someone would toss her a bite of steak or fish. But she was fussy and would eat only bites that had been specifically cut off for her.

One day, a group of us went fishing in the mouth of the Congo River, where we had great luck catching three barracudas. Mine was a nine-pounder, and the Congolese guide was anxious to land it. I could have done it, but he was so eager I handed him the pole. Steven hooked a five-pound perch and proudly reeled it in. Although the hotel would prepare any fish its patrons caught, we decided to take ours to nearby Vista and share them with Niles and Wisemans, our colleagues who were vacationing there. They had caught the other barracudas.

A fish fry on the beach would be the perfect ending to a fun-filled day. Grandpa filleted Steven's perch and grilled it with some of the barracudas over the fire. Dorothy's cook, Bavula, pan-fried the rest. Soon, the delicious aroma of fresh fish sizzling over the coals filled the air. Tata Bavula ranked high in Steven's and Glen's estimation, as he knew how to dry fish heads. Now they would have trophies to show their friends from their first fishing trip on the Congo River!

Long walks along the beach, working on our tans (we didn't know then that the sun's rays were so harmful), building sand castles, chasing crabs as they scuttled into their holes, riding the waves at Tonde Beach, and even watching the sun sink into the Atlantic Ocean provided hours of fun and relaxation. We were having a delightful vacation.

One afternoon we followed the beach, walking from the Mangrove Hotel to Vista. At times, the tide, determined to catch up with us, sent us scurrying to avoid getting our shoes and clothes wet. There were rocks to clamber over, an old lighthouse to inspect. In years gone by, it had guided sailors, warning them of dangerous rocks; but now it was no longer in use. We climbed the stairs to the top and looked out the windows to the wide Atlantic Ocean. Another year when we vacationed at Vista, we found an owl nesting in the lighthouse with her little family of fuzzy owlets.

Steven and Susan Walking the Beach at Vista

Adventures in Africa

Prior to 1960, Moanda and Vista had been favorite vacation spots for Europeans. Then came independence, and many people fled the country, never to return. Homes no longer occupied were now for sale. With colleagues Niles and Wisemans, we decided to explore the area a bit and look at some of the abandoned houses at Vista. Our part of Congo offered very little as a desirable vacation site. Maybe Vista would be the answer.

Overlooking the ocean stood a house with a huge baobab tree in the front yard and another down on the shore. Peeking in the windows, we could see the house would be adequate for two or three families to share on vacation. We were excited and could scarcely wait to return to Leopoldville and share our discovery with others. In due time, our Stateside mission headquarters purchased the house.

For several years, many of our families spent delightful vacations at Vista. Your parents have happy memories of the good times we shared there as a family. However, memories are all we have as the mission finally had to sell Villa CBZO, the name everyone called the house. CBZO was a French acronym which meant Baptist Community of Western Zaire. Our missionary presence in Congo had dwindled. The house was constantly broken into by thieves. The incoming tide continued to eat away the cliff on which the house sat. Even before we returned to the States for retirement, the path from the house to the shore had eroded badly, making the descent difficult. The huge baobab on the shore had fallen over, its shallow roots no longer able to support its massive girth. It reminded me of a fat old elephant lying there waiting to be carried out to sea by the tide. If the baobab still stands in the front yard, you would find your parents' initials carved into its trunk. Could it speak, that tree would tell us a lot about the different kids and adults who spent happy vacations there, making sure their initials were preserved for posterity.

I'm feeling nostalgic about a very special place, so this is it for tonight.

Much love, G'ma and G'pa

Partners in Crime

Dear Mireille and Matt,

They couldn't have picked a worse time. It was an August day in 1967 when your dad (fifteen years old) and three friends unthinkingly got into big trouble. A few weeks earlier, mercenaries (professional soldiers paid to fight for an army other than that of their own country) had attacked for a second time the cities of Kisangani and Bukavu in eastern Congo. Tempers were short, and folks were on edge, wondering what might happen next. Would there be more fighting? Now, on this day in mid-August, some angry people sacked the Belgian Embassy in downtown Leopoldville. It was this same day that four boys, at loose ends, bored and unaware of the events in town, decided to right what they considered a wrong.

Our mission station, built on the banks of the Congo, had a beautiful view of the river. On one side of the property was CHANIC, the Belgian owned shipyards. Each dry season, a large sandbar appeared in front of the station and was visible until the rains began again in September. CHANIC, putting in a dry dock to service riverboats, dredged the sandbar, then dumped the sand in a corner bordering on mission property. A fence was then erected along what previously had been mission riverbank frontage. The dry dock would allow CHANIC to make repairs below the waterline of a boat. A riverboat now blocked what had been a beautiful view of the river. The boys were highly indignant.

Earlier that summer, Steven and Kevin read a book about some British POWs. Digging a tunnel under the fence that separated them from the rest of the world, those intrepid prisoners made their way to freedom. Although we didn't know of Steven's and Kevin's escapade until many years later, these teenagers, after reading the book, were inspired to dig under the wall that separated mission property from the home of the Belgian director of CHANIC who lived on the other side of us. Although the gate to their yard was frequently open, walking through it was too tame for a couple of boys with big imaginations.

Reading the book about the prison break was their inspiration for what happened next, but their real motivation had more to do with moral indignation, your father says.

Before the boys left on their mission, they stopped first to check Grandpa's toolbox. Seeing his wire cutters, one of the boys picked them up, and the four started toward CHANIC. They could have walked right through the front gate, but going in through a hole cut in the fence would help make things even, they thought. They ambled toward the area where President Mobutu's boat was being re-outfitted. Guards approached. The boys split. Steven and Kevin walked calmly to the exit while Glen and Roger ran along the river towards the rapids. In hot pursuit, the guards captured the runners, and the two boys were taken to the nearby police station.

Realizing that the others had not walked out the gate with them, Steven and Kevin went to tell Grandpa what had happened. They drove to the police station where two scared, sheepish looking boys were waiting. A policeman held the guilty wire cutters. The boys weren't trying to sabotage the shipyards, they were just venting their frustration that CHANIC had obstructed our view of the river by building a dry dock in front of mission property.

When everything was settled and the boys were free to go, the policeman, looking longingly at the wire cutters said, "I'll just keep these." And he did. I wonder if he still has them?

It would never be right to cut a hole in someone's fence, but it's definitely not recommended when an embassy has been sacked and people are nervous and easily excited! No more reading about POW exploits for these boys.

Love you, G'ma and G'pa

Kinshasa Was Never Like This

Dear Grandchildren,

Passports and visas in hand, the four of us boarded a flight to South Africa. Classes had finished in Kinshasa for the school year, and we were taking advantage of vacationing in another African country. Arriving in Johannesburg was like stepping into another world. The clean streets were one of the first things we noticed. Even the major streets in Kinshasa were frequently littered with trash. Unfortunately for native South Africans, the wretched system of apartheid was still in effect. While Africans suffered many injustices, special privileges were granted to others living there, particularly those of European descent. The country was still under British control.

It was a chilly Saturday afternoon in July when we stepped from the plane in Johannesburg. Susan, wearing flip-flops, needed a pair of shoes. We didn't know that shops closed at 1:00 PM on Saturday and didn't open again until Monday morning. She endured icy feet until we were able to buy shoes two days later. South of the equator, the seasons are opposite to what we know in the States. Coming from tropical Africa, we found South Africa beautiful, but cold. It was winter there! Not as cold as winter in America, of course, but cold to us.

Grandpa had arranged to have a car waiting at the airport, and, after clearing customs inspection, we were on our way to Durban, a lovely city on the Indian Ocean. We had to get used to driving on the left side of the road with the steering wheel on the right-hand side of the car. The roads were paved, many of them hedged with scarlet poinsettias—quite a change from the elephant grass that bordered Congo roads! Except for the major roads in our part of Congo, none were paved. Prosperous looking farms were owned by Europeans. Nearby were smaller homes for African workers.

Seeing Durban for the first time had us gawking at the tall buildings, shops with beautiful merchandise, and even a Laundromat.

Stores were well stocked, and it was fun to wander from one to another and window-shop.

Our nicely furnished "holiday flat" was just what we needed for a perfect vacation. The only thing lacking was a potato peeler. Can you believe that was one of our first purchases! Preparing some of our meals was something we looked forward to. We adjusted quickly to a young boy coming daily to sweep and scrub the kitchen and bathroom. A maid came each morning to make the beds. Being pampered was foreign to us, but we had no trouble getting used to it.

With the availability of fresh produce, shopping for groceries and cooking was fun. We ate head lettuce till it came out our ears! And fresh tomatoes . . . much more tasty than the small tart ones we bought from the vegetable vendors who came to our door in Kinshasa. We decided we wouldn't buy any green beans or spinach on this trip. Those were always available at home . . . now we were on vacation! We would indulge our taste for veggies that we could rarely buy in Kinshasa. Steven loved drinking fresh milk, and Susan avoided it when possible.

We shared in meal planning and preparation. Each of us chose to make either the main dish, vegetables, salad or dessert. We allowed ourselves fifty cents each (South African) for our share of the noon meal. It was a challenge to see how to spend it. We didn't have to spend it all, but we weren't to go over that amount. Any money left over went into a kitty for the trip to Kruger Park. One morning, Steven bought a pound of fresh peas and another of tiny new potatoes for twenty-two cents. The kids gained experience in both shopping and cooking and had fun doing it.

While traveling in different African countries, we had developed a taste for curried dishes. Each country had their specialty. There was a large Asian population in Durban, and we learned they liked curries with potatoes in an extremely hot sauce. My ears burned from the heat, and I drank lots of water to put out the fire! One afternoon we visited an Indian market where curries of different strengths were displayed in wooden barrels. Various shades of yellow and red, each barrel had a sign giving the name of that particular curry. We knew that "Mother-in-law" and "Hell Fire" were bound to be hot!

Even though the coast on the Indian Ocean side of South Africa is quite protected, we found it cold and windy in July. Surfers didn't seem to mind, however, as they rode the waves to shore, then dashed back into the water again and again. Susan especially enjoyed the beach, but we agreed that the waves at Tonde Beach in Congo were more fun. Bouncing on the trampolines and trying out different rides in the amusement park was good entertainment.

All the beaches were segregated—with signs stating who could swim there: Whites only, Asians only, Coloreds only or Bantus only. Since the same water lapped the shores, it seemed ridiculous, but that was the rule in South Africa until the early 1990s. We even experienced discrimination in reverse when non-white restrooms were all we could find on the beach.

Before leaving Durban, we spent a chilly evening playing miniature golf. Miserable with the cold, we looked forward to getting back to the comfort of our flat. As luck would have it, both Grandpa and Steven knocked their golf balls into the box at the end of the game and rang the bell, thereby winning a free game apiece. With Scottish blood coursing in their veins, they couldn't resist taking advantage of their good luck. Hot chocolate warmed us a bit and we shivered only half as much during the next round.

There was much to see and do in Durban. A large aquarium was the ideal place to learn about marine life in the Indian Ocean. People were even instructed what to do in case of shark bite. We weren't about to lose our fingers to hungry sharks in an open tank and wisely kept them safely out of the water.

Snakes had always intrigued Grandpa, and, when he heard about a snake pit, he was eager to check it out. I, on the other hand, am not a herpetologist (check that in your dictionary!), and am uncomfortable around them, even harmless types. Although there is beauty in their colors and markings, snakes make me nervous. These poisonous reptiles, however, were safely housed in heavy glass cages. We were in no danger.

Vacations have a way of whizzing by. The two weeks spent in Durban ended much too soon, and we were on our way to Natal Lion Park, a small game park with a lion enclosure. We would have missed seeing lions had we not stopped there, as those in Kruger National Park eluded us. Within the enclosure, an overly friendly eland slobbered all over the car window, three haughty-looking ostriches strolled by, and a zebra stood still long enough for us to snap its picture with Steven. The lions were a lazy lot. One of them languidly waved a hind leg as though it were too much effort to stand up and look fierce.

The night was cold and our stay in a thatch-roofed motel was a chilly experience. Two years earlier, there had been three feet of snow in the area. Thawing out by a toasty fire in the dining room that evening, we almost hoped we would awaken to the beauty of snow in the morning. The price of the night's lodging included a big supper as well as breakfast the next day.

In the morning, still cold (but no snow), we drove through Northern Transvaal where the orange orchards reminded us of southern California. The fruit looked so delicious we stopped and bought a "pocket," as the vendor called a bag of oranges, for the ridiculous price of thirty cents. When we counted them, there were thirty-one sweet, juicy oranges for us to enjoy! Citrus honey on breakfast toast was also a delicious treat.

When we arrived at Kruger Park, rangers stopped us to see if we were carrying any meat. There was evidence of hoof and mouth disease in the park. Passing inspection, we checked into the rest camp, set our suitcases in our room, and were off to see the animals. And what a lot of them there were—tall elegant giraffes, impalas, elephants, several species of antelopes, Cape buffalo, zebras, and wart hogs. Wart hogs amused us, running with their brushy tails upended like a flag in the breeze. Baboons at water holes were a nuisance, climbing on the car, begging for handouts.

Beautiful birds with gorgeous colors flew throughout the park. Large, black birds with puffy red wattles passed the time of day in the middle of the road. If we pricked the wattles with a pin, would they deflate, we wondered? We came to a fork in the road where a large triangular road marker built of rock pointed the way to different towns. A bird the size of a hen turkey walked along the top of each three sides as if to help us choose our direction. All he needed was a bill cap and white gloves and he would have been a perfect traffic director.

"You can get out of your car at your own risk," another sign read, "but you must be accompanied by a guide to go down to the water." Immediately, an African, musket in hand, hustled to the car to escort us to the river. We were grateful for his protection, especially when we saw five hippos sound asleep on a sandbar!

One evening, a park ranger gave a slide presentation showing how crossbow and darts are used to immobilize animals long enough for them to be marked and give other data. One bull elephant, later found in Zimbabwe, was being tracked in his wanderings to see if he would later rejoin the herd. As the narration was in Afrikaans we had to rely on the slides to inform us how this system worked.

Our vacation was about over, and we were on our way to Johannesburg for the return flight to Kinshasa. There are gold mines right at the edge of the city, and we wanted to visit one. Because permission had to be requested two weeks in advance, we settled for a view of the mines from the top of a tower instead. Still, that gave us a magnificent view of the city and surrounding suburbs. Susan had never ridden a double-decker bus before and she was enchanted with the experience.

We had a few South African coins left over to spend before catching our flight. Steven bought a glass of milk, Susan spent hers on a comic book, and Grandpa bought a newspaper. Reading United States news from a South African viewpoint was interesting. Talking with a family at the airport I mentioned how much we enjoyed speaking English while we were on vacation. "Oh," she replied, "You don't speak English; you speak American! And you're on holiday, not vacation!"

It had been a great "holiday." This was the last vacation our family would spend together in Africa, as Steven would graduate from high school in a few months and return to the States for college. Though there were similarities between Congo and South Africa, apartheid was a repressive system. With all the problems Congolese faced, they enjoyed a freedom black South Africans did not. Blacks and whites studied together in our schools. People in government, business and offices held responsible positions. Congolese and ex-patriots in Kinshasa enjoyed a camaraderie we did not experience in South Africa.

God had given us a relaxing, restful time in a beautiful country. We were returning to Congo with its many problems, but it was home. We were glad to go back.

Love to our grandkids, G'ma and G'pa

Tragedy on the Kwilu

Dear Grandchildren,

Sometimes, something really tragic happened in Zaire, and this was one of those times. What was supposed to be an afternoon of fun and relaxation ended in disaster.

You may remember that Vanga is one of our upcountry mission stations. It's situated on the banks of the Kwilu River. We spent a vacation there one year. One afternoon, we spent a couple of delightful hours floating downstream on inner tubes, pulled along by the current until we reached the station dock. It was an exhilarating experience, an activity that was fun and cooling on a hot, tropical afternoon.

It was a year or so later, another hot, sunny day when a group of five missionaries and six children decided it was time for a float trip down the Kwilu. They donned their swimsuits, gathered inner tubes for everyone, and drove to the place where they always began the float. They had been in the water only moments when disaster struck. Some in the group were still on the riverbank getting ready to go in the water.

Suddenly, without warning, three hippos surfaced in the water amid the floaters. A Haitian volunteer medical student was tossed in the air by a hippo which grabbed her with its jaws as she fell, crushing her chest. Another grabbed one of the children by the foot. It was a real tug of war as one of the pilots grabbed the child by the arm to rescue her from the hippo. They were pulled under the water three times before he was able to use both feet and kick the hippo in the mouth. Only then did it let loose. Another pilot was also bitten on the foot.

Everyone was in shock as they swam to the shore, aiding those who had been attacked. It must have seemed forever until they were safely out of the water. They rescued the dying woman, who in her last year of medical school was volunteering for a few weeks at the Vanga hospital. Only the morning before, at a hospital staff prayer breakfast, she had stated that she wanted to dedicate her life to God to serve him through medicine. Painful as the experience was, it was a reminder that life is fleeting and everyone needs to be ready to face eternity at any time.

It was well-known there were hippos in the Kwilu River. There was even a small sandbar known as Hippo Island. The hippos often rested there, but they had never been seen in the part of the river where people floated on inner tubes. For several years, the Vanga folks had enjoyed floating down the river with no problem. However, as those involved in the horrible experience pieced things together, they believed they knew what had happened.

The three hippos were a father, mother, and baby who were startled by people swimming in the river. To protect their baby, the parents did the natural thing by attacking the swimmers. Hippo Island was upstream from where our people were swimming, and that likely was where the hippos were headed when the attack occurred.

Because of their size, hippos appear slow and clumsy. I was reminded of those we had seen on vacations and never dreamed they could be vicious. There was the one munching grass on the banks of the Nile River at Paraa Lodge in Uganda. We had walked right by it with no fear. In South Africa, a ranger had hurried to the water's edge to "protect" us from those sleeping on a sandbar. We had never before had reason to fear hippos. Now, however, we had a totally different opinion of these wild animals—never share their bathtub!

Love, and stay away from a hippo's habitat.
G'ma and G'pa

You Can't Get There from Here

Dear Grandchildren,
Traveling from one place to another in Congo was often a challenge. Outside the city, there was no bus service, and few people owned a car. In the area where we lived, traveling to the interior meant that people crowded onto a truck heavily overloaded with passengers, goats, chickens, manioc, drums of fuel, and whatever else they could pile on. It seemed that room could always be made for more passengers and the things they needed to have transported. Sometimes, there were serious accidents and people were injured or killed. Or the truck might break down en route and people could be stranded for days.

I remember seeing a truckload of tomatoes overturned on a hilly, dirt road and a student telling me, "*mbongo zifwidi*," meaning "dead money, all our hard work has been in vain." Because of the truck accident, the people had no other way to get the tomatoes, now rotting in the tropical sun, to market. The women who had planted and tended the gardens got nothing for their hard work, and the village people had lost a badly needed source of income.

On another occasion, several missionaries and church leaders had gone to a meeting at Kikongo on the Wamba River in the interior. Very few rivers in Congo have bridges, and the Wamba was no different. People and vehicles crossed from one side to the other on a motorized raft. A few days later, the delegates walked down to the river, expecting to cross to the opposite shore, where cars were waiting to take them back to Leopoldville. Imagine their chagrin to discover the raft had sunk. It was beneath a half-submerged truck of cement. The load had been too heavy for the raft to support its weight. Villagers in dugout canoes came and poled them safely across the Wamba. There's more than one way to get from here to there!

There was only one paved road leading downcountry from Kinshasa to Matadi, and just one leading upcountry from Kinshasa to Kenge. All others were narrow, dirt roads, often bordered on either side by tall elephant grass.

Once a day, a train carried passengers between the port city of Matadi and the capital city of Leopoldville, while another left the capital en route to Matadi. The train was an important link for people living near the railroad. The two years we lived at Banza Manteke, we relied on it for our mail, building supplies, and meat. One time, Grandpa arrived at the train station in Leopoldville with a box of baby chicks he was sending to Kimpese. Unfortunately, the train had pulled out a few minutes earlier on its way downcountry. "No problem," said the station agent, "just drive to the next village and you can put them on the train there." So Grandpa did just that.

When we first went to Congo, the main road was still unpaved. Traveling by train from Banza Manteke to Leopoldville, as both were called at that time, was more pleasant than jolting for several hours in a car or pickup over a dusty, bumpy road. Although the train ride took several hours, there was a dining car, and eating lunch on the train helped to pass the time. People who couldn't afford first or second class tickets sat on wooden benches, several to a seat, surrounded by their bags and baggage in another car. Those who didn't have suitcases tied their belongings in a large cloth.

The building of the railroad in the late 1880s opened the interior of Congo to commerce. In the early years, it took two days to travel by train from Matadi to Leopoldville, a distance of about two hundred miles. The train stopped overnight at the small town of Thysville, today's Banza Ngungu, before continuing the next morning to

Leopoldville. Thankfully, we missed that experience as the trip was made in one day long before we moved to Leopoldville.

The Congo River, one of the world's longest, was an important travel source. Fisherman in their dugout canoes plied the river for economic reasons as well as a way to provide food for their families. Riverboat travel took people all the way from Leopoldville to Stanleyville, today's Kisangani. Although the river made its way far beyond Stanleyville, riverboat travel was not possible further inland due to the rapids, just as the same was true between Leopoldville and Matadi. The trip upriver took nearly two weeks, but was several days shorter on the return trip due to the pull of the river's current.

Often, the boat docked along the shore at night, then continued on its way the next morning. Barges were tied on behind the boat at different towns along the way. By the time it reached its destination five or six barges trailed the boat. Life on the barges was similar to that in towns. People bartered or sold produce, fishermen caught fish and smoked it. Others smoked eels and elephant meat to be sold in the markets in Leopoldville. Women did laundry and laid it out to dry if they could find a spot to do so. People chatted and fussed; children ran in and out, getting in everyone's way. The riverboat was like a floating city. We never made a boat trip on the Congo River, but Steven did, and you will have to get him to tell you his experiences.

When we returned to Congo in 1961, a year after the country received its independence, much had changed, especially travel. Roads were deteriorating; there were gas shortages. It was getting more difficult to get from one area to another. Then God sent help in a very practical way. Missionary Aviation Fellowship (MAF) arrived in Congo. They came as support personnel to aid the various mission groups by flying missionaries and African coworkers from one station to another. Airstrips were built at different stations to allow the little Cessna aircrafts to land and take off.

One year, we had a group of church leaders from the United States who came to visit the work on our stations. One man, upon seeing the small plane, wanted no part of flying—he would travel in the pickup. After bouncing for several hours over Congo roads, the Cessna looked more airworthy than he first thought. He made the return trip to Leopoldville by plane in forty minutes.

Sometimes, bizarre and totally unexpected things happened. Once, the pilot broke his landing gear at Moanza, one of our upcountry stations. Radio contact was made with another MAF pilot, asking if he could fly from his post in central Congo to help out. He first stopped at one of our stations to pick up an African pastor and a missionary who needed medical attention. Airborne and without warning, the tip of the propeller flew off, causing the pilot to make a forced landing. Where? At the nearest airport? No, he landed the plane safely on a dirt road out in the middle of nowhere! People walking by didn't seem the least bit concerned about seeing an airplane in the middle of the road. They appeared as nonchalant as if that were a common occurrence. The pilot and his passengers spent a miserable night sitting in the plane's cramped quarters while a tropical downpour rained from the skies.

The next day, two United Nations helicopter pilots rescued the passengers. Later, all the pilots returned to the downed Cessna where they used a hacksaw to saw off both ends of the prop so they would match. Airborne again, they flew the plane to Leopoldville. There's more than one way to get from here to there!

God's protection and care were certainly evident on another occasion when a MAF pilot was practicing takeoffs and landings prior to going into strange airstrips. On the third takeoff, the engine stopped as the plane climbed over the tall trees at the end of the strip. The pilot had only a few brief seconds to get the engine started again, but he was unable to restart it. The airspeed dropped quickly and the plane came down through the trees sideways, cartwheeling and breaking apart in several places. The pilot had taken two Africans with him so they could see how their village looked from the air. The plane was totally demolished, yet the three men walked away from the accident with only a few bruises.

As miraculous as that was, they discovered that five dozen eggs sitting in flats on the back seat of the plane had remained in place even though they were not tied down. Not one egg was cracked or broken. The next morning at a service of thanksgiving the African pastor stated that God's guardian angels had their hands on the contents inside the plane.

The pilot saw God's intervention as the miracle, an indication of how much he cared for the three of them. Although he spared neither the plane nor the expense involved in its loss, he spared the three men. Our friend said it was a beautiful reality that God cares about us and knows us as individuals.

The day of the accident, in many different places, people were praying for God's protection in the day's operation. God answered in a marvelous way!

Till the next letter,
Love from your G'ma and G'pa

Hostel Living

Who? Me? A Houseparent?

Dear Grandchildren,

When we left Zaire in 1975, we weren't sure if we would be returning to Africa following our year's home leave. Before going on furlough, the church leaders asked Grandpa to train a Zairian to assume directorship of the Christian Center. Since we knew we would not be returning to that work, we wondered if International Ministries had something else for us.

Grandpa was in another state speaking in some churches about the work in Zaire when I received a telephone call from our mission headquarters in Valley Forge. They requested that following home leave we return to Zaire as houseparents in the missionary children's hostel. Acting as a surrogate parent for a house full of instant teenagers was not high on my list of job preferences. If there was anything I knew I never wanted to be, it was that. The children's parents lived and worked in the interior, or as we called it "the bush." Their children lived in the city during the school year to attend The American School of Kinshasa, affectionately known as TASOK.

To my dismay, when I called Grandpa to share this news, he was quite pleased with the idea. But not Grandma. She knew she did not want to be a hostel parent. Ever! But God has his own way of changing our thinking. One morning, as I was reading my Bible, I read something that made me pause and read it again. As I did, I asked, "God, are you trying to tell me something?" In this scripture, King David was speaking to Solomon about building the temple: He said: "Be strong and courageous and get to work. Don't be frightened by the size of the task for the Lord my God is with you; He will not forsake you. He will see to it that everything is finished correctly." 1 Chronicles 28:20 TEV

As I thought about David's advice to Solomon, I prayed that God would help me make the right decision. After Grandpa and I talked and prayed together, we felt God was showing us our next area of service. It was to be a four-year term at the children's hostel in Kinshasa, Zaire's capital city.

Missionary kids always called their parents' colleagues uncle and aunt, so Uncle Murray and Aunt Marj became houseparents to a neat group of children. At times, they tried our patience, but we have many good memories of what fine kids they were. For me, it was the most difficult term of the more than thirty years we lived in Africa, but I never once doubted that we were in the place God had for us at that time. (However, had anyone offered me an airline ticket and asked if I'd like to go home, it might have been difficult to refuse!)

There were a lot of great times the next four years. Some were exciting and fun, some tested our sense of humor and resolve. It wasn't easy for the children to be separated from their parents for weeks at a time, yet God enabled all of us to live and work together and have lots of memorable experiences. We'll share some of them with you in future letters.

Love you all,
G'ma and G'pa

Someone's in the Kitchen With...?

Dear Mireille, Matt, Aaron, Nicole, Zach, and Kalli,

Preparing three meals a day for the hostel kids took a lot of planning and energy. Since the school did not have a cafeteria, and it wasn't practical for the children to come home for lunch, we prepared a hot meal and took it to school. Several non-hostel students arranged to eat with us as well. We prepared lunch for thirty to forty children.

Naturally, a lot of funny things happened in the kitchen. There were also some that weren't so funny, but we muddled through. It was only later we could look back and laugh. A sense of humor was a definite asset in the hostel.

God surely wanted to teach me humility, for there were times I had to admit that the cook wasn't the only one who made dumb mistakes. We got into some real predicaments in the kitchen . . .

One of my early kitchen disasters as a hostel parent was that of making chocolate icing. Cupcakes were on the lunch menu, and it was my responsibility to see that they were iced. I got out all the ingredients and set to work. The icing needed more milk than seemed right, but I kept adding it until the icing was the proper consistency. Finally, I took a taste. Blecch! How ghastly! It's not a good idea to use baking powder in place of powdered sugar! The glass jar was clearly labeled baking powder, but my glasses were somewhere other than on my nose, and my mistake was discovered too late to rescue the icing. That was one disaster we couldn't recycle.

Tata Matelenge, one of the cooks, made his share of kitchen disasters. One day he told Lois that Mama Sharp was smart when she wore her glasses. And Mama Sharp found out later what happened when Matelenge left the cornmeal out of the cornbread she intended to use in cornbread stuffing!

The air-conditioned storeroom at the hostel was the ideal place to keep a supply of sugar and flour for our daily use. Noticing one day that the supply was getting low in each barrel, I asked Azanga to refill them. And just to make sure it was done properly Matelenge went along to help. Azanga brought two one-hundred-pound bags, one of sugar, one of flour . . . and together the men managed to empty the flour into the sugar barrel and the sugar into the flour barrel. "Oh, Mama. Guess what?" was the first I knew of the latest kitchen disaster.

Finally, we sifted our way through the sugar/flour mess. It was fortunate that Congo sugar is much coarser than the American variety, for the flour sifted through the sieves leaving the larger grains of sugar. However, the flour had a definite sweet taste, and the kids were asking, "Why is the bread so sweet?" We never wasted anything in the hostel if it could be helped, and we were not about to dump the sweetened flour. Sugar and flour were not always available and they were too expensive to throw away.

Matelenge tried to make donuts, but there was no way the dough was going to rise with all that sugar-flavored flour. By adding lots of milk and baking powder to the donut batter, the mess made passable pancakes although one of the girls wondered why they smelled like yeast. Sometimes we were a bit sneaky about recycling kitchen disasters!

Mishaps in the kitchen tested our sense of humor as well as patience. How well I remember the incident of Kinshasa's largest hamburger bun. As Tata Matelenge was going on vacation, we needed to be sure there was enough bread in the freezer during his absence. He had started the bread dough, sufficient for ten loaves of bread, and had it rising in a bowl the size of a large dishpan. While I was busy making Grandpa's traditional anniversary cherry pie, Matelenge dreamily greased the bread pans. Can you guess what happens when you open the door of a preheated oven, ready to bake a pie and discover a huge mound of bread dough rising? This great mass of dough had started to bake. It looked like an enormous hamburger bun!

Tata Matelenge chided me for not checking first to see if there was anything in the oven before I turned it on. He was right, of course, so I bit my tongue and said nothing. Recycling the dough was a real challenge.

Having read somewhere that no bread is so bad it can't be used as toast, I had him make the mass into loaves. It was edible as toast . . . not very good toast, mind you . . . but edible.

Brownie pudding was on the lunch menu one day, but as luck would have it, Tata Matelenge was home in bed with a bad back. Making the dessert was up to me. Perhaps I could be excused for the disaster that day, as having to make ten loaves of bread took a lot of time and energy. I wasn't used to kneading thirty cups of flour by hand into bread dough. We usually made bread for the hostel's use, as the local bakery often had difficulty getting flour.

We always sent the noon meal to school, as our workmen didn't like to go home after dark, and darkness falls about six o'clock in the tropics. I'm not sure what went wrong that day, but when the lunch things came back to the hostel most of the brownie pudding was

Kinshasa's Largest Hamburger Bun

uneaten. Hmmm. I tasted it. The brownie part was fine, but the pudding? Bitter! I had left out the sugar.

In a couple of days, Tata Matelenge was back in the kitchen making a golden cake. It's now or never, I thought, and with a pitcher of milk in one hand and the mixer in the other, I determined to render the brownie pudding into something edible. Blended together, the golden cake and brownie pudding were supposed to have a marbled effect. Instead, the pudding sank to the bottom with the cake on top. We decided to serve it anyway. The kids thought the pudding cake was great. I smiled my Mona Lisa smile and never said a word! Would you say that the "proof is in the pudding?"

Food disasters weren't the only challenge we had in the kitchen. We learned how to recycle a lot of things rather than throw them away. Because items such as Jell-O and Kool-Aid absorb moisture in the tropics, we learned how to use them anyway. We had several boxes of Jell-O that wouldn't gel after they got damp, and it took too much Knox gelatin to make them useable. By adding Jell-O to equally damp pre-sweetened Kool-Aid, we had a very refreshing drink. Some of the kids were a bit suspicious though, when they noticed bits of Jell-O floating in the pitchers.

One time, another hostel mother was faced with several boxes of chocolate pudding, which, being in the tropics, had absorbed the taste of cardboard. She knew the pudding was safe to eat, but figured the kids would never eat it. She made it one evening and set it out for a snack during study break. She told the children that the pudding didn't taste good and that only those who really wanted it were to take it. Everyone else leave it alone. With those instructions most of the kids ate it and said it was good!

It often seemed that if things were going well in the hostel a crisis couldn't be far off. Two weeks prior to vacation one year, things fell apart right at dish drying time. We finally got through Friday and Saturday with a bit of calm restored, then Sunday morning came.

I was in the kitchen finishing the last touches for dinner before leaving for church. A student came to pick up one of our boys to take him on an outing for the day. This fifteen-year-old friend had a forged driver's license stating his age as nineteen. There was no way that boy could be nineteen. It was easy to get a driver's license—just pay a bribe at the motor vehicle office. The boy's parents arrived, verifying their son's age as fifteen. The hostel had strict rules about our kids riding only with legitimate drivers. By the time we got everything sorted out, Aunt Marj was pretty uptight. People were not being honest in what they were telling me, and I was upset.

After we returned from church, I searched for the seasoned flour and onion soup mix prepared ahead of time for roast beef gravy. All we could find was cinnamon sugar and flour, which Vera was sure I didn't intend to use in the gravy. With a sinking feeling I tasted the peach pie made earlier that morning and learned what had happened to the gravy mix.

The next afternoon at Bible study, Mollie said she thought they should pray for Marj, for any hostel mother who sweetened peach pie with onion soup mix surely was in need of prayer! Amen!

Have fun in the kitchen—but watch what you're doing!

Love, G'ma and G'pa

Ingenuity Pays Off

Dear Grandkids,

The dictionary says that a corsage is a small bouquet of flowers worn on a woman's wrist or shoulder. Each year, the junior class at TASOK honored the senior class members with a banquet. It was customary for the guys to give their dates corsages. While ordering a corsage in the United States is easy, it was impossible in Kinshasa, where there were only one or two flower shops, and none of the employees knew how to make a corsage. Now there was a challenge for the hostel moms.

One year, flowers were bought in town, then stored overnight in a refrigerator until the next day when the women planned to make them into corsages. Unfortunately, the refrigerator had problems, and when we opened the door, there lay the flowers, every one of them frozen! How awful! Grandpa and two of the women made a quick trip to town to look for more. The choice flowers had been bought the day before, but by buying the few still available and by filling them out with frangipani blossoms from trees on the station, we made pretty corsages for the girls.

The frangipani is a tropical tree that has five-petaled blossoms in delicate shades of rose, pink, yellow, or cream. In Hawaii, they are used in leis to welcome people who come to the islands with a tour group. In Congo, little children put them on the end of a thin reed and watch them whirl in the wind as they run. While these blossoms would be considered exotic in the States and certainly worthy of a corsage, our hostel kids didn't consider them corsage material. Frangipani trees were for climbing.

A dress up occasion such as the junior-senior banquet always sparked the interest of the younger kids. They gathered in the living room to watch as the girls came out in their pretty dresses. There were a lot of good natured comments and teasing as the boys, also dressed up, pinned the corsages on their dates. The following week, the sophomores and freshmen had a dinner, and the older kids made a big deal of sitting down in the living room to watch the younger ones as they left for the evening. That year Grandpa's suit coat went to two banquets so we called it his "dinner jacket."

Trying to make corsages often tested our ingenuity. On one occasion, we tried to order flowers from South Africa, but there was a war going on somewhere and Zaire's telephone line had been cut. Or so we were told. The woman from whom we had ordered flowers locally sold most of them to someone else, probably because they offered her more money. With only the few we were able to buy in town, someone suggested we drive to the cemetery where there were always flower vendors. Can you imagine buying flowers for corsages at a cemetery? We did, and, with frangipani and other flowers we managed to find on the station, we made sixteen corsages. The girls had made their banquet dresses and had given us scraps of cloth from them. We felt quite clever that the colors coordinated so well.

Probably the most exciting corsage experience happened our last year as hostel parents. We had a good friend in the American Embassy who ordered flowers for us from South Africa. We needed to make sure the flowers would arrive from Johannesburg in time for us to make them into corsages.

On Wednesday evening before the Friday banquet, we received word that a helicopter pilot with Gulf Oil would hand carry the flowers that night, arriving in Kinshasa at 2:00 AM Thursday. Since the local telephones didn't work, we drove to the Gulf compound and asked if the kind gentleman bringing the flowers could put them in water for us. Yes, we were assured, that would be possible providing he didn't fall into the water first himself from sheer weariness. With all those flowers, people must have wondered if he were going to a funeral or a wedding!

The next morning, after we picked up the flowers, we made a tent in the air-conditioned storeroom at the hostel to keep them fresh. Those flowers were not going to freeze in the refrigerator! That afternoon, several of us got together to make the corsages. One of the women brought asparagus fern from her house. My gardenia bush conveniently put out one blossom at the right time. Others brought star jasmine or whatever flowers they had that would be appropriate in a corsage. There was even pretty ribbon to tie on the finished products. The corsages looked quite professional when we finished. A lot of folks worked together to make the evening memorable for the girls and their dates. That year we didn't even have to use frangipanis, much to everyone's delight.

One of the boys asked for pointers on the proper way to pin a corsage. I had him practice on me. Then his date arrived wearing an off the shoulder dress. Before Jim got the bewildered look off his face one of the hostel moms came to his rescue and pinned the corsage on his date's dress.

While on the subject of flowers, I wanted to tell you about the wedding of one of our former "mish kids," the name we called children of missionaries. Your parents are former mish kids. Just as a lot of people worked together to make corsages special for the girls, the same thing was true about the wedding.

The groom's mother arrived from the states, bringing with her eleven boxes of cake mix for the wedding cake. Atop the cake, a miniature bride and groom wore wedding finery just like that of the bridal couple. Martha, the bride's mother, attached red hibiscus blossoms to all the chairs and platform for the outdoor wedding, which was at Kimpese, a two hour drive from Kinshasa. Grandpa and I stopped along the way and picked field orchids and added ours to those that others had brought.

For several mornings prior to the wedding, the bride's mother had picked gardenia blossoms, kept them in the refrigerator and had bowls of them everywhere. They were beautiful. The bride had requested flowers, flowers, flowers. She definitely had her wish on her wedding day.

We'll write again in a few days.

Love to all,
G'ma and G'pa

Hostel Moms Making Corsages for the guys to Give to Their Dates

Off to the Boonies

Dear Grandkids,

During the four years we were houseparents in the children's hostel, two other mission groups also had hostels. Sometimes, the three hostels combined outings to nearby areas. Frequent holidays were declared by the Zaire government to celebrate different political events. This was fine with the kids, as it meant a day off from school. It was also possible the hostel parents could be persuaded to plan a trip somewhere.

A few miles outside the city of Kinshasa was the small village of Kinsuka, where most of the men earned their livelihood by fishing. A narrow one-way bridge, barely wide enough for a truck, connected the village to a tiny island. Gravel and sand were dug there and transported across the bridge for construction in Kinshasa. Beneath it, the Zaire River swirled and foamed over huge boulders, forming dangerous rapids.

The bridge was not only narrow, it had no guardrails, and in places the curb was missing. I'm not sure which was worse—walking across the bridge during dry season when the river was low, or during rainy season when it was high. Either way, looking down on the rocks and water was scary for anyone afraid of heights. Especially your grandmother.

The president had announced a holiday for some reason, and the hostel set off for a picnic at the Kinsuka rapids. Even carrying picnic supplies, the children had no problem crossing the bridge to the island. Its sandy beach was the perfect spot for a wiener roast. The kids swam, worked on their tans, relaxed and enjoyed a carefree day. Some of the girls even shampooed their hair. You'd be surprised how clean brown river water can get your hair.

When it was time to return to the hostel van, I was reluctant to walk back across the bridge. I had barely recovered from crossing it to the island. Everyone started out, oblivious to the foaming water and boulders below. Keeping to the center of the narrow bridge, I looked straight ahead and inched my way across, not daring to turn around. I distinctly heard a gravel truck behind me. If the driver had honked for me to hurry up, I likely would have leaped over the side in sheer panic. Bless the driver . . . he patiently let me plod along at a baby step, snail's pace until I safely crossed the bridge.

Even though I hated to walk across the bridge, picnicking at Kinsuka rapids was a great place for the kids. One year, there was a big political holiday, and the three hostels planned to spend the day there. As we were leaving for the rapids, we learned soldiers were guarding the bridge, allowing no one to cross. Since neither the island nor the gravel pit had anything to do with the army that seemed ridiculous. No one lived on that tiny spot of land, and the gravel pit was no threat to national security. But the soldiers, impressed with their authority, insisted that swimming in the river was a no-no, and swimming *definitely* was not allowed on a political holiday. Crazy! At least your grandmother was spared having to cross that scary bridge again!

However, Kinsuka wasn't the only place to picnic. Everyone drove to Ngombe, a village farther down the river, and we spent the day swimming, playing soccer in the sand, tossing Frisbees, and relaxing.

One year, two hostels planned an overnight camping trip to Green Lake, a small body of water, probably spring-fed, several miles from town. It was out in the middle of nowhere, surrounded by grassland and a few termite hills. The water was crystal clear, but the reflection from a few surrounding trees made it appear green. Since trips to Green Lake were rare, the children couldn't wait to be on their way.

Sometimes, the hostel bought halves of beef, cut up the meat and froze it for future use. The ribs were saved for a campout event. While the boys hunted firewood, the girls gathered wild flowers for the tables. Everyone was excited to be at Green Lake. They made every effort to make it a memorable occasion.

Potatoes baked in the coals while Grandpa barbecued the ribs. There's something about cooking outdoors that gives a wonderful flavor to food. Everything tasted delicious. The kids had fun tossing the rib bones into the darkness . . . just like in medieval days, they said.

At bedtime, thirty of us spread our sleeping bags on the ground and went to sleep, happy and contented, under a beautiful, starry Zaire sky.

Although I expected pranks and mischief during the night, even the middle school boys were on their best behavior.

What a wonderful time we had—in spite of miserable sunburns. On the return trip to town, the van got stuck in the sand, and everybody had to get out and help push. But no one cared—it was all part of the fun.

During our first year as houseparents, we worked with another missionary couple until they returned to the States on home assignment. After that, volunteers were recruited to work with us. Bill and Vera's year as volunteers was finished, but before they returned to California the kids wanted to have a farewell picnic for them at Kinsuka rapids. It was to be a surprise. The children planned a menu of barbecued chicken, potato salad, and baked beans. We were ready to leave when Bill, who didn't like the river anyway, decided he would stay home and write letters. It took some fast talking to get him to join us without giving the surprise away.

It was May that year, well past the rainy season, and the river was low. The huge rocks, normally covered in water, were exposed, giving the children hours of fun scrambling over them as they jumped and slid into the water.

While we were eating our picnic, a Zairian boy, eight or nine years old, watched from a distance. The children prepared a plate of food for him which he readily accepted. Surely he had never eaten potato salad ... or baked beans ... or barbecued chicken before. His diet included *sakasaka*, (manioc greens) and *luku*, made from manioc flour. Any chicken he had eaten would have been cooked in palm oil. He must have wondered about the strange food the *mindele* ate.

When we finished eating, we stacked the paper plates planning to take them back to the hostel for disposal. Without a word, this little boy walked over, picked up the plates, took them down to the river, washed them, and returned them to us. Probably he had never seen paper plates before and didn't know they were disposable. Washing them must have been his way of saying thank you. We were touched.

One September, before the rains started, the three hostels planned an overnight campout on the Zaire River beyond the village of Ngombe. As soon as the children were home from school, we loaded all the gear—sleeping bags, boiled drinking water, supper of potato salad, baked beans, hot dogs, hamburgers, plates and silverware. Tata Matelenge even made donuts and cinnamon rolls for breakfast on the beach.

The moment we arrived at the river, the kids scattered, either to cool off in the water or to select their campsite. There had been no rain for several weeks, and the river was low, leaving a wide, sandy beach. The kids had fun scrambling over the big boulders, which were always covered by water during the rainy season. The sandy stretches of beach were a great place for Frisbee or soccer games.

Even though there were forty-five of us, there was space for everyone to set up camp. The high school boys settled on a spot near the water, while the middle school boys retreated a few feet away from them, tossing their sleeping bags nearby. The high school girls located their camp near some big rocks and trees. One of them even brought a hammock and stretched it between a couple of trees. That year six of the younger girls were away from home for the first time. Some weren't sure about sleeping under the stars. Susan, having finished college, was back in Zaire working as a teacher's aid at TASOK. She and some of the older girls camped with the younger ones.

And the hostel parents? Where did they sleep? Near the food, of course. It needed to be protected from hungry kids who might possibly walk in their sleep!

Happily, there was no wildlife to disturb us other than one small snake that someone captured in a glass jar, then let it go the next day when we left. I've no idea whether it was poisonous or not, but with me snakes have always been guilty until proven innocent. We knew there were crocodiles in the Zaire River, but no one saw any on that trip.

Each little group of campers kept a fire going during the night. From time to time, someone woke up long enough to toss on another piece of wood. There was no moon that night, but the sky was full of stars, and I fell asleep trying to count them.

Daylight came at six o'clock, and, by then, most of the kids were wide awake, hungry for Matelenge's donuts and cinnamon rolls. The sleepyheads had to forget about catching any more "zzzs." (At the hostel, Saturday breakfast was always available between seven and nine o'clock. One of our boys, not wanting to ever miss a meal, regularly arrived in the dining room at seven, ate his breakfast, then went back to bed for a couple of hours.) By the time we got home that afternoon, everybody was tired but happy. And would you believe, by 9:15 that evening everyone had gone to bed!

When President Mobutu's wife died, he proclaimed a three-day holiday. That year, eleven of our fifteen children were from down-country. The Kimpese station contacted us by radio inviting us to bring everyone down for those few days. The children were excited about the break from school, impatient to be with their parents again. They eagerly helped get lunch ready.

However, the four middle school boys were in trouble. Before we could leave, they had to scrub, mop, and rewax the floor in their hallway, a project that kept them occupied for two and a half hours. Earlier, bent on mischief, they had dragged all the furniture from one of their rooms into the hall, badly scraping and scratching the recently waxed vinyl tile floor. Housemothers took a dim view of such mischief.

At last, we were on our way, headed downcountry to Kimpese. An hour later, we arrived at Sona Bata, stopping to eat our lunch with one of the families whose two sons were in the hostel. Leaving the boys and one of the hostel kids whose family lived upcountry, we were on the road again, arriving two hours later at Kimpese.

Parents and children were delighted to have this unexpected time together. The falling rain didn't dampen their welcome, nor did it dampen the pizza delivery to the homes where we were staying. Like many Americans, the hostel kids thought pizza was one of the five major food requirements! Our host families had prepared a pizza supper. There couldn't have been a better choice.

Kimpese was the site of a large hospital, staffed by missionaries from Europe and North America. While we were at Kimpese, the Canadian volunteer couple who worked with us in the hostel wanted to learn about Canadian Baptist work among Angolan refugees. Refugees were again crossing the border into Zaire after hiding in the forests in Angola for many months. These poor people were caught between two political factions. Many of them, sick and destitute, had found their way to the hospital. Due to the war in Angola, the Canadian missionaries had moved to our area as the refugees spoke Kikongo, the same language as the people with whom we worked in lower Zaire. In Zaire, the Canadians continued their work of evangelism, education, agriculture, and medicine with the Angolan refugees.

While most of us were enjoying the holiday that gave us a break from hostel life, Grandpa was sick with malaria, probably as a result of the overnight camping trip to Ngombe. About all he could do was sweat, chill, and be miserable. Poor Grandpa!

Till next time . . .

We love you,
G'ma and G'pa

Gobble, Gobble, Gobble!

Dear Brenner and Sharp Grandchildren,
The hostel arrived back from the coast shortly before dark one Sunday afternoon in late November. As the kids left the van, traces of sand, a happy reminder of a fun-filled Thanksgiving weekend, trailed them into the building. Now there were ice chests to clean, sleeping bags to shake out, grubby laundry to deal with.

We had just returned from a few days at Nsiamfumu, a small African village along part of Congo's fourteen miles of coastline where our mission had a guesthouse overlooking the Atlantic Ocean. Nsiamfumu, or Vista as it was also called, was a favorite vacation spot for our missionary families.

The hostel parents had never undertaken a trip such as this with the children, but Thanksgiving vacation was coming up. The three downcountry kids could go home, but it was too expensive for such a short period of time for our upcountry kids. They would have had to fly home in the little Cessna aircraft. An enthusiastic "thumbs up" from the parents gave us the response we needed to get organized for the trip. The children were excited—Thanksgiving at the ocean would be a first in hostel life!

The girls planned the menus, and all week the hostel kitchen hummed with activity. We prepared meals ahead as it was both difficult and expensive to find what we might need at the coast. We made chili, baked beans, spaghetti sauce, and muffins. Matelenge made loaves of bread, hot dog rolls and hamburger buns. We wouldn't dream of going away without his cinnamon rolls. A near crisis arose when the pita bread recipe got lost, but Aunt Marj muddled through. Guessing at the ingredients I managed to produce acceptable pita bread. Pizza was high on the children's list of favorite food, but they liked tacos, too. Making tortillas was a time-consuming job. The children stuffed pita bread with taco filling. It didn't fall out like it did in tortillas, they said.

By the time everything was made, the freezers were full. Since it would take twelve hours to drive to the coast, we took the kids out of school a day early. It was rainy season. We splashed through puddles the entire way to Kimpese, our first stop, where we ate supper and stayed overnight with missionary families. The resourceful mother of one of our boys even donned her swimsuit and protected our supper beneath an umbrella as she trekked from one house to another to bake pizza in her colleagues' ovens.

In the morning, we were up for an early breakfast, had picked lemons for lemonade and a fish dinner and were on our way, The downcountry kids were spending Thanksgiving vacation at Kimpese with their parents. We would pick them up on our return from the coast.

A few sprinkles left over from yesterday's rain splashed against the windshield; low clouds hung over the hills. Egrets and cattle shared the grassland. Great clumps of bamboo arched across the road, making a green canopy for us to drive under. Especially surprising were the mango trees—ripe fruit hung down within arms' reach.

Mango trees at the hostel were huge, and one had to be good at tree climbing to pick their luscious fruit.

As we drove to the Matadi ferry that would take us across the mighty Congo River, the Baptist hostel van passed the kids from the Methodist-Presbyterian hostel. They were also en route to Nsiamfumu and had spent the night at Matadi. In good fun, they wanted to cross the river before we did. They almost made it, and were actually on the ferry, when an overly eager soldier, no doubt hoping for a bribe, made them get off, insisting they go to the police station. Ultimately, the soldier was reprimanded by his commanding officer, but by then the Baptists had gotten ahead.

Due to heavy rains, the river was high and the current so strong that in midstream the ferry barely moved. Thirty minutes later, we were safely on the other side, thankful to be on solid ground once more. In later years, we were able to cross the river by suspension bridge, thanks to the engineering expertise of the Japanese.

Along the way, we stopped at a village and bought bananas for a banana break. Congo bananas were the sweetest, most flavorful we had ever eaten. After we returned to America, it took me a year to enjoy eating bananas again as those we bought in the States had so little flavor.

We stopped at Boma, a port city on the Congo River, where we ate our sandwiches in the cool shade of huge, old trees. It's at Boma that the pavement abruptly stops. We jolted the rest of the way to the coast over a bumpy, washboard road. Two hours later, we arrived at the vacation house. As soon as the kids could break away from carrying sleeping bags and ice chests, they were down on the beach.

If we thought we might get away from Kinshasa crowds, we weren't that lucky. In addition to the thirteen of us from the hostel, seven more from Kinshasa wanted in on the fun. Susan was with that group, as she was a teacher's aid at TASOK that year. We had kids sleeping on the porch, in the living room, in the bedrooms. Very cozy! Very crowded! We had to be careful where we stepped.

What is Thanksgiving without turkey? They were unavailable in the grocery stores, but through the kindness of an American Embassy friend, we were able to purchase two from the commissary in Kinshasa. What a treat! In the guesthouse were two stoves; one used bottled gas, one was electric. They both worked, but there was one drawback—neither of the oven doors closed tightly. We simply propped the doors shut with sticks, poking them in a crack in the cement floor. You get the idea that our accommodations were not posh!

Just before sunset Thanksgiving afternoon, both hostels gathered beneath the large old baobab tree on the cliff overlooking the ocean. Carved with many initials and names over the years, it was the perfect place to listen to the roar of the ocean, to sing, and to watch the sun sink into the Atlantic. I never got used to seeing the sun set in the Atlantic Ocean even though we were on the West Coast of Africa.

That evening, twenty-one of us sat around the table, enjoying a traditional American Thanksgiving dinner in the heart of Africa. Much of the meal had been prepared earlier at the hostel, ready for our special dinner. Even "pumpkin pie" made from *lengi*, an African squash, tasted authentic a continent away from the real thing. Sitting around the table everyone shared what they were thankful for. We were so blessed.

Watching the Sun Go Down at Nsaimfumu

Next morning, fishermen brought *capitain,* an ocean perch, for a fish dinner fixed by Chef Uncle Murray. The kitchen crew made *frites* (French fries). Another feast! We walked to nearby Tonde Beach, where the weather was marvelous and the waves so much fun that the kids played all day, taking time out only to eat turkey sandwiches for lunch. A former mish kid who was a mechanic with Gulf Oil had part ownership in a boat. He took several of the kids and Grandpa and Susan water skiing—a fun way to end the holiday.

That evening, everyone pitched in to leave the house clean for the next folks who would come down to enjoy a few days at the ocean. Up at 4:00 AM the following morning, we devoured Matelenge's cinnamon rolls with coffee, and took off for Matadi. It was urgent that we arrive there before noon, as gas stations were not open Sunday afternoon. We arrived at the river in good time, then waited nearly an hour for the ferry to work its way across the river to fetch us. It was well before noon when we docked at Matadi, but to our chagrin we learned that no one was selling gas. Come back on Monday we were told. This was Zaire! Our friends at the Swedish Mission generously let us buy gas from them and

Thanksgiving at Nsiamfumu/Vista

we continued on our way to Kinshasa. The alternative may have been having a bunch of noisy teenagers camped on their doorstep overnight!

Stopping at Kimpese, we ate a sandwich picnic, picked up the three downcountry kids and were on our way home. Jim and June treated us to fresh lemonade when we stopped at Sona Bata for a few minutes. En route from Nsiamfumu to Kinshasa, the children were excited and happy about the few days they had spent at the ocean. They sang and sang—everything from camp songs to popular music to Zairian hymns. They also whistled the Zaire National anthem. Piercingly! They never did sing the words (which they all knew), just whistled it.

What a treat to arrive back at the hostel to find supper waiting for us. Susan had arrived by plane a few hours earlier and had prepared our evening meal, a nice welcome to finish off Thanksgiving vacation.

Those few days at Vista with our hostel kids were a memorable experience. Would we do it again? Yes, we would—only not right away!

Love to all,
G'ma and G'pa

What Next?!

Dear Grandchildren,

While Grandpa and I were hostel parents, we had a unique experience that was definitely not the usual daily fare of living in Zaire. TASOK, The American School of Kinshasa, had hired a new school superintendent. The school board suggested we meet his flight arriving at Ndjili airport, fetch him and bring him to the hostel, where he would have lunch with us, giving him opportunity to meet some of the students. That sounded like a good idea, and we were glad to oblige. None of us knew what excitement a simple airport run would produce.

Grandpa and I were off to the airport, and in due time the new school director arrived. Getting through customs at Ndjili was always a nerve-wracking experience, as eight or ten young men, each eager to handle one's luggage through customs, descended en masse on unsuspecting travelers. *"C'est moi, Felix le chat,"* (It's me, Felix the cat,") proclaimed one young man anxious that we choose him. It helped that we could speak both French and Lingala, and, in short time, we were able to assist the director through immigration with a minimum of delay.

Driving through the streets of Kinshasa with its erratic drivers and countless pedestrians, the new director must have wondered where this job he had so recently contracted would lead him. As the mission station was on the opposite side of the city, he had plenty of time to ponder his decision. Grandpa negotiated the traffic like the pro that he was, and we were well on our way to the hostel when he stopped suddenly. We were now out of the heavy traffic, driving down tree shaded streets.

Crossing the street in front of us was an unbelievable sight. A large, monitor lizard, a least four feet long, was definitely out of its environment. Normally, these big lizards are meat eaters, but the only other one I ever saw was in the top of a tall palm tree indulging his diet with palm nuts. Not this fella. He was searching for something, but we didn't know what. Grandpa got out of the van and looked at this creature ambling blissfully along Avenue Albert.

I'm not sure what possessed Grandpa, but he evidently decided this animal would be interesting for the hostel kids to observe. Putting his foot on the lizard's neck he hoisted it up by the tail and carried it to the van. The new superintendent, whose experience in Zaire was limited to about forty minutes of driving from the airport to that particular spot, must have wondered if too much tropical sun had affected your grandpa's brain. Grandpa suggested one of us would have to hold this fierce looking creature.

"Well," said Kinshasa's latest arrival, "I'm not going to hold it."

"Well," added your grandma who had never eyed a monitor lizard that closely before, "I'm not going to hold it either."

"All right. Marji you drive and I'll hold it," said your unflappable grandpa.

And that's how we proceeded to the hostel with the lizard on the floor of the van, Grandpa's feet firmly holding it down. Unfortunately, our latest acquisition did not have good manners and it did what any scared lizard would do under the circumstances. It pottied. Arriving at the hostel the van had an unmistakable nasty odor.

When the kids heard we had arrived with both the new superintendent and a monitor lizard, guess which received top billing! One of our boys, wearing steel toed boots, could feel the pressure of the lizard's jaws when he put his foot in its mouth. Hearing the commotion, the hostel workmen came to investigate. Seeing the lizard, and with everyone talking at once, they noisily said we had to give it to them. Grandpa told them he planned to take it to TASOK and give it to the

Monitor Lizard Biting Steel Toed Boots

science department. "Well, then, you have to give us a goat," they insisted. They were not joking; they couldn't have been more serious.

We learned that these lizards are highly prized by men as they are a delicacy which they rarely get to eat. But only men may eat them. It's taboo for women, as they are told they won't be able to bear children. This belief, of course, assured more for the men.

Grandpa left the monitor lizard with the science teacher where it was of great interest to the students. They weren't the only ones who found it interesting. The school workmen insisted they be given the animal. And that's what happened when the science department was no longer able to provide it with food. Instead of returning it to the forest, the teacher gave it to the school workmen who killed it and had a feast. The hostel workers were indignant and mad when they learned the others had eaten the hapless lizard which they felt was rightfully theirs.

The unlucky animal never suspected its fate as it ambled along a tree shaded Kinshasa street.

Love to all, and should a monitor lizard cross your path just say "hi" and keep moving.

G'ma and G'pa

Hostel Kids Decorating Cookies

Christmas in Africa

Frog Legs for Christmas?

Dear Mireille and Matt,

When we grow up and think of Christmas, we often associate it with those remembered from our childhood. Growing up in northwestern Ohio, I could always count on snow for Christmas. There were grandparents, aunts, uncles, and cousins to share the special dinner at our home. And later, we children ran to the snow-covered pasture to play fox and geese or flopped in the snow and made snow angels. Since the equator runs through Congo, snow at Christmas was never an option. Hot weather, rain perhaps, and a breeze riffling the fronds on the palm trees were more like it in Congo.

A tropical Christmas, our second in Congo, stands out in my memory. We were living downcountry at Banza Manteke and had been invited to spend Christmas vacation at Vanga, an upcountry mission station on the Kwilu River. We had been in Congo only a year and looked forward to seeing the mission work at each of our eight stations. Grandpa loaded the Chevrolet Carryall with our luggage, and we were on our way. Traveling in the bush, we always spent the night at one of our mission stations. Luxuries like Holiday Inn or Econo Lodge were unknown. Besides, it was more fun at a mission station.

The main road connecting the capital city of Leopoldville to Matadi, the port city two hundred miles away, was unpaved at that time. Banza Manteke lay between them, and we bounced and jolted over the dusty road from our home to Sona Bata, the first stop on our trip. While there, we toured the schools and hospital, never dreaming that Susan would be born in that same bush hospital eighteen months later! The highlight of the evening was the donut and sticky bun party with all the missionaries on the station. In the morning, fortified with a delicious breakfast of pancakes, the Sona Bata folks waved goodbye to us as we left for Boko, the newest of our mission stations.

If we thought the road to Sona Bata was bad, we were in for even worse jolts and bumps. That road was a cinch compared to the sandy route to Boko. We were at a loss to know if we should drive slowly and hit the bumps at fifteen miles an hour or if we should zip along and just hit the tops of them. No matter which, we hit 'em all! In spite of the dreadful road, the scenery was awesome. The rains had perked up the forests, and the hills were incredibly green. We stopped along the road, spreading a tarp on the ground, to eat the lunch the Sona Bata folks had fixed. Looking down into the valley below, we heard voices as people called to one another, yet the foliage was so thick we could see no one.

The wide Kwango River loomed before us at Popokabaka, but where was the bridge to take us to the other side? Not to worry—we would be ferried across. This prompted four-year-old Steven to ask where the fairies were! Grandpa drove onto a two-car raft set atop three flat boats powered by motors. This craft did not look seaworthy, but it transported us safely across the Kwango, and, a few minutes later, we were on the road again for Boko.

We were in Bayaka country, one of many tribes found throughout Congo. These people were small in stature, partly due to poor diet, not as progressed as some tribes, quite poor and often hungry. Their homes were built of sticks plastered with mud and had thatch roofs and dirt floors.

After a jolting, dusty, twelve-hour drive to Boko, it was good to arrive and be greeted by our colleagues. Among them were our good friends Scotty and Dolores who were stationed there to build a hospital. The day that Scotty and his crew of Congolese workmen started building, six people died in the dirt floored, thatched roof and mud-walled structure, which served as "the hospital."

How easy it is for us to get a drink of water or take a bath. Just turn on the tap, and water comes pouring out. It's not that simple at a bush station. One of the missionaries had put in a hydraulic ram to get water piped up a very steep hill so the mission could have running water. We wanted to see this unique water system and made the descent down lush green trails to the base of a hill where a crystal clear stream made its way. The guys waded into the falls and took showers!

The following morning the Scotts and Sharps left Boko for the all-day drive to Vanga. Throughout the day, we crossed five rivers, each of them by *bac* (ferry) of some sort. Whether driving onto a flimsy-looking motor driven raft, or poled across the river by chanting Congolese, or swept across by cable and the river's current, we had breathtaking views of the rivers and the accompanying shorelines. What an experience! For those still fairly new missionaries it was stuff to write home about!

When we stopped to eat lunch, some men appeared and gave us a gift of four eggs. They were Christians from the Moanza area, another of the upcountry mission stations. In all the years we lived in Africa, we never ceased to be amazed at the generosity of a people who had so little, but who shared so willingly from their meager resources. We were happy we still had sandwiches that we could share with them.

After hours on the road, it was a relief to finally arrive at Vanga on the banks of the Kwilu River. We were meeting some of our colleagues for the first time. Jerry and Lee and their four children were guests as well. The previous year, we had spent a few months with them in Belgium in French study. This tropical Christmas would be memorable, unlike any I had ever known in snowy Ohio.

The first night we were at Vanga we were awakened from a sound sleep by a loud thump on the metal roof. We sat up in bed. Had some wild animal suddenly pounced on the house? No, nothing quite so exotic. But there was an avocado tree by the house, and a big one had dropped on the roof, waking us. Our hearts stopped pounding and we went back to sleep.

In the morning, we canoed across the Kwilu to Konzi. Although the village wasn't visible from Vanga, we heard women and children calling to one another before we docked at the shore. Walking along the trail to the village, we met women carrying large enamel basins of writhing, wriggling caterpillars on their heads. These varicolored creatures would be dried in the sun and provide protein in the local diet. Our arrival brought lots of chatter from the children as they watched our every move. Each evening at Vanga, we could hear the sound of Konzi drumbeats on the night air.

On Christmas Eve, we joined the Congolese in a special worship service and singing of Christmas carols. Although the carols were familiar, the languages were not, as people sang this beautiful music in their mother tongue—Kituba, Kihungana, Kimbala, Kikongo. In earlier years, Congolese and missionaries had translated the carols, and now, even though we were far from our homeland and families, we were singing the same music with new friends. Following the carol sing, the missionaries served tea and cookies to those who remembered to bring a cup. No one had enough cups to serve all the carolers, and the nearest Wal-Mart where one might buy them was a continent away.

Before going to bed Christmas Eve, Steven hung up his stocking along with Carol and Joanie, daughters of our host couple. Christmas morning, discovering that Santa had found his stocking, Steven exclaimed, with a touch of awe in his voice, "Well! Santa Claus didn't leave switches!"

On Christmas morning, we worshiped again with the Congolese. Later, we gathered in one of the missionary homes to open gifts (we had earlier drawn names) and share a wonderful dinner together. With twelve children and fourteen adults, there was much joy and fun around the table. Folks had saved goodies sent from the States for this special occasion. Our colleagues were quickly becoming "family."

The Vanga hosts had planned many interesting things for us to see and do. A new church was under construction at Kimbata, where there was also a small lake. We would go there for a picnic and swim. Kimbata was on the opposite side of the river from Vanga. The men drove fifteen miles to the nearest ferry, where they crossed the river, then drove another fifteen miles to Konzi to meet us. We had crossed the river earlier by dugout canoe and waited for them to arrive. There wasn't enough room in the vans for all of us to make the trip at the same time. It was a "long way around Robin Hood's barn" but eventually we all got to Kimbata for the picnic and swim.

The antics of *mindele* (white people) always drew the attention of Congolese children. Whether we were swimming, eating lunch, or just visiting, children stood nearby chattering back and forth, noting our every action. A bit disconcerting and a habit which I never enjoyed, but I reminded myself that maybe in their culture they were not being rude. After all, what could be more exciting than watching a *mundele* eat her sandwich! It lent variety to village life!

It was impressive to see three large church buildings under construction in the area. Impressive because the local people were erecting their churches without outside financial help. No mud and thatch building materials for these churches—they were being built of durable stone. At one of the churches, we learned that as members walked the trails to worship services they stopped and picked up large rocks and added them to the growing pile of building materials at the church site.

While at Vanga, we enjoyed watching the river traffic. A boat arrived every twelve days bringing mail. One evening we heard the boat whistle, and, under a beautiful full moon, we went down to the beach to watch the activity. These were wood burning boats and usually pulled two or three barges behind them. Once, as we watched a boat head downstream to Leopoldville, the current was so swift the boat had to turn around and head back upstream so it could dock and offload its cargo.

The few days at Vanga left us with some memorable experiences. We liked to watch the schoolgirls go down to the river in the afternoon to swim. They always stayed near the bank, and while half the girls made "whoomping" noises in the water with their hands, the other half played in the water. After awhile they switched. There were crocodiles in the river, they said, and this sound scared them away.

One evening, Grandpa and a couple of men went out in a dugout canoe hoping to come back with the makings for a frog leg supper. While the frogs had no reason to fear losing their legs, there was a positive note to the adventure. Our friend mentioned this escapade in a letter to her mother. Several weeks later, when the mail boat arrived there was a tinned ham for her in the mail sack! Her mother was sure her daughter and family were meat deprived.

Christmas vacation was nearly over and it was time to move on, but our second Christmas in Congo was an experience we would never forget.

Love, G'ma and G'pa

Merry Christmas In the "Zoo"

Dear Grandchildren, One and All,

Being houseparents in the children's hostel was a demanding responsibility. It was Christmas vacation, and the children had gone home to spend the time with their families in the interior. Although Grandpa and I had been to Kenya before, we had never been there at Christmas. We, too, needed a break from the hostel. Kenya was the ideal place to forget about the duties connected with maintaining a home for the children while they were away at school. Sam and Mary Etta were houseparents in another hostel and they needed a break as well. Two weeks' vacation in Kenya was a must. "Nairobi, here we come!" was our rallying cry.

We planned to fly to Nairobi via Air Zaire, more commonly known by most "expats" as *Air Peutêtre* (Air Perhaps). One never knew—perhaps the flight would leave, perhaps it wouldn't. An expatriate is someone who lives abroad. To be assured of getting on the flight, the four of us arrived two hours early at Ndjili Airport. Air Peutêtre was in no hurry to leave. So we fussed and fidgeted, waiting for the plane to take off. Nine and a half hours later, we were finally airborne.

Due to the plane's late departure from Kinshasa, it was 3:00 AM by the time we got to our hotel. Unfortunately, we had been booked into the wrong rooms, and it took another hour before everything was straightened out. We were dead tired, but I wanted a bath anyway. The water gushed from the faucet! What wonderful pressure! How many hours had I waited for a trickle of water from faucets at the hostel? This was sheer delight! Maybe I wouldn't sightsee while we were in Kenya. Maybe I'd spend my vacation taking baths!

It was nice to be in an English speaking country again. It was fun to shop in stores that were well stocked. The streets were clean. Beautiful flowers bloomed everywhere. We liked reading the newspapers in English. All over the city, there was outward evidence of Christmas with lighted trees and folks singing or playing carols and hymns.

Late one afternoon, Grandpa and Sam rented a car for our trip to the game parks. We had eaten sandwiches at noon, and Mary Etta and I dressed up, hoping to have dinner at a nice restaurant that evening. On our way there, the car lights went off. The guys fiddled with this and that, but the lights stubbornly refused to come back on. As the car rental agency was closed for the night, we couldn't return the car and get another. In the dark, we found a gas station where a man who considered himself a mechanic tried to get the lights working again. He had no luck either. The guys decided to return to our hotel using the blinkers to alert other drivers, when for no apparent reason, the lights came back on. By then, it was 9 PM. We were hungry. We were tired. We were no longer in the mood for dinner. What a disappointing evening. Passing Colonel Sander's Kentucky Fried Chicken we ate our "nice dinner" there. Bless the Colonel. He had made his way to Africa! We had never shared Christmas Eve with him before.

Christmas Day we were off to Amboseli Game Park, stopping along the way like good tourists to take pictures of animals. Long before we arrived at the park we counted eighteen giraffes on either side of the paved highway. Masai men, decked out in their dirty red blankets, herded their cattle. Inside the park, rhinos and lions eluded us, but there were herds of wildebeest, Thomson's gazelles, zebras, and elephants that kept us exclaiming. If ever an animal looked as though a committee designed it, it's the ostrich. In spite of their beady eyes, long, skinny neck, and equally skinny legs, they are built for speed. Sam tried to outrun it, but the ostrich had no trouble winning first place.

Off in the distance, we saw one lone elephant and drove off the road for a closer view. The old boy lifted his trunk, flapped his ears and headed our direction to show us who was boss. Sam put the car in reverse—and backed into a hole, right up to the axle. We sat very quietly and held our breath until the elephant, deciding we were harmless, lumbered off. When we could breathe again we got out of the car, lifted it out of the hole, and continued on our way content to view elephants from a safer distance.

Although Christmas Eve dinner at Kentucky Fried Chicken was a letdown, Christmas dinner in Amboseli was a beautiful, tempting array of salads, meats, vegetables, and desserts. Only one thing was wrong. It didn't feel like Christmas. We missed Steven and Melanie and Susan. (Susan hadn't met Mike yet.) Christmas is family time; we were wistful for ours.

Back on the road after dinner, we stopped at waterholes, hoping to see more animals as they came to drink. Sun bleached bones were mute evidence that more than one animal had become dinner for others.

Christmas in Africa

Lifting the Car from a Hole
Elephant is in background, then ambles off.

By the time we left Amboseli and got to the paved highway, it was dark, but there was no problem with the car lights. We stopped to switch drivers—and the lights went out. No amount of fiddling made any difference. In desperation, the fellows wired one headlight to the battery and we "popeyed" back to Nairobi. Irate drivers kept blinking at us to dim, and then put up their brights when they drove even with us. By the time we got back to Nairobi we'd had it with that crazy car.

Later in the week, we took the overnight train to Mombasa on the coast where we found lodging at Kanamai campground. Grandpa and Susan and I had stayed there four years earlier. December is a busy tourist month, and we were lucky to find a place to stay. Our cottage with housekeeping privileges boasted the creature comforts of a three-burner gas plate, a refrigerator that shocked us when we touched it, and cold running water. Fishermen came to the cottage to sell fresh fish, and Grandpa fixed us some yummy fish dinners.

With the Indian Ocean right outside our cottage door, we enjoyed long walks along the beach. Other beaches are prettier than Kanamai, but it can't be beat for beachcombing. Cowrie shells in delicate hues of yellow, pink, lavender, and blue had washed in with the tide and lay scattered in the sand.

Some distance from shore lies a coral reef. At low tide, we walked out to it and were amazed at the variety of marine life. One day, we went to a nearby game reserve, where we were rewarded with our first view of sable antelopes. Mean looking Cape buffalo roamed the reserve as well.

On New Year's Eve, Mary Etta and I enjoyed our dress up dinner when we went to Red Lobster for authentic seafood. Grandpa remembers ordering a lobster casserole rather than the whole lobster after seeing the difference in price. Our dinners were delicious, and our taste for seafood satisfied.

The days passed swiftly, and, all too soon, our two-week vacation was over. We returned to Nairobi and did a bit more shopping: parts for Joel's motorcycle, elastic bandages for John, tennis shoes for Phyllis, paring knives for the hostel—and a big basket to carry everything in for the return trip to Kinshasa.

What a delightful vacation it had been. We'll tell you about other Christmases in Africa in another letter.

Love to all, G'ma and G'pa

How 'Bout a Swim on Christmas Day?

Dear Aaron, Nicole, Zachary, and Kallianne,

It was the week before Christmas, and, all through the hostel, no children were stirring. They had all gone to their homes in the interior to spend the holidays with their parents. Grandpa and I looked forward to a few days of vacation at the mission guesthouse down on the coast at Nsiamfumu. Your mom had graduated from college a few months earlier and was employed as a teacher's aide at TASOK. We were glad she could spend Christmas with us. But before we could leave, there was work to do.

With only a day and a half to get the hostel clean again, the two hostel moms sailed into high gear, and with the help of the workmen, cleaned screens and windows, mopped floors, laundered bedding and remade beds. Even dead mosquito remains had to be washed off the walls, as many an unfortunate insect had met its demise where one of the kids had swatted it.

We were packed and ready to leave bright and early on Saturday morning, optimistically hoping to make the trip to the coast in twelve hours. Stopping at Sona Bata for a quick cup of coffee with Clarks, we continued to Matadi where the ferry would take us across the wide Zaire River. It was not uncommon for the ferry to break down, and of course, this was one of those times. We waited and waited. Three hours we waited, as did a lot of other people, but finally Grandpa was able to drive the van onto the crowded ferry. Forty-five minutes later, we arrived on the other side of the river.

Sometimes, you have to look beyond bad roads and travel delays to enjoy the surprises God has for you. At the ferry, several showy flamboyant trees, dressed in bright orange blossoms, lined the road. The sunset over the Zaire River giving color to the drab Matadi hills that night was awesome. Only God's hand could create such beauty.

Having crossed the river, we drove to Boma on paved road; but, just outside the city, the pavement ended. From there down to the coast, it was a snail's pace drive over a washboard, dusty road. The twelve-hour trip had stretched into fifteen hours, and by the time we arrived at the guesthouse, we were too tired to do more than make the beds and crawl in. But a good night's sleep does wonders. In the morning, we were eager to decorate the small artificial Christmas tree someone had left for others to enjoy. Even in the tropics, we liked to observe traditions from our childhood.

A former "mish kid," at that time a mechanic with Gulf Oil, joined us for Christmas dinner. Gulf was drilling for oil off Zaire's coast. Wayne brought cauliflower and green peas, both a treat for us, and we contributed roast chicken, dressing and dessert. In my haste to leave Kinshasa, I had forgotten the sage and poultry seasoning for the dressing, but a previous vacationer had left oregano and curry powder in a cupboard. You just improvise when you don't have what you need.

Wayne took us water skiing in his boat one afternoon. Susan and Grandpa got right up without any problem, but I kept bobbing around like a cork and finally gave up. However, my attempts to water-ski gave a cluster of Zairian children something to howl over. Never had they seen such a funny *mundele*.

The Gulf helicopter pilot gave us a noisy hop over Tonde Beach one afternoon, where we looked down on people enjoying the sun and waves. Our favorite spot for riding the waves, Tonde was a couple of miles from Nsiamfumu. Walking from one beach to the other, we often gathered shells and "hully gullies." Now, flying, below us we saw two enormous black kettles abandoned in a field of elephant grass and scrub trees. They were the kind my dad used for scalding hogs on butchering day, except these were more than twice as large. We could only imagine why they were there. Cashew nuts were grown locally. Maybe the cashews were heated in the pots to burn off the poison before they would be safe to eat.

Sometimes, fishermen came to the guesthouse with fish to sell from their day's catch. And sometimes, we caught our own. Grandpa and Susan often fished off a point near the guesthouse and caught several nice rock bass and a stingray.

We were going to toss the stingray until some Portuguese teenagers came by and told us how to prepare it. To our surprise, it was good eating, too. Grandpa often got his line tangled in the rocks. It was Susan's job to swim out and unsnarl it. If anyone ever earned a medal for rescuing tangled fish line, it was your mom. One day, Wayne and Grandpa fished successfully for barracuda in the Zaire River. Delicious fish dinners were a treat.

During the years we lived in Congo, the country changed its name from Belgian Congo to Republic of Congo to Zaire. Today it's known as Democratic Republic of the Congo. It was still called Zaire when we spent Christmas at Nsiamfumu. People often spoke of it as the land of three Zs—Zaire the country, Zaire the River and zaire the money. The day after Christmas, President Mobutu announced that, henceforth, the five and ten zaire bills would no longer be valid currency. New bills would replace them. Imagine if we were told we could no longer use five and ten dollar bills. Chaos would result. And it did there too.

For months people had been hoarding those bills, which meant there were few in circulation. Businesses with large payrolls had difficulty getting money to pay salaries. All flights in and out of Kinshasa were cancelled for several days to prevent hoarders from bringing trunks of those bills to the banks or from taking them out of the country, hoping to exchange them at banks in Europe. We made four trips to the bank hoping to exchange our zaires for the new bills, but, of course, the bank had none. Meanwhile, the banks took the old bills, registered them and announced they would be replaced with new bills. The few people who did get payment received no more than a tenth of what they turned in. We didn't get anything for ours. Driving from the bank back to Nsiamfumu, we stopped at a couple of markets to buy fresh fruit and vegetables. The women didn't have new bills and neither did we—they weren't selling and we couldn't buy.

In spite of the chaotic days after Christmas, we enjoyed the days of rest and relaxation of our ocean vacation. But it was time to return to Kinshasa and become hostel parents again. The return trip was uneventful, that is if you call waiting five hours for the ferry to take us across the river to Matadi uneventful. It was good we hadn't left Nsiamfumu a day earlier, as the ferry had stopped running that afternoon. Now, twenty-four hours later, the ferry was repaired and a great crush of people waited to cross.

Women with huge basketloads of manioc greens suspended from their foreheads by straps, firewood carried on their backs in baskets suspended in the same fashion, made them look like beasts of burden. They had slept overnight at the river, then waited in the hot sun the next day for the ferry to take them across the river in order to sell their produce. When the ferry finally arrived, everyone rushed to get on. Grandpa, driving the van, was one of the first, but Susan and I joined the throng of people pushing to get on. Two or three women fell in the water. Susan and I gripped hands, swept along in the crush of people. There wasn't an inch of empty space on that ferry! Finally, we reached Matadi. What a relief to have our feet on solid ground again.

Until the next letter . . .

Love you, G'ma and G'pa

You Won't Find Snow on the Equator

Dear Matt and Mireille,

Our seventeenth Christmas in Zaire was totally unlike others we had known. Catching an Air Zaire flight from Kinshasa, Grandpa and I flew to Mbandaka, situated on the equator, to spend the holidays with your dad. He had taught English with the Peace Corps for two years in Zairian high schools and was now regional representative in Equator Province. He was responsible for the large group of Peace Corps volunteers who served as teachers in several area high schools.

Despite spending more Christmases in the tropics than in cold climates, I wanted a Christmas tree. I cut a branch from a mimosa tree already decorated with lovely pink blossoms. After two or three hours in Zaire's tropical heat, the blossoms drooped. Mimosas were not a good substitute for evergreens.

Still, I was determined to have a tree. We finally cut two palm fronds, slit them at the base and tied them together giving a three-dimensional effect. There might not be snow in Mbandaka, but there were snowflakes on our tree. Your dad produced scissors and we cut fancy ones from paper. Our tree glowed not from tiny lights, but from candles placed on pedestals on either side. The city of several thousand people was without electricity at that time. While it wasn't an authentic Christmas tree, our experiment with palm fronds was quite acceptable.

The four Peace Corps volunteers in Mbandaka were invited to share our dinner. While in town one morning, the women were approached by a man with two incredibly scrawny chickens for sale. Now there is nothing scrawnier nor tougher than a Zaire fowl. We decided to tenderize them in crushed papaya leaves, which have a tenderizing enzyme. To our dismay, we discovered that the skin nearly dissolved! Nevertheless, we stuffed those birds.

Not only was the city without electricity, there was no propane gas available either. Everyone cooked outside on small charcoal grills. Charcoal, made locally by women, was a steady and reliable source.

Unsure how long my pioneer spirit might prevail, Grandpa took a piece of sheet metal and from it fashioned a charcoal stove which he placed in the stove oven. There, over the coals, we roasted those scrawny chickens, baked the dressing, the squash, and the small tinned ham we brought from Kinshasa.

The seven of us had just finished eating when a large truck stopped in front of the house and four more Peace Corps volunteers climbed down. They were teachers from the high school at Tondo. Jolting in the back of a truck over bumpy roads was preferable to spending Christmas Day in Tondo they said. Seven hours later in what should have been a three-hour trip, they arrived hungry and dusty. They quickly finished eating the leftovers from our dinner and joined us for dessert.

The Mbandaka volunteers brought chocolate cake and pineapple upside down cake. To this was added our pumpkin pie made from *lengi*, a tasty squash we could buy in Zaire. The entire dinner had been prepared over charcoal fires and was delicious.

That evening, we sat around the tree singing Christmas carols in the glow of candles. Sharing that special time with those young volunteers who were far from their own homes and families, Grandpa and I felt privileged to be a part of their Christmas on the equator. Our Savior's birth had brought us together. It was a Christmas we will never forget.

Much love,
G'ma and G'pa

Caw, Caw, and Just Becaws

Dear Brenner Grandkids,

It was the day before Christmas, and, all through our house, there was plenty of stirring. Grandma was getting ready to stuff two turkeys for Christmas dinner which would include fifty-five people the next day. The number kept growing. In addition to those living on the mission station, two of our families who lived in the bush were in town. They were invited. Other folks worked in Kinshasa, but had no colleagues with whom to share the day. They shouldn't spend the day alone. Then there were two evangelists from New Zealand who were away from their families. Christmas would be a lonely day for them. They accepted our invitation. Like the energizer bunny that keeps going and going, our number kept growing and growing.

While I chopped celery and onions, Grandpa was involved with feathered creatures as well. The American School of Kinshasa (TASOK) was located on our mission station at that time. In front of the classrooms stood a tall kapok tree in which a pair of crows was raising its young family. These birds were different from the common black variety we find in the United States. These were black and white. Grandpa, aided and abetted by a couple of the kids, climbed the tree and stole the three babies, intending to raise them as pets and teach them to talk. They were almost ready to leave the nest.

To our house marched the bird snatchers, each one carrying a frightened, squawking young crow. Circling overhead, and protesting this outrage, the parent birds followed their every step. The three hapless babies were deposited in a cage on our back porch while a pair of very angry crows set up surveillance in the avocado tree right outside the kitchen door. They continued to scream their distress. In the meantime, the chief nest robber went off to town, leaving your grandma to contend with the racket. She was not pleased.

Susan, then eleven years old, came home from a party shocked and indignant to find the baby crows caged on our back porch. She cried and turned on the dramatics. "How would you like it if the birds came down and took Steven and me away? . . . It's stealing, that's what it is. . . . Now no one will like us anymore because we took the birds and they'll never come back to nest." And so it went. And I would have liked to! By then I was coping with the turkey stuffing, frantic birds, my anger, *and* Susan's melodramatics. My thoughts were not exactly about Christmas. The parent birds continued their protests until dark that night, awaking Susan at 6:30 the next morning when they started all over again.

Susan cared for several birds while we were in Congo (most of them died) and, after she got over her anger and indignation about the crows, she took good care of them. She fed them and let them out to exercise, but they didn't live long. Sadly, one morning she found hers with its feet in the air lying dead in the cage. The other two survived only a day or so after that.

By the time classes resumed after Christmas vacation, most of the students had forgotten about the crows, but the birds never nested in the kapok tree again.

I rarely see or hear a crow today that I'm not reminded of that incident when the parent birds "cawed" so desperately for their children.

Now then, don't rob any bird nests!

Love to all,
G'ma and G'pa

Diff'rent Strokes for Diff'rent Folks

Dear Grandkids,

During the years we worked in the purchasing service, there were some interesting experiences at Christmas that showed us how differently Africans and Americans view the giving of gifts. I've told you about Mama Nsukami Suzanne, the elderly lady who "adopted" Susan when she realized they had the same name.

It was Christmas one year when she limped her way to our home to bring us a gift of spinach, green beans, and fresh peanuts. She had raised the peanuts in her tiny garden, but from her meager resources she had bought the beans and spinach at the market. As we visited together, enjoying cookies and tea, hers heavily laced with sugar and milk, she waggled a foot in my direction. She had borrowed the flip-flops she was wearing, she said, from the lady who lived across the street from her. The ones I had given her last Christmas were now worn out!

I had purchased a headscarf and cloth for a new wraparound skirt and blouse and wished her a Merry Christmas as I gave them to her. Clapping her hands twice in acceptance, Suzanne bobbed a little curtsy, telling me *ntondele* (thank you). When she was ready to leave, I handed her a basket with several food items—sugar, tea, rice, milk powder, mackerel, a couple of onions. Carefully she looked them over, and asked, "Isn't there any margarine?" We always gave her a bit of money to buy anything we had missed, but she never could resist asking for something else!

Late one Christmas Eve, Grandpa and I had gone to the candlelight Communion service at church and we didn't get home until 1:15 Christmas morning. As we walked to the house, Grandpa said he thought he'd like some eggnog. That seemed like a good idea, so, while he found carols to play on the tape recorder and turned on the tree lights, I went into the kitchen to make eggnog. Then we heard a voice at our front door. From the darkness someone called, "*Ko-ko-ko.*" That's the same as someone knocking in our culture. Now who could possibly be at our door at 1:15 in the morning, we wondered? There stood the night watchman saying, "*Bonne fête, bonne fête!*"

When someone says that they're asking you to give them a gift. In this case it meant, "Where's my Christmas present?" The night watchman had been quite creative as he had taken a palm frond, braided the individual leaves together, then worked bougainvillea and frangipani blossoms into the whole thing. It was quite impressive. We had to admire his ingenuity. This was his offering preceding his request. Even though we thought it was a poor time to be asking for a gift, the night watchman saw we had returned home, and what better opportunity! After all, he was awake and we were too. "Strike while the iron is hot," was his thinking.

One Christmas, prior to making a trip to the stations in the interior, the Congolese director of the mission (the general secretary), asked the purchasing service to buy and prepare gifts for those who worked at the station. There were about fifty who came to work each day in the different offices. Grandpa went shopping in town and returned with sugar, rice, tea, milk powder, and tins of mackerel. We began weighing and bagging food in preparation for the special event.

The day before Christmas, all the workers assembled at the chapel to sing carols and receive their gift. It wasn't long before we were informed there was a "little problem." People from the Education Department had not been invited to the party because the government paid them. All the other workers were paid by the mission, and they refused to accept their gifts until the "little problem" was taken care of. Certainly the government would do nothing for those who worked in the Education Department, so they must be included in the station gift as well, we were told. To us it seemed they thought a gift was something owed them, not something freely given. When we felt annoyed with people over this attitude, we had to ask ourselves if God were just as disappointed with us when we seemed unappreciative of the many gifts we received from him.

The following Christmas, there was a much better spirit. Everyone who worked at the mission station was included in gifts that year. There were more than eighty to prepare for. Outside the little chapel* we sang carols and listened to the Christmas story read in Lingala, Kituba, French, and English, the languages used in the different offices. Cookies and sodas were enjoyed together.

The new general secretary announced that the gift they were about to receive was a symbol of love, that the mission lacked the money to give everyone a big gift, but that what was given was an expression of love. That year, no one refused their gift of beans, rice, and tins of fish. As soon as the party was over, Luyinda and I sold twenty-seven large sacks of manioc that had arrived on a truck from Vanga the day before. We needed to sell the manioc right away as it would have spoiled by Monday, the first day everyone would have returned to work.

One of the most unique Christmas experiences I remember was the party my Bible study group gave for young women at a handicapped center. Most of them were fairly young, but crippled in their feet or legs. Some had had polio as a child. Others had a condition known as clubfoot, a congenital deformity in which the foot is twisted and turned inward. Several wore leg braces. Some were in wheelchairs, but all had the use of their hands. These young women were employed by the handicapped center to embroider tablecloths, napkins, and doilies. They also made authentic little figures of Congolese in various poses, such as a woman pounding manioc, men poling a canoe, a mother with a baby tied to her back, a drummer playing a drum.

Our group had made sewing kits to give to the women. The kits were filled with needles, scissors, embroidery floss, hoops, and a thimble. In their excitement at receiving their very own sewing kit, the girls cheered and clapped. We also gave each one a Lingala New Testament, then read the Christmas Scripture together and sang carols.

Knowing the Congolese love of cookies and cakes, we went prepared with party fare. We had made dozens of cookies for the party, and in addition, we gave each young woman a plate of them to take home. Despite our forethought, these young ladies were a step ahead of us! Each one took her napkin and began filling it with as many extra cookies as she could! What a party. They were having a grand time, and we were too.

This was the first time any of us had ever met these women. My Bible study group had heard about them and we wanted to give them a party. It was a great opportunity to share that just as God had sent Jesus as his gift to the world, we also wanted to share gifts with them.

Christmases in Africa were usually very different from those we had known in the States, but God made each one of them special for us in some way.

Merry Christmas!

Much love from G'ma and G'pa

*Sims Chapel, Kinshasa's oldest building, is a landmark in the city. It was built in the late 1800s and named for Aaron Sims, an early pioneer missionary doctor. Originally it had a thatch roof. It is used regularly for meetings and worship services.

The Twelve Days of Christmas

(in Zaire/Congo)
with Apologies to the Original Author

Dear Grandkids,
Now then, everybody sing!

On the first day of Christmas your grandpa gave to me
A red tailed parrot in a palm tree.

On the second day of Christmas your grandpa gave to me
Two bongo drums and a red tailed parrot in a palm tree.

On the third day of Christmas your grandpa gave to me
Three fruit bats, two bongo drums and a red tailed parrot in a palm tree.

On the fourth day of Christmas your grandpa gave to me
Four chimpanzees, three fruit bats, two bongo drums and a red tailed parrot in a palm tree.

On the fifth day of Christmas your grandpa gave to me
Five ripe mangos, Four chimpanzees, three fruit bats, two bongo drums and a red tailed parrot in a palm tree.

On the sixth day of Christmas your grandpa gave to me
Six saucy monkeys, five ripe mangos, four chimpanzees, three fruit bats, two bongo drums and a red tailed parrot in a palm tree.

On the seventh day of Christmas your Grandpa gave to me
Seven lions roaring, six saucy monkeys, five ripe mangos, four chimpanzees, three fruit bats, two bongo drums and a red tailed parrot in a palm tree.

On the eighth day of Christmas your grandpa gave to me
Eight hippos swimming, seven lions roaring, six saucy monkeys, five ripe mangos, four chimpanzees, three fruit bats, two bongo drums and a red tailed parrot in a palm tree.

On the ninth day of Christmas your grandpa gave to me
Nine drummers drumming, eight hippos swimming, seven lions roaring, six saucy monkeys, five ripe mangos, four chimpanzees, three fruit bats, two bongo drums and a red tailed parrot in a palm tree.

On the tenth day of Christmas your grandpa gave to me
Ten women dancing, nine drummers drumming, eight hippos swimming, seven lions roaring, six saucy monkeys, five ripe mangos, four chimpanzees, three fruit bats, two bongo drums and a red tailed parrot in a palm tree.

On the eleventh day of Christmas your grandpa gave to me
eleven choirs a-singing, ten women dancing, nine drummers drumming, eight hippos swimming, seven lions roaring, six saucy monkeys, five ripe mangos, four chimpanzees, three fruit bats, two bongo drums and a red tailed parrot in a palm tree.

On the twelfth day of Christmas your grandpa gave to me
Twelve hostel children, eleven choirs a-singing, ten women dancing, nine drummers drumming, eight hippos swimming, seven lions roaring, six saucy monkey, five ripe mangos, four chimpanzees, three fruit bats, two bongo drums and a red tailed parrot in a palm tree.

Love to all, and Merry Christmas!
G'ma and G'pa

A Christmas Goodbye

Dear Aaron, Nicole, Zachary, and Kallianne,

I didn't see Alexander lying on the floor and tripped over him, startling both of us. It was Christmas, and we were house-sitting for friends. One of our responsibilities was to care for their several animals, among them Alexander, a huge Alsatian shepherd. In spite of his size, Alexander required a bit of TLC (Tender Loving Care). He had to be fed each bite with a large wooden spoon. Once a week, we had to open those massive jaws and toss a liver pill down his throat, rubbing it to make sure the pill went down. Alex may have been a guard dog, but he had his eccentric moments. Bulbul, a Welsh Corgi, didn't have any idiosyncrasies. Although short-legged and a tad overweight, he and Alex were good buddies.

The night before I stumbled over the dog, bruising my kneecaps, Susan, Mike, and Aaron landed at Ndjili airport via Lufthansa. Grandpa persuaded the gate official that he needed to get into the baggage area to help his family through customs. A few minutes later, there were hugs and kisses all around, and Grandma was finally able to hold her first grandchild, six-months-old Aaron. Back at Shangalele, our friends' home, we talked far into the night. We had a lot of catching up to do. Despite his schedule being upset, Aaron took in his new surroundings and adjusted to all the changes.

The next morning, the day before Christmas, we ate breakfast on the veranda overlooking the grounds, beautiful with a variety of flowering tropical plants. This would be our last Christmas in Zaire (Aaron's very first anywhere), and we looked forward to spending it at Matadi with Martha and Leon. James and June who were teaching in the high school at Sona Bata would be there as well. By now, our children and those of our colleagues were grown up and back in the States, but with Susan, Mike, and Aaron's visit, we anticipated a Merry Christmas.

We didn't leave Kinshasa until noon, and it was dark long before we arrived at Matadi. The road was winding and twisting, and we made some wrong turns before finally finding Emmerts' house. We arrived somewhat grumpy, but Martha's tasty homemade soup soon restored our spirits. Christmas Eve, everyone hung their stockings. The next morning, it was fun to open them, as well as the gifts we had made for each other.

Church members were building the Emmerts' house, which would become a guest house for the church when finished. What an undertaking that was! *Matadi* means rocks, and the city was well named. Lacking the equipment we would use in the United States, the men dug the hill by hand and later pounded the rocks into small stones for building. Wheelbarrow loads of dirt were used to extend the sloping front yard. Martha had planted hundred of trees and bushes—one day the rocky hillside would be beautiful. She set out ten plants for every one that survived. Although they flourished during the rains; in dry season, water had to be hand-carried to keep them alive.

After Christmas, we drove to the coast to spend a week at Nsiamfumu. The trip was not without its perils, however. Leaving Matadi, we discovered a hole in the fuel tank, poked there by the rocky ascent to Emmerts' house. Toothpicks are good for more than cleaning teeth, however, and one took care of the flow. Ingenuity is necessary when you're not near a garage! Zipping along the dirt road between Matadi and Boma, we suddenly saw smoke billowing out from under the hood. We bailed out quickly, threw dirt on the fire, stuck another toothpick in the tank to stem the stream of diesel fuel, and we were on our way once more.

Just as we turned onto the road leading to Nsiamfumu the hood flew up. Not to worry—it's not the same as driving on the Los Angeles freeway. We seemed to be the only car on the road. Ever resourceful, Grandpa tied the hood down with cord, as it had sprung when it flew up. By then, our car looked like a true Zairian vehicle. If it's true that "getting there is half the fun" we definitely had fun that trip.

We swam and rode the waves at Tonde Beach, picnicked at Star Beach, got sunburned, fished, and bought *capitain* from a fisherman who came to the guesthouse with his catch. We coped with frequent electrical and water problems and cheered Aaron when he cut his first tooth on New Year's Day. Murray climbed the big baobab tree overlooking the ocean and carved Aaron's name and date. Mike and Susan's names are there as well, as Mike added theirs to the growing list. If erosion hasn't caused the tree to tumble into the ocean, you would find all our names there today.

Years earlier, when Susan was a baby, we drove to Zongo Falls near Sona Bata where the water gushing over the cliffs was a spectacular sight. Back then, she wasn't much older than Aaron, and I carried her down the hill tied on my back just like the African mothers carried their babies. At that time, I never dreamed that someday we would return to those same beautiful falls and that she would be there with her baby. The road had not improved in the nearly thirty years since we had first gone to the falls. If possible, it had even more potholes than the route between Matadi and Boma. However, we negotiated it without anymore toothpicks in the fuel tank.

What a grand time we had for the three and a half weeks Susan and family were with us in Zaire. Mike had seen where she grew up, met many of her "aunts and uncles," gone to some of the places she remembered from her childhood, and had experienced life in a totally different culture from that which he knew growing up in California.

We wished Steven and Melanie could have spent that special time with us as well, but we had to be satisfied with the pictures and video they sent of Mireille. She would be ten months old before Melanie would put her in Grandma's arms at the Atlanta airport.

Our last Christmas in Zaire was quite different from others we had spent in the country. But what a wonderful and memorable time it was!

Till the next letter,
Love from G'ma and G'pa

The Purchasing Service

Oh, The Perils of Purchasing

Dear Grandkids,

After Congo gained its independence from Belgium in 1960, systems in the country began to break down. Many people didn't realize that freedom to govern themselves would mean a lot of hard work. Under the colonial system, people expected the government to provide everything for them. Some wanted the benefits of independence without having to accept the responsibilities that went with them. The roads were one of the first systems that broke down.

Our people working in the interior were having a hard time getting the necessary supplies to operate their programs. Schools and hospitals needed building materials, food, and medicine. Aviation gas for the airplane and fuel for trucks were increasingly difficult to get. With roads deteriorating due to lack of maintenance, trucks frequently broke down en route to and from the city. It became very expensive for people to go to Kinshasa to purchase their supplies. It also took a lot of time for them to travel to the city to do their shopping.

To help our colleagues living in the interior get the supplies they needed for their work, a purchasing service was organized. Grandpa and I were asked to oversee it. Each morning, Grandpa went to the radio room for the inter-mission broadcast and received the orders from folks in the interior. Through this broadcast, we were able to keep up to date with what was happening on our different stations as well. After churches, schools, hospitals, and missionaries gave their orders, Grandpa then went to town to buy the supplies.

One day, we were asked to load the seven-ton truck with aviation gas and helicopter fuel for the evangelistic program at Moanza. They also needed school supplies, bicycles for the rural medical dispensary and hospital nurses, 100 pound bags of flour, and tins of powdered milk for the schools. Another time, we loaded the truck with several tons of cement for the building program at Kikongo. Personal belongings for the new builder and his family bounced along on the same bumpy load. A barge load of building supplies and medicines destined for Vanga was delayed when the riverboat broke down. The boat's propeller had broken on a sandbar, and it was weeks before it was repaired. Purchasing supplies and sending them had its problems.

The money constantly devalued, which meant Grandpa needed to take a lot with him when he went shopping. Thieves, knowing that people carried large sums of money, constantly watched for opportunities to steal while people's attention was diverted. One of their tricks was to puncture tires. While you repaired them, the thieves (two often worked together), would steal your briefcase with money.

Dr. Dan had written a medical book which was on sale at a bookstore in town. Nearly $900 worth of books had been sold and Grandpa was asked to pick up the money. When he returned to the van, he discovered a tire had been slashed. The thieves were waiting, at a distance, of course, ready to move in and grab Grandpa's briefcase, but he outsmarted them. With the $900 safely inside his briefcase, Grandpa sat on it while he calmly changed the tire! I figured he was the only person in Kinshasa who ever changed a tire sitting on his money. A few days later, he returned to the van and found another tire slashed. As he was changing it, he looked up and saw a thief peering in the van window. Grandpa stood up, wrench in hand, and started after the guy. The man knew he better get out of there fast and took off on the run.

Most shopping trips were made without too much hassle. We just learned to be very alert and not take unnecessary chances. Purchasing supplies for people in the interior and sending them to the stations had its perils, but it helped our colleagues do their work.

Till next time—G'ma and G'pa

Bugs, Bugs, and More Bugs!

Dear Matt, Mireille, Nicole, Aaron, Kalli, and Zach,

Relentlessly, white ants indulged their insatiable appetite for paper and cloth, and at times, even the rafters which supported the roofs of buildings. Just as Jesus said we would always have the poor with us, that's the way we felt about termites. There was no getting rid of them. White ants were definitely a way of life in Congo.

At the purchasing service where Grandpa and I were working, there was a large container that had arrived with ocean freight a few months earlier. It was the size of a semi truck, such as we see on highways in America. The freight company did not want the container back, and it seemed the ideal place to store the medical text books which Doctor Dan had written and published. The books were worth several thousand dollars. In addition, another missionary had worked with a Congolese, and together they had written books in the Kikongo language. These were stored in the container as well, safe from the ravages of white ants. Or so we thought.

One day, we received an order from a doctor for six hundred copies of Dan's book. Unlocking the container to fill the order, we discovered to our horror that it was not termite proof. The ants had come up from the ground, made their way through the flooring and were prepared for a royal banquet. While we were taking care of our business, they were taking care of theirs.

We dreaded opening the cartons of books, lest we discover termites had totally ruined them. White ants have a nasty habit of eating their way through every page, decorating each one with cutout work. They have no respect for your important papers, for bolts of cloth or for anything else they can devour. As they invade your fabric and paper, they build tunnels on their march to indulge their appetite. Chomping their way through fabric, it looks similar to cutout embroidery—minus the fancy needlework. Of course, it's not just one piece of material that is damaged, it's the whole stack. We were fortunate. The greatest damage to the things in the container was to the cartons in which the books were stored.

There was still a big problem. How would we protect the rest of the books from the ever marching ants? We had to take all the cartons outside, check them carefully to be sure there were no ants lurking inside, then build new platforms on which to store the books. We set the platform legs in cans of oil in the hope of preventing the termites from climbing to their dinner table.

White ants were often sneaky, especially where wood was concerned. The rafters in a large storeroom had to be replaced one year as they were eaten so badly there was danger of the roof giving way. The outer part of the rafter looked fine, but inside, the termites had completely eaten the wood, leaving only the outer shell intact. A hard wood, such as mahogany, was usually used for rafters and was treated with creosote to help make it termite proof.

It's not likely you will ever have to deal with termites, but in hot, tropical countries they are a real menace. They may just be sitting up at the dinner table, knife and fork in hand, ready to enjoy a banquet!

Love to all,
G'ma and G'pa

Excitement on the Kwilu

Dear Grandchildren,

Situated on the banks of the Kwilu River, Vanga is one of our upcountry mission stations. In a month, we were to leave for a year's home assignment in the States. Before that, however, the missionaries at Vanga wanted to show us how the supplies we bought through the purchasing service helped them in their work.

We were enjoying a leisurely Saturday morning cup of coffee with John and Sue when one of his workmen ran frantically to the house yelling, "*Tata John! Tata John! Tracteur me vila!*" "What do you mean, the tractor is lost?" John asked. Catching his breath Kabamba gasped, "*Yo me dinda!*" "It drowned?" John questioned. "*E, yo me dinda na nzadi!*" (Yes, it drowned in the river!) John sprang from his chair, grabbed the keys to the Isuzu Trooper, we all hopped in, and John sped to the river. A leisurely Saturday morning abruptly ended with Kabamba's news.

Down at the river, the tractor was nowhere to be seen. One of John's workmen, charged with the Saturday morning job of driving the tractor to the river to be washed, had failed to set the brake. It had rolled into the water and had sunk from sight. Dozens of men and boys had gathered, excitedly discussing the best way to recover it. A tractor disappearing into the Kwilu River was not an everyday occurrence!

John put on swim trunks and waded in. In a few moments he found it, but how do you get a submerged tractor out of the water? With heavy rope, he tied one end to the tractor and the other end to the winch on the Trooper. The men grabbed the rope and began straining and pulling... straining and pulling. John cranked the winch, but the tractor didn't budge. More straining, more pulling. Still no luck. The men wrapped ropes around a huge tree to get more leverage as they struggled and pulled. Gradually, the Trooper inched backwards, pulling, pulling... Congolese have a custom of shouting in unison when they need to coordinate their movements: Rrrrrr, pah! Rrrrrr, pah! Now, with each pull, the men shouted together tugging and

Pulling John's Tractor from the Kwilu River

straining on the ropes. Finally, the front end of the tractor was visible. Then a bit more . . . and a bit more. Cheers went up as ever so slowly it edged forward from its watery grave.

It had taken two or three hours of hard work before the tractor was finally rescued. It kept John busy the next morning cleaning and drying it out. For the folks from Kinshasa, it was a never-to-be-forgotten experience!

John, one of our "mish kids," was building a new hospital at Vanga. His parents were our colleagues. John and Steven had known each other since they were little boys. They later graduated together from TASOK. Now, John was back as a mission builder, living on the same station where he had spent part of his childhood.

John gave us a tour of the new hospital under construction. What an opportunity to see how the materials Grandpa had sent were being used. Tons of cement had gone into the foundation and water storage tanks. For the workmen, there were tools, nails, and more nails. Whitewash would be mixed with colored powdered paint for hospital walls. Reinforcing iron would strengthen the building. Corrugated metal sheets were sent for the roof. There was lumber for rafters, trusses, and furniture. Most of these supplies had been purchased in Kinshasa, then sent to Vanga by truck, riverboat, or airplane.

The old hospital, in use until the completion of the new building, also received many supplies through the purchasing service. We ordered medicines, fuel, food, mattresses, and blankets. We sent crates of White Cross supplies purchased or made by women in our churches in America: bandages, hospital gowns, baby layettes, nurses uniforms. These were neatly stacked on shelves in a storeroom, ready to be used by the staff. Dan and Miriam gave us a tour and explained the medical work. The purchasing service played an important role in helping our colleagues in their work.

Outside Miriam's house, we saw a few women lined up with baskets and basins. What were they bringing, we wondered? We had to check this out. It was grapefruit! They brought the fruit to Miriam, and she paid them with clothing. They were especially anxious for children's clothes. Since the nearest stores were miles away, many women preferred payment in clothes to cash.

Vanga grapefruit is the best we have ever eaten. Just the right tartness and juiciness, it has one drawback—the seeds. Lots of seeds. A friend remarked that God surely intended Vanga grapefruit to reproduce! While we were houseparents in the children's hostel, Miriam occasionally sent grapefruit to us in fifty-gallon drums. As the drums had to travel by truck over impossible, at times impassable, bumpy dirt roads, she protected each layer of fruit with wood shavings from the carpentry shop.

It was encouraging to see how buying and sending supplies to our colleagues in the "bush" helped them in their work, but there was one more treat in store for us. They were taking us on a float trip on the Kwilu River. That sounded like fun to these city folks. We knew there were hippos in the river and wondered if we would see any. There was even a place they called Hippo Island. John drove upriver some distance, then everyone donned an inner tube and lazily floated back to Vanga. What fun! It's just as well we didn't see any hippos that day. In an earlier letter we told you about the tragic event that happened a few years later when people were floating on the Kwilu River.

The weekend had been great. We had seen how much folks on the bush stations depended on the purchasing service. We had enjoyed seeing our colleagues again. We were impressed with the new hospital buildings under construction. No one had planned the tractor episode, but it certainly added to the weekend's excitement. Now it was time to leave Vanga and return home.

To make the trip from Kinshasa to Vanga, we had driven the paved road as far as Kivamva, then parked the van at the Congolese pastor's house. John and Sue met us there in the Isuzu, a four-wheel drive vehicle, practical transportation on Congo roads. For the next two and a half hours, we bounced our way to Vanga. On the return trip, the MAF pilot (Missionary Aviation Fellowship) flew us to Kivamva in twenty minutes. Twenty minutes! What a difference from the time-consuming, bumpy road travel three days earlier. Flying was certainly a lot quicker and smoother way to travel in the bush.

We greeted the Kivamva pastor and his wife, thanked them for keeping the van safe, and were on our way to Kinshasa. What a lot we had to talk about on the way home!

Love to our grandkids,
G'ma and G'pa

Traveling by Canoe on the Kwilu River at Vanga

Kaleidoscope III

Policemen on Patrol

Dear Matt, Mireille, Nicole, Aaron, Zach, and Kalli,

I doubt that anyone who ever lived in Zaire left the country without at least one run-in with the police. We used to entertain one another with the latest story. The police in turn likely shared stories with their friends about the *mindele* they stopped and the crazy stories they were told. During the years we lived in Kinshasa, we had our share of police experiences.

One of our favorite stories happened to a colleague who was driving down one of Kinshasa's major streets. Lee was stopped by a policeman when he blew his whistle at her. Even though the population of the city numbered four or five million at that time, there were no working traffic lights in the city. Traffic was directed by policemen standing in the middle of a few intersections. An upraised arm was the equivalent of a red light and drivers were supposed to stop. With arms outstretched the policeman motioned the cross-traffic to proceed.

A few of the main routes had six or seven streets converging at a central location known as a *rond-point* (traffic circle) like spokes of a wheel. They dated from the days Zaire had been a Belgian colony. Belgians had decorated the traffic circles with shrubs and flowers. Some were built on a mound with an enormous saucerlike dish in the middle in which flowers were planted.

On the day that Lee was stopped by a policeman, the saucer no longer held flowers. But, right in the middle of it stood a policeman directing traffic. Not seeing him in the flowerpot, my friend drove through the intersection, only to hear a sharp whistle. She stopped and waited for the policeman to climb down and approach her car.

"Madame," he said, "You have committed a grave infraction. Did you not see me as I raised my arms to change the direction of traffic?"

"Oh, yes." admitted my quick-thinking friend. "I saw you up there, but I thought you were King Baudouin!" (king of the Belgians; in this case, a statue)

Fortunately, the policeman had a sense of humor, laughed and waved her on after reminding her that the next time she drove through that intersection to be sure and look for him (in his flowerpot!) directing traffic.

Not all traffic policemen were gifted with a sense of humor, and some were irritating, hoping you would pay a bribe so they would let you go. We had one unpleasant experience that wasted the entire morning.

Grandpa was sharpening some drills on his emery wheel one Saturday afternoon when a tiny speck of metal flew into the cornea of one eye. He spent a miserable weekend until he could see a doctor Monday morning. By then, scar tissue had begun to form, and the eye was infected. The doctor sent us to an ophthalmologist who used a slit lamp and special knife to remove the metal speck. The specialist was leaving for Belgium in a few days, yet he was still in Zaire when Grandpa needed him. God knew we were going to need that doctor's skill.

En route to the hospital to see the specialist, I heard a police whistle. I was driving on the main street, but at one place another road angled off to the side. Hoping for a bribe, the policeman told me I had committed a grave infraction (infractions were always "grave") by not signaling I would continue driving on the main street. I didn't need to signal, but he wanted us to give him some money so he would let us go. We would have to go to the police station he said. (Translation: Give me some money and you can be on your way.)

While he very slowly copied *everything* from my driver's license and car registration card I reminded him it was urgent that we get to the hospital to see the doctor. By this time, the metal had been in Grandpa's eye more than two and a half days, and we were quite concerned. Finally the policeman finished writing, got in the car with us and said we would have to go to the police station to pay a fine. (Still hoping for that bribe.) I told him we must go to the hospital first, and then we would go to the station. He suggested to Grandpa that we could forget the whole thing for $10.00.

It took the doctor an hour to remove the particle from Grandpa's eye. When we returned to the car an irate policeman was waiting for us. We were wasting his time he said and keeping him from his work. Besides, we hadn't even asked him to go into the hospital with us!

I asked him to direct us to the police station so we could go pay the fine. He had been a back-seat driver all the way into town, but now he seemed reluctant to continue to the station. No doubt thinking that we would tell the police chief that he had asked us to bribe him, he suddenly changed his tactics. He ordered me to take him back to where he had stopped us originally, all the time telling us what a good man he was. I was wasting his day, he said, keeping him from doing his work.

A few days later, I drove the wrong way around a *rond-point* that had six or seven streets emerging from the center. I fully expected a policeman would discover the error of my ways and haul me off to the police station. But none did, and as a friend commented, "They're never around when you really do something deserving of a ticket."

There was an unwritten rule in Kinshasa that when driving down the boulevard at night, cars should turn off their lights. The reason, we were told, was that the street lights provided sufficient light. Perhaps it was also thought that this would save car batteries. Near where we lived, the main street also had the same kind of lights as those on the boulevard. There was one big problem. Several of the light poles in our area had been knocked over by motorists. Since they had not been repaired, they no longer gave light to drivers. Sections of the street were dark.

One evening, Grandpa, a colleague and I were returning home from a meeting. Since so few streetlights were still working Grandpa turned on the car lights. Tweet! Tweet! Oh, no! A policeman had whistled us to stop. We were reminded, of course, that we had committed a grave infraction. Asking what that might be, we were scolded for driving with our lights on. Grandpa explained that since so many of the poles had been knocked over and the lights were no longer working, he had to turn on the car lights in order to see. That was no excuse. It was a rule, said the policeman, that where there were light poles you did not drive with your car lights on. Logic had nothing to do with it.

We knew what the policeman was waiting for. Not getting money pressed into his palm, he asked Grandpa what he thought he should do. "You're the policeman," said Grandpa. "That's for you to decide." The policeman looked doubtful. He had never heard that answer before. Maybe this *mundele* didn't understand. He tried again. "You have committed a grave infraction by driving with your lights on. What do you think we should do about this?" "I think," said Grandpa, "that you should let me go so I can take these women home." The policeman agreed and we were on our way.

I wonder if the policeman related the incident to his family when he got home and if he shook his head at the crazy white man who didn't understand he was supposed to hand over some money so he could be on his way.

That's enough police stories for this time. Be sure to always drive with your lights on!

Love you, G'ma and G'pa

It's Raining, It's Pouring!

Dear Grandkids,

Seasons in tropical Africa are opposite from ours in the United States. When we're wishing for cooler weather during our hot summer months, it's cool and hazy, dusty and dirty in Congo. Sometimes the sun didn't come out until early afternoon. That time of year, the dry season, is called *sivu*. The cooler weather was a relief, but people looked forward to the rains returning to clear the air and settle the dust. It never rained in July, although a drizzle one year prompted folks to refer to it as the drip-dry season.

Usually the rains started in September, but another year it might be October before they began. When we saw water hyacinths floating down the Congo River, we knew that the rains had started in the interior and that our rains wouldn't be far behind. The first rain was almost always preceded by a big wind that blew leaves and dust everywhere. Twigs and dead branches littered the ground. A film of dust covered everything in the house.

Where we lived overlooking the Congo River, it widened into an area a couple of miles across. We knew it as Stanley Pool. Years earlier, the Belgians had named it to honor Henry Morton Stanley who explored much of Congo in the late 1800s. When President Mobutu came into power, he authorized a return to authenticity, and many places that had been named by the Belgians reverted to their original African names. At that time, the Congolese renamed Stanley Pool, calling it Ngaliema Bay in honor of Chief Ngaliema. He was the one with whom Stanley actually negotiated for the property on which our mission stands today.

I loved watching the Congo River during a storm. The sky darkened with an almost unnatural light, palm trees bent in the wind, their fronds blowing straight out from the trunk. Mango and avocado trees dropped their fruit, and people scurried to seek shelter from the oncoming rain. Woe to the fisherman in his dugout canoe should he be caught on the water. In heavy storms, the wind blew the rain horizontally, and we had to rush to close the windows. Otherwise, we had a mess to mop up. Stanley Pool appeared calm before it reached the rapids on its rush to the Atlantic Ocean, but during a storm, wind whipped the water into a continuous display of whitecaps. Then, usually placid Stanley Pool churned and foamed in fury. It was fascinating to watch. Sometimes I thought the wind might blow me into the next province!

Once, after a big wind and rain storm, I looked out the kitchen window and watched Susan and four little pals parade past. They had found a large umbrella plant, broken leaves from it and were wearing them on their heads. They had found their own unique way to deal with the rain.

In 1961, a year after Congo received its independence from Belgium, the American School of Leopoldville opened. We called it TASOL then, but today it's TASOK, the American School of Kinshasa. That year we were blessed with early rains. In order to get the school started, our mission offered the use of one building. It was painted red and dubbed "the little red schoolhouse." Phil and his workmen renovated it into classrooms and restrooms, and everything was ready for opening day. All we lacked were the desks.

On that first day of school, a torrential rain poured from the skies. Forty-five kids and their teachers huddled inside classrooms to escape the rain. Unfortunately, the desks hadn't arrived yet, but some tables and benches destined for the Christian Center were found, and soon everyone had a place to sit. When the rain slackened an hour or more later, the truck arrived with the new desks, and classes proceeded on schedule. That was quite a beginning for the opening day of a brand new school.

Grandpa taught math in our home that year to two high school girls. Several more classrooms were built on the mission station to accommodate the growing school population. Later, the school moved to its present campus at another location. Our colleague Scotty built much of the high school and faculty housing. In succeeding years, the student body grew to 550 in the mid-seventies. TASOL/TASOK had many more opening days of school, but none of them compared with that very first one in 1961 when forty-five kids and their teachers met for classes in a tropical downpour.

When we were houseparents in the children's hostel, the first rain of the season always brought out the wildness in the kids. Looking toward the river, the sky growing darker by the minute, they knew that first rain was on its way. They were ready and waiting, eager to get soaked.

The main problem in hostel living was the struggle we faced with lack of water. The trickle coming from the faucets made it difficult to get enough water to do laundry and prepare meals. Tubs were set out on the porch to catch rainwater. At least that could be used for flushing toilets.

When the skies finally opened and the rain poured down, most of the kids ran pell-mell, arms wide open to embrace the cooling rain. They yelled and hollered, thoroughly enjoying the drenching. Some poured water over themselves from the tubs (there went the flushing water!), then ran dripping wet into the hostel. It was a glorious time. A few even helped mop up the mess. That first rain was something else!

The end of *sivu* with its coming rains heralded the arrival of spring. It might be fall in the United States, but it was spring in Congo. I loved that season, as, after only one or two rains, the grass turned green again and trees began to blossom. Ironwoods and jacarandas spread a purple carpet under their branches. The orchid trees and frangipanis blossomed in a variety of colors. Flamboyants, a blaze of color in villages and along Kinshasa streets, let us know spring had truly arrived.

One of my favorite trees was a mock almond that stood outside our dining room. It was the only tree I ever saw in Congo that took on autumn colors as trees do here in America. The large, colorful leaves dropped off, making way for the new ones. All curled up, they looked like little green candles until they opened out. Susan's swing hung from that tree and the swinging motion caused all those green candles to rotate. Quite a sight!

The rains were refreshing, bringing new life to a hazy, dusty, dry landscape. Now the women could return to their gardens and plant peanuts and manioc again. Even though the days were much hotter now, we had the rains to look forward to. They cooled things off, at least for a little while.

Should it rain and you've nothing better to do, run outside and let it splash all over you!

Till the next letter. Love you,

G'ma and G'pa

What? No Television? No Video Games?

Dear Grandchildren,

Without television, videos and DVDs, whatever did your parents do for fun in Congo?

The "mish kids" were a creative bunch, always coming up with new ideas of something fun to do. They never lacked for imagination and they always had playmates, as there were several children living on the station. Neither the hot weather of rainy season nor the cooler temperatures of dry season ever dimmed their exuberance for living each day to the fullest.

For a while, they were stamp collectors, trading stamps with one another and putting them in albums. Sometimes it got a bit noisy with their deciding what would be a fair exchange for a particular stamp. Steven has kept his childhood love of stamp collecting into his adult life and still collects today.

Bicycle races were always a challenge. Each bike had a name; Steven's was Bluebonnet. Why he named it that, I'm not sure since we're not Texans, but the bike was indeed blue. Smaller than the others, Bluebonnet had balloon tires and a reputation for speed. As the bikers pedaled furiously toward the finish line, the other kids lined the driveway to cheer them on. Bluebonnet was definitely a favorite; everyone wanted to ride her. By the time Steven was in high school, he had outgrown his faithful bike, and another replaced it. Later, motocross captured the kids' interest. Even though none of them had motorcycles, several had seen the races and they turned their bike fun into motocross maneuvers.

Living in the tropics, we didn't have snow, but that didn't keep the kids from "sledding." The hill behind one of the houses was the perfect place for this pastime. Flattened pieces of cardboard boxes made ideal sleds. With a push from behind and amid squeals of laughter, they went flying down the hill. It wasn't long before someone hit upon a better idea. There were numerous palm trees on the station, and someone discovered that the wide end of a palm frond made a perfect sled. The more flights down the hill, the slicker became the frond. The kids had hours of fun sliding down the hill, then dragging the frond back for the next person to take a turn.

Another activity that kept the children occupied for weeks was building Matchboxville. The toys came in a box about the size of a small box of matches and ranged from cars to trucks, tractors to trailers and everything in between. As their interest in Matchboxville grew, they were given a room where they could set up this wonderful village and leave it until the next time they were ready to play. They built roads, added houses and other buildings. There was even the First Baptist Church of Matchboxville. During those tense days following the Congolese Army revolt after independence in 1960, the children spent many hours playing with these toys.

For a short time, the children turned their attention to gardening. Although they dug a small plot of ground, planted seeds, and watered them, they weren't cut out to be gardeners. Their interest waned when the seeds took longer to sprout than they had anticipated. There was a song about a little boy who was chided because the seeds he planted hadn't sprouted: "No, no it won't come up. Your carrot won't come up." Our kids couldn't wait for seeds to sprout and grow either—they were off to more exciting adventures.

In the years prior to independence, several of our children attended the Belgian schools. We took them swimming twice a week at Mampeza after their classes finished. Chanic Shipyards, which neighbored mission property, owned the pool, and the director gave us permission to use it. It was stream-fed with water coming in one end and exiting the other. We had never seen a pool like that. Steven learned to swim in it. None of us ever got sick from swimming there, so evidently it was safe. Several years later the American school built a pool at the campus which became the favorite place to swim. Until then the kids looked forward to a swim and picnic supper at the Funa Club on Friday afternoon.

Many Tuesday evenings, everyone fixed a picnic supper and drove up the hill where Stanley Monument overlooked the Congo River as it widened into Stanley Pool. Years earlier, the Belgians had honored Henry Morton Stanley for his exploration of the Congo by naming this area for him. In 1972, the Congo government, in its desire for authenticity, renamed them Mount Ngaliema and Ngaliema Bay after the chief with whom Stanley negotiated our mission property.

There was an immense bronze statue of Stanley, pith helmet on his head, arm upraised, looking out across the river, the other hand resting on a staff. The statue disappeared in 1972 during the authenticity era, and there was much speculation, none of it complimentary, concerning its fate. There were also several larger-than-life statues of Congolese: a fisherman, porter, workman that still stand today.

With a cool breeze blowing in from the river, Stanley Monument was a great place for a picnic. Eating our sandwiches with colleagues as the last rays of sunset disappeared, looking for the Southern Cross in a star-studded sky, and watching the children play tag gave us a sense of peace at the close of a busy day. We watched Sputnik, Russia's first earth-orbiting satellite, wink its way across the night sky. Another time, we surprised the hostel kids with watermelon, the only year it was sold in the stores.

There was a favorite place on mission property, which the children liked to explore. It was behind some buildings in a tall grassy area. Eating sandwiches there, perhaps they had visions of trekking through the wilderness like early explorers. The children's hostel had not been built yet, and Susan was incensed that this special place was to become the site for it. "They're just ruining the mission," she lamented one day when she learned what was to happen.

While Congolese workmen were digging the foundation for the hostel, Steven came home one day bearing a large bone which looked as if it had belonged to a human in its other life. Knowing that Congolese would be greatly upset if this were true and they learned about it, we told him to take it back. "Oh, yes," said dear old Tata Mbaki who had worked forever at the mission, "they used to bury people there." If other bones were dug up, we never heard about it, but at least one leg bone was back where it belonged!

One summer, the children invented their version of blind man's buff. Pushing slides, jungle gym, and merry-go-round together they had to jump from one to the other without touching the ground. Blindfolded "It" had to catch them and identify them while they were on the equipment. They all had crazy names. Susan's was Super Spud, her initials being S S.

While the children never had TV to watch when they were growing up, they have a wealth of happy memories of the fun and imaginative things they did. We hope you will too.

Love to all, G'ma and G'pa

Stanley Monument

Thanksgiving Is More Than Turkeys

Dear Grandkids,

In October or November, our churches held a special service called *Matondo*. The name comes from the Kikongo verb *tonda* which means to thank or to be thankful. You may remember my writing in an earlier letter that one way to express thanks was to say *ntondele*. The "n" equals our pronoun I, so the word means I thank you.

Matondo services were always a very joyful occasion, and, in remembering them, four things stand out vividly in my mind: the music, the offerings, the way the churches were decorated, and how hard those wooden benches became after sitting on them for three or four hours!

If a church did not have sufficient funds to put up a permanent building but was still worshiping outside under a palm thatch shelter, even that humble place of worship was decorated for the occasion. Men cut palm fronds, tied them together and attached them to the limbs which supported the thatched roof. To give the structure a festive appearance, colorful bougainvillea blossoms were tucked into the fronds. Bright yellow or red canna lilies also added much color to the church. God's sanctuary reflected their love for him.

We loved the music. In addition to the local church choirs, others came from different churches throughout the city. Some of the choir directors had a flair for the dramatic and waved their arms vigorously as they led their group. Women waved small palm branches and swayed to the rhythm of the music as they sang. Choirs ignored the pastor's request to sing only one anthem by remaining seated as they sang their first number. Only as they stood to their feet to sing was that considered their anthem!

Sometimes ten or more choirs came to sing at the Matondo service. You can understand why the pastors wanted to limit how many anthems they sang. Often, the music was written by the choir directors. One of the best choirs we ever heard was a group of men from a nearby prison. They weren't criminals, but were in prison for minor reasons, some because they had not paid their taxes.

We often said that since God loves a cheerful giver, he must love the Congolese a lot. Offerings were a joyful affair. How dull and uninteresting the taking of an offering in our churches would seem to them. While one of the many choirs sang, accompanied by a guitarist or two, drummers beat out a rhythm on tall drums as we all marched forward to place our offering in large enamel basins. As we swayed to the music and clapped our hands, it was two steps forward and one back. Deacons counted the offering on the spot as it was given and the amount announced.

At the village of Ngombe, the young, innovative pastor had a fresh idea for receiving the offering. He had found a large wheel, which he attached to a pulley and rope. The spokes were liberally decorated with bougainvillea blossoms. As the offering was counted, the wheel was raised and lowered and the group that had given the largest offering was cheered.

Sometimes, there was a contest between the women and the men to see who would give the largest offering. It wasn't a good idea to give it all at once, for then one wouldn't be able to march forward a second time. At one service, a man placed a live goat, feet tied together, in the basin, thereby dashing the women's hope that they would be declared the winners. Goats were not cheap, and selling one would give the men a much larger offering than the women could possibly give.

After all the choirs had sung, and thirty minutes had passed taking the offering, there was still the sermon to be preached. Those hard, wooden benches had to be endured for yet another forty-five minutes. Still, there was that warm Pepsi Cola to look forward to at the end of the service.

Till the next letter, G'ma and G'pa

"I Think That I Shall Never See..."

Dear Grandkids,

An avocado tree, tall and straight, dropped its fruit on our metal roof one night waking us from a sound sleep. Hearts pounding, we sat straight up in bed. "What was that?" When we realized it was only an avocado, we lay down and went back to sleep. We put one on the scales once and it weighed almost two pounds. Our dog, Satchmo, had the shiniest coat of any dog around. He loved avocados.

What a variety of trees there are in Congo. We knew the African name for some of them such as *wenge* (ironwood), used in making beautiful furniture, and *nkamba* (mahogany). All our furniture was made from mahogany. If we didn't know the name of a tree, we gave it one. There was the tall, red seed tree at the entrance to the mission station in Kinshasa. It surely had an authentic name, but its small red seeds were all the definition it needed. Wood carvers used ebony to carve animals and figurines to sell to tourists. We knew to scratch the bottom of a carving to see if it was really ebony or if the carver had used black shoe polish to make it look authentic.

The rains started in September turning the dry, dusty country green again. A coat of dust had covered everything. With the coming of the rains, ferny-leafed ironwoods and jacarandas greeted us with soft purple carpets beneath their branches. Not to be outdone, the mimosas dressed themselves in fluffy pink blossoms. The flamboyants burst out in oranges, reds and yellows. What a brilliant display they made, lining each side of the dirt road leading into Nsona Mpangu. We loved spring in Congo.

Because it had low, easy-to-climb branches, frangipani trees, often called "frangipangi" by the children, was a favorite with them. Congolese children liked to thread the five-petaled blossoms on a thin reed and run with them in the wind. The creamy white, pink, or delicate yellow flowers had a heavy perfume. If someone broke a branch climbing the tree, milky sap oozed from the break. More than one child had a broken bone or sore knees after a fall from a frangipani. I remember one afternoon when two boys, at different times, fell from a frangipani tree. One broke a leg, the other an arm.

We called another tree the orchid tree. Its speckled white blossoms bordered by deep maroon were like miniature orchids. The leaves were perfect for putting under a piece of paper, which, when rubbed with a crayon or pencil, produced an interesting leaf design. Poinsettias grew several feet tall, their red leaves adding color to the landscape. Unlike the ones grown in hothouses in the United States, ours never bloomed at Christmas. When trees bloomed during the rainy season, it was like an artist's palette of colors.

Kapok trees reminded me of cottonwood trees where I grew up in Ohio. A good breeze was all it took for the kapok to float lazily down to the ground. It was also the perfect nesting place for a family of crows whose children met a sad demise one Christmas. I wrote about that in another letter. During *sivu* (dry season) the mock almond shed its colorful leaves. When the new ones appeared, they looked like green candles before they opened. The nuts were good to eat, and Miriam shelled some for me when I promised to bake cookies.

Congo's climate is too hot for most fruit found in the United States, but citrus trees love the hot, humid climate. Instead of buying a few bananas at a time as we do in America we often bought a stalk of them from a vendor who came to our house. After we returned to the States, I learned there is no banana that equals one from Congo. It took nearly a year before I could honestly enjoy eating the ones we bought here. Congo bananas have far more flavor.

I dreaded mango season. The fruit was wonderful to eat or use in desserts, but people who climbed the trees never, ever tidied up the mess they left. Sticks and leaves and rotting mangos scattered on the ground were not their concern. Once, when we had just hired someone to rake the yard, two men came and proceeded to climb the tree. With so many mango trees on the station, why did they have to choose the one in my yard? I asked them to find another tree, as I had just paid someone to clean the yard. They were deaf. However, one of the men had left his shoes at the foot of the tree. I picked them up and took them inside. "Oh, Mama, don't do that," he said. When he came down I handed him the rake—and he redeemed his shoes.

Fruit bats also loved mangos, and many a night we heard them enjoying their banquet. They have a long face like a moose and a two to three feet wingspan. Ugly critters that they are, they do love mangos. Their call sounded like someone hammering on an anvil.

We were surrounded by a variety of palm trees. The coconut, skinny and tall, kept its fruit at the topmost fronds where it was difficult to reach. A coconut harvester climbed the tree with the aid of a rope made from sturdy fibers woven together. Securing the rope behind his back and around the tree the man flipped the rope up as he hoisted himself, inching his way bit by bit. Reaching the top, he took his machete and whacked at the coconuts until they fell. It was an extremely dangerous job and sometimes the rope broke and the man fell breaking many bones. Some were paralyzed from such a fall. Boys liked to take rocks and pound at the outer shell until it broke apart, then opened the coconut to enjoy its delicious meat.

One of the major food sources in the Congo diet comes from a palm tree which bears large clusters of fibrous nuts, orange in color and rich in vitamin A. Many of their foods are cooked in this oil called *ngazi*. Most of us learned to prepare African dishes using palm oil. A Congolese with a dry skin problem sometimes rubbed *ngazi* on his/her arms and legs.

The fan palm, also called traveler palm because it holds water in its center, is one of the prettiest palms. Its fronds spread out like a lady's fan. Another palm grows a bushy "flower" which Congolese burn, then use the ashes to treat ringworm. This is an infection which is transmitted to humans from infected pets or sandboxes. It's easily treated so you don't need to feel icky about it.

In another letter I told you about the baobab tree, which was one of my favorites. Its branches looked like roots reaching for the sky, but the blossoms were especially intriguing. We could almost see them open and unfold, as though a time camera were on them. Mangrove trees grew along the Congo River on its rush to the Atlantic Ocean. Those trees were also fascinating as their intertwined roots grew above water, then bent back into the water like an upside down U.

I never developed a taste for guavas, though a lot of people enjoyed them. They made good jelly, and the kids especially liked to climb the trees to get the fruit. On occasion, we could buy mangosteens in the market. They have a hard, reddish-brown rind that, when peeled off, reveals a succulent, sweet fruit. The "packaging" of the mangosteen is neat, as it protects the fruit, keeping it clean until it's opened.

One tree, the *nsafu*, has a fruit that is unlike anything you have ever eaten. The purple outer skin is paper-thin while the meat is the color of an avocado. It's about two inches in length. Pour boiling water over the *nsafu* and it's soon ready to eat. Remove the skin, salt or sugar it or serve it with a bit of mayonnaise, and it's a tasty snack. Although it took a long time before I could honestly say I liked them, today, just thinking about *nsafus* makes my mouth water. I'm hungry!

It's lunchtime—

Love to all, G'ma and G'pa

Long Ago and Far Away

Dear Grandkids,

The year is 1878. Can you imagine what it's like to leave the comfort of your home and say goodbye to your family and friends whom you might never see again? Your destination is Belgian Congo and you're traveling there by ship, for these are the days before air travel. You've felt God's call to share the Good News with people in that land. You don't know their language, you don't know their customs, and you might die of malaria or other tropical diseases. You don't know what dangers you might face. Still, you go because you firmly believe this is God's will for your life . . .

The first missionaries in what became Belgian Congo landed at the port city of Matadi on the Congo River. From there they trekked inland nine miles since ships could not get around the rapids in the river. They followed a path up a steep hill to the village of Palabala in the Crystal Mountains. There they negotiated with village chiefs to establish the very first mission station in the entire country. There they began their work. The gospel had come to Congo.

Those first missionaries were from England, sent out by Livingstone Inland Mission. After three or four years, they were unable to continue their work and asked American Baptist Foreign Mission Society to take over. Some of their missionaries stayed on to work with ours.

Fast forward now to 1978, one hundred years after those first missionaries arrived. A big celebration was taking place at Palabala to commemorate one hundred years since the first missionaries arrived to bring the gospel to the Congolese people.

Grandpa and I drove from Kinshasa to Kimpese, where we stayed overnight. Getting that far, even on the paved road, had its problems, as we had to take enough fuel with us for the return trip. Zaire was in the middle of another gas crisis. There was none to be bought at any station between Kinshasa and Matadi, a distance of two hundred miles.

Thirteen of us left Kimpese for Palabala at 5:30 the next morning. Zairians and Angolans, who also wanted to go to the celebration, rode with us. Zaire and Angola shared a common border in that part of the country. En route to Palabala, we noticed several new refugee villages. Angolans were spilling over into Zaire at the rate of 1000 to 2000 refugees a month. Caught between the Cuban backed guerrillas and the Angolan army, many had hidden in the forests for two or three years. They were hungry, homeless, destitute and in need of serious medical attention. Since most were from the Bakongo tribe, they spoke the same language and shared a common culture with the people who lived in our part of Zaire.

After a jolting two-hour drive over bumpy, dusty roads we arrived at Palabala. Church members welcomed us. They had prepared breakfast for all the guests and we were given a choice of coffee or tea plus a roll with a bit of sardine inside. I asked for coffee, but I finally concluded that my drink was smoky tea. All water had to be carried up hill and heating of water and cooking was done over charcoal fires in the open air.

Some people had arrived the day before and had slept that night in the little church. Among them were our friends Scotty and Dolores, who joined the wall-to-wall sleepers. They set up their camp cots and for a bit of privacy placed a bench at the foot of their cots. During the night they awakened and discovered two people, had spotted the bench and were curled up on it, sound asleep. Forget about privacy!

Since the little church could not hold the great number of people who had come for the celebration, the service was held in a cleared banana grove. Villagers had made benches for the occasion, and desks were carried from the school. The banana grove offered little shade and most of the *mindele* had sore noses and sunburned necks after sitting several hours in the hot sun. Entering the outdoor sanctuary, each person was given a leaf from a palm frond. These were collected and counted later. That's a nifty way to know how many people attended! People must have been busy counting those 1500 palm leaves, the number estimated of those in attendance.

Several of the early missionaries died at Palabala and were buried in the little cemetery. In preparation for the celebration, a memorial had been built over it. It was in the shape of a semicircle stage with a large wooden cross in the back and steps leading to it. On either side of the steps an African artist had made life-size ceramic likenesses of people hearing the gospel message in 1878 and 1978.

Recognition of nine elderly chiefs, among them a woman, was one of the most interesting parts of the service. Each wore their symbol of chieftainship, a woven raffia hat amply decorated with talons of some kind. Some of the men wore ancient frock coats or swallow-tailed coats. Had some long-deceased early missionaries left those relics? And where were those coats when I needed them? I had used a bathrobe pattern as a point of departure when I made a frock coat for Steven when he played

Ceramic Representation of People Hearing the Gospel in 1878 and 1978

in Arsenic and Old Lace at TASOK. Each chief wore a *nlele* (cloth) wrapped skirt fashion under his/her coat. Two men carried a rod of some sort, another symbol of their chieftainship.

At each end of the row of chiefs stood a guard holding a sword. Throughout the four-hour service, they remained standing, their swords held at attention, point end up. Even in all that heat, one of the guards wore a Navy wool pea jacket.

Former students were recognized, starting with those who had been in our schools between 1878 and 1900. There were five or six in that group, among them some of the chiefs who had been little children in the early 1900s. Three choirs were on the program and each was reminded to sing only one song. A men's choral group found it impossible to heed that request and popped up three times to sing when the master of ceremonies took a breath. Women's choirs from Sona Bata and Bandalungwa weren't

Old Chiefs at Palabala

even on the program, but they had come for the celebration determined to sing. Of course they were squeezed into the service. You can understand why it lasted four hours!

We were in Kikongo-speaking country, and most of the service was in that language. Pastor Lubikulu gave the morning message in Kikongo, which was then translated into French. He closed his sermon by saying that if a baby breaks something he is not scolded because he is not responsible, but an older child is treated differently because he knows better. Even so, before the missionaries came with the message of salvation, the people knew about God, but not about Jesus, They didn't know they needed salvation. Now we know, said Pastor Lubikulu, so God holds us responsible for our acceptance or rejection of him. Another pastor referred to Palabala as "the Bethlehem of Zaire."

Unfortunately, the pastor in charge of the offering thought we needed another sermon. Offerings were usually a joyful occasion with people dancing two steps forward and one step back to place their gifts in a large enamel basin. It seemed to me he called attention to himself rather than the offering.

After a long four-hour worship service in the hot sun, it was nice to go back to the church where the women had lunch ready for the guests. Rice, *kwanga* (manioc), beans, chicken, and fish cooked in palm sauce had never tasted so good.

What a fascinating weekend it had been. To be present at the 100th anniversary of the opening of the Congo to the gospel of Jesus Christ was an experience we would never forget. Those men and women who had braved sickness and despair, separation from their families and unknown dangers had persevered with God's help and shared their love for Jesus with others. Now, a hundred years later, thousands of people had come to trust him as their Savior through that faithful witness.

Since I've written to you about Palabala, there's something else I'd like to tell you that has nothing to do with the 100th anniversary. In the late 1400s, Portuguese sailors discovered the mouth of the Congo River and sailed upriver a few miles beyond Matadi. There they were stopped by rapids. At this point, the river narrows into a gorge where the water spews high in the air as it crashes over immense boulders. Unable to sail any farther, the sailors landed and inscribed a rock with their names and date.

That rock is still there today, but most people never see it as it's quite inaccessible. You have to be very eager to go there as the long hike down the mountain from Palabala to the river is extremely tiring. A year after we arrived in Belgian Congo, we were eager to see that historic site and drove the dusty road to Palabala. That was the easy part. Hiking down the mountain in the blazing sun with three-year-old Steven on his dad's shoulders was not. We picked our way down the steep mountainside, grabbing a small bush or tree now and then for support. My legs felt like rubber. They shook so I could hardly walk. While it was worth the effort to see that bit of history, the thought of going back up the mountain left me weak-kneed all over again.

While Steven was in college, he came back to Congo for a visit. He wanted to go to Palabala and make the trip down to the river again. It was a struggle getting there, but in spite of shaky legs was worth it. Fishermen were drying tiny shrimp and sardines on the rocks. We wondered how old gnarled, stunted baobab trees growing out of the rocks could get enough moisture and soil to survive.

The moment came when we had to climb the mountain back to Palabala. It looked formidable. Susan got tired waiting for me and struck out on her own, but she wasn't sure of the path and at times thought she was lost. The roar of the river drowned out her voice when she called to us. Finally, we all made it to the top, thankful that the sky was overcast this time.

It had been fifteen years since we made the first trip, but this time Steven made it on his own—he didn't have to be carried on his dad's shoulders. Maybe some day you will get to see this bit of history. Be sure to take a walking stick!

Shortly after I started writing this book, I came across one of Charles Schulz's *Peanuts* cartoons. Snoopy is sitting on top of his dog house, typewriter in front of him writing a story.

He types: *It was*

Writer's block takes over and Snoopy leaves his dog house.

Returning to his typewriter, he tries again: *It was a dark*

With no inspiration, he forsakes his typewriter once more.

At last, Snoopy resumes his place and adds: *It was a dark and stormy night.*

Finally, Snoopy confesses: *Good writing is hard work!*

My sentiments exactly!

There are more letters I could write, but these are enough to peak your imagination. I have to stop somewhere! You will have to ask your parents those things you've wondered about as you've read this book.

All the years we lived and worked in Congo, we were always aware of God's love for us and the help and strength he gave us in the good times when everything went well, and also his presence during the difficult times. We were privileged to know many fine Congolese who were positive and thankful for the way God sustained them during their difficult situations. We were blessed to be a part of their lives and those years.

Much love to each of our grandkids,

G'ma and G'pa

Trust in the Lord with all your heart. Never rely on what you think you know. Remember the Lord in everything you do, and he will show you the right way.

Proverbs 3:5–6, Good News Bible